NICK STELLINO'S
GLORIOUS ITALIAN COOKING

Nick Stellino's Glorious Italian Cooking

ROMANTIC MEALS AND MENUS FROM CUCINA AMORE™

West 175 Enterprises Inc.

LIBRARY OF CONGRESS CATALOGING-IN-PUBLICATION DATA
STELLINO, NICK.
NICK STELLINO'S GLORIOUS ITALIAN COOKING / NICK STELLINO.
P. CM.
ISBN 0-9583354-3-5
1. COOKERY, ITALIAN. I. CUCINA AMORE (TELEVISION PROGRAM)
II. TITLE.
TX723.S796 .1996   95-49960 CIP
641.5945—DC20

PRINTED IN THE UNITED STATES OF AMERICA
1 2 3 4 5 6 7 8 9 10

THIS BOOK IS PRINTED ON ACID-FREE PAPER.

DEDICATION

I dedicate this book to my wife, Nanci, my guiding light and inspiration. I think of myself as a lucky man who has won the lottery twice in his life: once when I met Nanci, the second time when we married!

ACKNOWLEDGMENTS

This book would not exist without the beautiful stories and the teaching of my mother, Massimiliana Boccato, and my father, Vincenzo Stellino. As for that rascal of a brother, Mario, I want to thank him for his steadfast support and his belief in my abilities. I'm thankful to my wife, Nanci, for successfully mediating my ego and my temper throughout the most difficult moments of this project.

I'd also like to thank the following people: John McEwen, the visionary who brought us all together; John McLean, the grammatical authority on all schools of thought, but especially those relating to little green bits; Carl De Santis for his brilliant legal counsel; Christine Andrews Rylko, for her gentle leadership in every area of the Cucina Amore project (may she always get the gnocchi she deserves); my senior food assistant Jenny Steinle, whose testing and cooking of my recipes is always flawless; Marlene Lambert, for dedicated research, keeping the book organized through endless changes, and competent assistance in the kitchen; Pattye O'Connor, who communicates my message to the public with unequaled personal color and the loyal heart of a true Texan; Connie Lunde, for persevering to create the images and book design that make my words sing; to John Duff, for his glorious publishing insight. Special thanks to the entire West 175 Enterprises team, Pam Brown, Melissa Dungan, Debra Runnels, Danielle Clark and Don Ely. Last but definitely not least, Robert Zimmer and Mauro Pazienti for giving me excellent advice on wine selections.

CONTENTS

Introduction
FROM MY HEART TO YOUR KITCHEN
2

Antipasti
APPETIZERS
5

Zuppe e Insalate
SOUPS & SALADS
23

Paste e Risotti
PASTA & RISOTTO
49

I Secondi
ENTREES
95

Contorni
SIDE DISHES
147

Dolci
DESSERTS
173

Ricette Fondamentali
BASICS
211

INDEX
233

From My Heart To Your Kitchen

"Nick, try to remember that life is an adventure and, if you can, try to follow your dreams."

I remember having breakfast with my father one wintry Saturday morning while my mother and brother, Mario, were still asleep. Dad was smoking his typical morning cigarette, surrounded in a cloud of thick white smoke, sipping a cup of freshly brewed espresso. He was staring out of the kitchen window toward an imaginary horizon.

I sat next to him, clutching a mug of hot cocoa, dipping one of my mother's homemade cookies between gulps. My father's thoughts were somewhere far away that morning. I felt his hand gently caressing the back of my head. Then he turned his face toward me and said with a soulful look in his eyes, "Nick, try to remember that life is an adventure and, if you can, try to follow your dreams."

I remember being puzzled, wondering what he meant. All I could think to do in response was to offer him a drink of my cocoa. He laughed, poured some in his own cup and together we ate the rest of the cookies. Like always, my mother's homemade cookies worked their magic. Even Dad started to smile.

As I look back in time, I see my life as a tapestry of little stories, chasing one another in and out of chronological sequence, but all connected by the common threads of family and food. Faces, times and places shine brilliantly, polished by the romantic recollection of my heart, woven inextricably with the wonderful, simple dishes that adorned my family table. Even when the rest of the world revolved frenetically around us, time rolled out slowly around our family meals. The Stellino family celebrated their dinner table as a sacred tribal meeting ground, a safe haven where we could take refuge against life's hectic pace. The love for food and its preparation, held together by a collage of little stories, is my family heritage. Today it has matured and become my life's passion, my dream and my adventure, in which I see my present, past and future.

While the world today seems to move more frantically than in my childhood, I still find myself repeating my family traditions around a dinner table. Seated with my wife and my friends, a little food, a little wine and the magic of my family recipes takes its course. The air is filled with laughter and stories. My past comes back and my present becomes more alive. Life comes full circle.

This is a book about cooking that comes from my heart. I hope that you will share a little bit of its magical moments in your kitchen.

"Faces, times and places shine brilliantly, polished by the romantic recollection of my heart."

ANTIPASTI

APPETIZERS

CROSTINI
Garlic Toast with Assorted
Toppings 8-9

MELONE CON PROSCIUTTO E GORGONZOLA
Canteloupe with Prosciutto and
Gorgonzola 10

PEPERONI ARROSTI
Roasted Bell Peppers in
Balsamic Vinegar 11

CARCIOFI SPADELLATI
Artichoke Sauté 12

FUNGHI FARCITI
Stuffed Mushroom Caps 13

CARCIOFI ARROSTI COL CAVIAL DI BOSCO
Artichoke Hearts with
Mushroom Caviar 14-15

PASTICCINO INGLESE
Savory Meat Pie 16-17

CAPESANTE CON SPINACI
Scallops with Spinach 18

PURÉ DI CECI AL LIMONE
Lemony Garbanzo Spread 19

PANE CON LE OLIVE
Olive Bread 20-21

Crostini

GARLIC TOAST WITH ASSORTED SPREADS

I've discovered that one of the most successful business-building techniques at Italian restaurants is bringing your patrons little dishes of appetizing finger foods before they order from the menu. It seems that there is nothing that encourages eating more than a tantalizing morsel to wake up the taste buds.

Crostini are always one of the most popular appetizers. There are endless variations you can make with your favorite ingredients to top the irresistible little slices of toasted garlic bread. Just always follow one rule: make plenty! They will disappear at a much faster rate than you had originally forecast.

SERVES 4

OLIVE SPREAD
2 ounces (½ cup or 60 g) pitted Greek or Sicilian black olives
2 teaspoons olive oil
2 teaspoons balsamic vinegar
1 whole head Roasted Garlic (see page 224)
1 tablespoon chopped fresh Italian parsley
¼ teaspoon black pepper

RICOTTA/GORGONZOLA SPREAD
¼ cup ricotta cheese
2 tablespoons Gorgonzola cheese
4 Roasted Garlic cloves (see page 224)
1 tablespoon chopped fresh Italian parsley

SUN-DRIED TOMATO SPREAD
6 oil-packed sun-dried tomato halves
¼ cup goat cheese
2 tablespoons mascarpone cheese
1 tablespoon chopped fresh sage

GARLIC TOAST
12 slices hearty Italian bread, cut ¼ inch thick
3 tablespoons olive oil
1 large whole garlic clove, peeled

For the Olive Spread

Place all the ingredients in a food processor and process for 30 seconds, until it reaches a spreading consistency. This topping will not be completely smooth. Transfer to a bowl and set aside.

For the Ricotta/Gorgonzola Spread

Purée the ricotta, Gorgonzola and garlic in a processor until smooth. Add the parsley and process until just mixed. Transfer to a bowl and set aside.

For the Sun-dried Tomato Spread

Process the sun-dried tomato halves in a processor until chopped into small pieces. Add the goat and mascarpone cheeses and process until well mixed. Add the sage and process until just mixed. Transfer to a bowl and set aside.

For the Garlic Toast

Place the bread slices on a baking sheet and brush both sides with olive oil. Place under a broiler for about 2 minutes on each side, until lightly browned. Rub one side of the toasted slices with the whole garlic clove. Before the bread cools, cut the slices in half if you are using a fat loaf of bread. Your toast should be about 2-3 inches (5-8 cm) in diameter.

Spread the toppings on the toast and arrange on individual serving plates so each guest gets one of each kind. Serve at room temperature.

"Tell me what kind of food you eat, and I will tell you what kind of man you are."

BRILLAT-SAVARIN

Melone con Prosciutto e Gorgonzola

CANTALOUPE WITH PROSCIUTTO AND GORGONZOLA

I first tasted a Gorgonzola sauce in a little restaurant near Padova. The strong Gorgonzola taste was used as a sauce for carpaccio (thin slices of raw steak). It inspired me to start on an aggressive experimentation program, trying to develop my own version of the sauce. Once I achieved that, I started looking for new matches for my "discovery." After a laborious series of mostly disastrous combinations, I finally stumbled upon this perfect match of culinary personalities.

This was a great relief to my wife, who still gets a bit exasperated when she smells the distinctive Gorgonzola aroma in my shopping bag after a trip to the market. By the way, prosciutto and melon are one of the most common appetizers throughout Northern Italy. If you don't like Gorgonzola, enjoy the recipe without the sauce.

SERVES 4

½ cup Gorgonzola cheese
2 tablespoons whipping cream
1 large cantaloupe
¼ cup Port wine
12 slices prosciutto, sliced paper thin
5 ounces (150 g) arugula leaves, washed and stemmed
⅛ teaspoon black pepper

Place ¼ cup of the Gorgonzola cheese and the cream in a small saucepan and cook over medium heat until the cheese has melted and the sauce has a smooth consistency. Remove from the heat to cool.

Slice the cantaloupe in half and clean out the seeds. Scoop out balls of cantaloupe, using a melon baller. Place the cantaloupe balls in a medium bowl and pour the Port over them. Marinate for 30 minutes, stirring frequently.

Place 3 slices of the prosciutto on each plate and top with the arugula. Mound the melon balls on top. Drizzle with 1 tablespoon of the sauce and sprinkle with 1 tablespoon of the remaining cheese. (If the sauce has cooled too much to drizzle from a spoon, just put it back on the heat and stir until it becomes thinner, about 1 minute.) Sprinkle with the pepper.

COOK'S TIP

An alternate and more traditional way to serve this dish, would be to cut the melon into thin wedges instead of balls, eliminate the Port wine marinade and wrap each wedge with a slice of prosciutto.

Peperoni Arrosti

ROASTED BELL PEPPERS IN BALSAMIC VINEGAR

SERVES 8

*8 bell peppers, halved, cored and seeded,
preferably a mix of red, yellow and green peppers
8 tablespoons olive oil
2 teaspoons chopped fresh garlic
1 teaspoon salt
½ teaspoon black pepper
1 tablespoon balsamic vinegar
2 teaspoons chopped fresh Italian parsley
1 loaf Italian bread, sliced, toasted in the oven and rubbed with garlic*

Preheat the oven to 500° F (260° C). Brush the pepper halves with 4 tablespoons of the olive oil, place skin-side-up on a nonstick baking sheet and bake for 15-20 minutes, until the skin is blackened. Transfer the peppers to a large paper bag, seal and let cool. Peel off the blackened skin, slice the peppers into strips and set aside.

In a medium bowl, mix the remaining 4 tablespoons of the olive oil, the garlic, salt, pepper, vinegar and parsley. Stir in the peeled peppers and let marinate at room temperature for at least 2 hours.

Serve the peppers in a beautiful bowl placed on a serving tray, with the garlic toast arranged around it.

COOK'S TIP

Create an easy, colorful salad by tossing 4-5 ounces (115-150 g) of mixed baby salad greens with the marinating juices from the roasted peppers. Put the greens on serving plates and top with a portion of pepper strips. Sprinkle with freshly grated Parmigiano Reggiano cheese and serve.

A Stellino family outing to a restaurant was always one of my most exciting experiences. One of the few establishments which passed my father's stringent quality tests was "La Scuderia" (The Stable), located next to Palermo's horse racing track. It was a very popular eatery, attracting many of the local journalists, actors and prominent political figures.

Of course, my father always wore his "dried prune face." This frozen look of disdain was maintained throughout the evening, a stern reminder to all restaurant personnel that Don Vincenzo would be judging every bite of food.

My favorite sight upon entering was a huge table of antipasti (appetizers). Its centerpiece was a long silver tray that contained the famous "Peperoni Arrosti." The following recipe is my rendition of this fabulous first course.

Carciofi Spadellati
Artichoke Sauté

You might not believe this, but as a boy I was afraid of artichokes. It all started as I was racing around my Grandmother Maria's garden after my brother, Mario. I fell right on top of some spiny artichoke plants and ended up hopping around the garden like a kangaroo, yelping with pain. Even now when I prepare artichokes, I can still hear my brother's laughter, appreciating my kangaroo imitation.

SERVES 6

4 tablespoons olive oil
1 ½ teaspoons anchovy paste
4 garlic cloves, thickly sliced
⅓ cup drained capers
¾ cup pitted Greek or Sicilian black olives, halved
12 fresh cooked artichoke hearts (see page 14 for cleaning directions),
cut into 1-inch (2.5-cm) cubes
or 2 (9-ounce) (250-g) packages frozen artichoke hearts,
thawed, ends of leaves trimmed and cut in half
¼ teaspoon red pepper flakes
¼ cup lemon juice
¾ cup Chicken Stock (see page 228)
¼ teaspoon black pepper
4 tablespoons extra virgin olive oil

Heat the 4 tablespoons of olive oil and the anchovy paste in a large sauté pan set on medium-high heat until sizzling, about 2 minutes. Once it begins to sizzle, break up the anchovy paste with a wooden spoon and stir it into the olive oil. Add the garlic, capers and olives and cook for 2-3 minutes. Stir in the artichokes and red pepper flakes and cook for 3-4 minutes to brown the artichokes. Pour in the lemon juice, chicken stock and pepper, bring to a boil and cook for 1 minute to thicken the juices. Transfer to a bowl and cool to room temperature. Stir in the extra virgin olive oil and serve.

You may also cover the dish and refrigerate overnight, but don't add the extra virgin olive oil until serving time. Before serving, bring to room temperature. Just before serving, stir in the 4 tablespoons of extra virgin olive oil.

Funghi Farciti
STUFFED MUSHROOM CAPS

SERVES 4

4 large portobello mushrooms or 16 large white button mushrooms
1 recipe Vegetarian or Roasted Stuffing (see page 214 or 216)
1 cup Tomato Sauce (see page 225)
½ cup Chicken Stock (see page 228)
1 tablespoon chopped fresh Italian parsley
2 tablespoons freshly grated Parmigiano Reggiano cheese
2 tablespoons Italian Bread Crumbs (see page 218)

Preheat the oven to 500° F (260° C). Remove the mushroom stems and discard them. Fill the caps with the stuffing.

In a medium bowl, mix together the tomato sauce, chicken stock and parsley and pour into an 11 x 13-inch (28 x 33-cm) baking dish. Place the stuffed mushrooms in the pan. Sprinkle the tops of the mushrooms with the cheese and bread crumbs. Bake for 15 minutes, remove from the sauce and serve. (The sauce is used for cooking the mushrooms only; some will be absorbed during the cooking time.)

Note: If you don't have a pan large enough for the portobello mushrooms, line a cookie sheet with aluminum foil and build up edges with the foil to hold the sauce in.

COOK'S TIP

The wonderful, meaty taste of portobello mushrooms lends itself to many uses. For a fast, easy appetizer or side dish, marinate portobellos in Balsamic Vinaigrette (page 38) or your favorite vinaigrette for 15-30 minutes. Cook in a large sauté pan with 2 tablespoons of olive oil until well browned, about 2-3 minutes per side. Serve whole or cut into slices.

My mother and father always had a kind of playful competitiveness when it came to personal renditions of certain dishes and this recipe is a good example. My mother's stuffed mushrooms always came out of the oven baked until golden, simmering in a bed of fragrant brown juices with the same meaty aroma as a hearty beef roast on a winter night. So, with my brother and me as the well fed judges, we pronounced her the winner.

In a gesture of pure appreciation for her accomplishment, my father took my mother's hand and with an uncommon display of open affection, kissed her gently.

Every time I make this dish I remember my parents holding hands like two teenagers.

Carciofi Arrosti col Cavial di Bosco
ROASTED ARTICHOKE HEARTS WITH MUSHROOM CAVIAR

Our friend, Tino il Parigino, was one of those people who lived out their dreams every moment of their daily life. To make it even more interesting, Tino's dreams changed frequently and his physical appearance changed with the dream.

For instance, during Tino's infamous French Period, he wore a beret slashing dramatically across his hair, a moustache trimmed to a pencil-thin whip curling around his nostrils and an oversized camel-hair coat flowing over his shoulders like a cape. In particular devotion to authenticity, and despite the fact that he didn't smoke, he took to lighting up unfiltered French cigarettes, I think solely to show off his graceful gift of flicking a cigarette lighter.

This French-inspired dish reminds me of Tino il Parigino and I dedicate it to the dreamer in all of us.

SERVES 4

2 lemons
2 quarts (2 l) water
4 whole artichokes
2 cups Chicken Stock or Enhanced Chicken Stock (see page 228 or 229)
½ ounce (15 g) dried mushrooms, such as porcini or shiitake
¾ pound (350 g) mushrooms, preferably portobello or crimini, chopped
4 garlic cloves, chopped
2 tablespoons chopped fresh Italian parsley
2 tablespoons freshly grated Parmigiano Reggiano cheese
2 tablespoons vegetable oil
¼ teaspoon salt
¼ teaspoon black pepper
¼ cup dry Marsala wine
2 teaspoons cornstarch mixed with 2 tablespoons chicken stock (slurry)

Squeeze the juice of the lemons into a bowl with the water, saving the lemon skins to rub over your hands to keep them from being discolored.

To clean the artichokes, cut the stem off, even with the bottom of the artichoke. Pull off the tough outer leaves by bending them backwards until they break off. Continue breaking off leaves until you reach the soft inner leaves. Cut away the remaining leaves at the point where they begin to curve inward. Discard the leaves. With a sharp knife, cut away all the tough green skin from the bottoms of the artichokes so the white fleshy part underneath is exposed. Scrape the fuzzy choke from the center of the artichoke bottom with a teaspoon. What you now have looks like a very shallow bowl, perfect for stuffing. (The choke can also be scooped out with a teaspoon after the artichoke hearts have been cooked.) Immediately drop the artichoke heart into the bowl of lemon water to keep it from discoloring. Repeat this process with the remaining artichokes.

Bring the chicken stock to a boil in a medium saucepan. Cook the artichoke hearts in the boiling stock for 5 minutes. Remove and set aside, reserving the stock separately.

Soak the dried mushrooms in the reserved stock for 15 minutes. Drain, reserving the stock separately, and chop finely. Combine all the mushrooms with the garlic and parsley, mix well, and refrigerate for at least 15 minutes.

Preheat the oven to 400° F (200° C). Place the cooked artichoke hearts in an 8 x 8-inch (20 x 20-cm) baking dish with I cup of the reserved stock. Top each heart with 1½ teaspoons of the diced mushroom mixture and sprinkle the entire dish with I teaspoon of the cheese. Bake for 15 minutes.

Approximately 5 minutes before the artichokes are done, heat the oil in a large sauté pan set on high heat until sizzling, about 2 minutes. Add the remaining mushroom mixture and cook for 2 minutes without stirring. If the mushrooms don't fit the pan in a single layer, cook them in 2 batches. Stir in the salt and pepper, and transfer to a medium bowl. Pour the wine into the same sauté pan, stir to dislodge the brown bits from the bottom and bring to a boil. Reduce the heat to simmer.

To serve, spread a layer of the cooked mushroom mixture across each salad plate and put a cooked artichoke heart on top. Pour the cooking liquid from the baking dish into the simmering wine mixture in the sauté pan. Return to a boil and season to taste with salt and pepper. Remove the pan from the heat and stir in the cornstarch slurry. Return the pan to the heat and cook until just slightly thickened, about I minute. Pour the sauce over the stuffed artichoke hearts, sprinkle with the remaining cheese and bring proudly to your table.

"A friend may well be reckoned the masterpiece of nature."

RALPH WALDO EMERSON

Pasticcino Inglese
Savory Meat Pie

This dish is the result of what I now recall as a "lucky crash."

As a sophomore in high school, my favorite mode of transportation was a small secondhand motor scooter (a gift from my father after a full year of pleading). It wasn't much to look at, but it beat walking and I used it with glee to explore every nook and cranny of historic Palermo. Unfortunately, on one of these motorized adventures, a mesmerized moment spent dwelling upon one of the city's treasures (well, the pouty lips of a Sophia Lorenesque beauty) resulted in my going full speed into a street curb.

As I stood there holding my dented scooter in one hand and a ticket for reckless driving in the other, I noticed a steady flow of people going into an old but sumptuous town house and coming out with food.

Serves 8 to 12

1 ½ tablespoons olive oil

1 pound (450 g) pork or turkey Italian sausage, removed from the casing

⅛ teaspoon cumin

⅛ teaspoon dried thyme

⅛ teaspoon cinnamon

⅛ teaspoon nutmeg

⅛ teaspoon red pepper flakes

⅛ teaspoon salt

⅛ teaspoon black pepper

1 teaspoon sugar

¼ cup dry Marsala wine

1 cup Chicken Stock (see page 228)

2 tablespoons tomato paste

½ cup frozen peas, thawed

1 recipe Pie Dough (see pages 222-223), chilled

1 teaspoon sugar mixed with 1 egg yolk

Heat the olive oil in a large nonstick sauté pan set on medium heat. Add the crumbled sausage and cook until browned, about 3 minutes. While the sausage is cooking, use the back of a wooden spoon to break it into smaller pieces. Drain the fat from the pan and return to the heat. (To remove as much of the fat as possible from the meat, I like to pour it into a strainer and press with the back of a wooden spoon to squeeze the fat out.)

Stir in the cumin, thyme, cinnamon, nutmeg, red pepper flakes, salt, pepper and sugar, and cook over medium heat for 3 minutes. Raise the heat to high, pour in the wine and cook, stirring, for 3 minutes. Add the chicken stock and tomato paste, stir well and bring to a boil. Reduce the heat to low and simmer, partially covered, for 30 minutes, stirring occasionally.

If you're using pork sausage, stir in the peas, then transfer the mixture to a bowl. With the turkey sausage, which can sometimes be a little tougher, transfer the mixture to a food processor and pulse 15 times to lightly chop the meat. Transfer to a bowl and stir in the peas. Cover the bowl and refrigerate the filling until cold.

Preheat the oven to 400° F (200° C). Cut ⅔ of the dough from the chilled pastry dough. Return the smaller piece to the refrigerator. Reshape the piece of dough into a flat, round disk with your hands and lightly flour both sides. On a floured work surface, roll the dough into a circle large enough to fit an 8-inch (20-cm) wide, 1-inch (2.5-cm) deep fluted tart pan with a removable bottom. Drape the dough over the rolling pin and carefully unroll it over the pan. Trim the edges, leaving a 1-inch (2.5-cm) overhang. Fill with the chilled meat filling. (It is very important that both the filling and the dough are well chilled or the filling will melt the butter in the pastry and cause it to be soggy.) Roll out the remaining ⅓ of the dough into a round large enough to cover the filling, with a ½- to 1-inch (12-mm to 2.5-cm) overhang. Lay the dough across the filling. Fold the edges of the dough back over the top of the meat pie and gently roll the rolling pin across the top of the pie to seal the edges. Poke a few holes in the top of the crust with a fork.

Bake the pie for 30 minutes. Remove from the oven and brush with a thick coating of the sugar and egg mixture. Return to the oven for an additional 5-8 minutes, until the top is golden brown. Serve immediately or reheat the next day.

To reheat, take the pie from the refrigerator, cover with foil and bake at 375° F (190° C) for 25 minutes. Remove the foil and bake for another 5 minutes.

Cook's Tip

For a less elegant, more rustic method of assembling the pie, use a large baking sheet instead of a pie pan. Divide the dough in half. Roll half of it into a large circle (approximately ¼ inch or 6 mm thick) and place on the baking sheet. Spoon the filling over the center, leaving a 1½-inch (4-cm) border all around. Roll out the remaining dough into a slightly larger circle and place it over the filling. Seal the pie by pinching together the overlapping edges. Bake according to the original instructions.

Going over to investigate, I found myself in the waiting room of "Il Portocino," an exclusive catering establishment that had serviced Palermo's high society for over a century, but whose location was kept secret.

This recipe is my rendition of my favorite dish from the menu of Il Portocino.

Capesante con Spinaci

SCALLOPS WITH SPINACH

I was travelling in France with my wife when I first discovered this dish. We were driving between Paris and Normandy on narrow country lanes that skirted ivy-covered farmhouses and thick apple orchards. It felt as if time stood still as we watched the land sliding past, the crackling sound of an old Edith Piaf song whispering from the radio.

As the sun started to disappear over the hills, I pulled the car to the side of the road and held my wife's hand to watch the last furious flash of amber glow. Sometimes real life is better than a movie. Then that country lane magically carried us to a working farm that also doubled as an inn.

What follows is my version of the dish we enjoyed that evening. I hope you'll use it to crown one of your most inspiring days.

SERVES 4

5 tablespoons olive oil
4 garlic cloves, thickly sliced
¼ teaspoon red pepper flakes
1 pound (450 g) fresh spinach leaves, washed, drained and coarsely chopped
Juice of 1 lemon
¾ teaspoon salt
¼ teaspoon black pepper
12 large sea scallops (approximately ¾ pound) (350 g), cut in half
2 tablespoons chopped shallots
½ cup white wine
2 tablespoons chopped fresh Italian parsley

Heat 3 tablespoons of the olive oil and the garlic in a large sauté pan set on medium-high heat until it starts to sizzle and the garlic begins browning, about 4 minutes. Add the red pepper flakes, a handful of the spinach leaves and the lemon juice and cook, tossing, for 1 minute, until the spinach is just wilted. Continue adding and tossing the remaining spinach until wilted. This should take about 3-5 minutes. Season with ¼ teaspoon of the salt and ⅛ teaspoon of the pepper. Arrange the cooked spinach in the center of 4 small serving plates.

Wipe the pan clean and heat 1 tablespoon of the remaining olive oil over high heat until it starts to sizzle. Season the scallops with ¼ teaspoon of the remaining salt and the remaining pepper. When the pan is smoking, add the scallops and cook for 1 minute on each side. Remove the scallops from the pan and arrange around the spinach on each serving plate.

Put the pan back on high heat and add the remaining olive oil and the shallots and sauté for no more than 30 seconds. Add the white wine, parsley and the remaining salt. Cook over high heat until reduced by half, about 1½-2 minutes, until it has a syrupy consistency. Spoon over the scallops and spinach and serve.

Puré di Ceci al Limone

Lemony Garbanzo Spread

MAKES 1½ CUPS

1 (15-ounce) (425-g) can garbanzo beans, rinsed and drained

2 garlic cloves

1 green onion, cut into 1-inch (2.5-cm) pieces

2 tablespoons fresh lemon juice

1 tablespoon extra virgin olive oil

¼ teaspoon salt

⅛ teaspoon black pepper

2 tablespoons plain yogurt

This traditional Mediterranean garbanzo bean purée has added zest to centuries of bread eating and enjoyment. You may also enjoy it as a dip for crisp vegetables.

Process all the ingredients in a food processor or blender until smooth. Transfer to a serving bowl. The spread will keep for several days in the refrigerator.

This is great spread on Olive Bread (see page 20)!

COOK'S TIP

Spice up this basic spread by adding your favorite spice or herb. Cumin or curry add wonderful flavor. Add chopped fresh herbs for a great herbal spread.

Pane con le Olive
OLIVE BREAD

One of my favorite errands to run for my mother was going to "Il Panificio," a bread shop presided over by Don Onofrio. A diminutive man with large hands, he always wore a white tank top and an ankle-length apron over wide black pants with a light dusting of flour over his tan skin. La Signora, his wife, ran the cash register and served the continuous flow of customers. I always arrived early to get the best selection of freshly baked breads. Don Onofrio always called me the "Picciriddu" (Little Boy).

It wasn't until many years later, when I lived in America that Don Onofrio told me a few of his secrets. What follows is my version of a childhood favorite.

MAKES 2 LARGE LOAVES
5½ cups all-purpose flour
1 tablespoon sugar
1½ tablespoons active yeast
2½ cups warm water
2 cups semolina flour
2 teaspoons salt
8 ounces (225 g) pitted Greek or Sicilian black olives, roughly chopped

In a medium bowl, mix 1 cup of the all-purpose flour with the sugar and yeast. Stir in 1 cup of the warm water. Don't worry if there are a few lumps, just stir until reasonably smooth. Cover and let stand at room temperature for about 15 minutes, until doubled in size and bubbly.

In the bowl of a stand mixer, combine 3½ cups of the remaining all-purpose flour with the semolina flour and salt. Add the remaining water and the proofed yeast/flour mixture. Mix well at low speed using the paddle attachment for your mixer. Change to the dough hook and knead for 8 minutes. (If you are making the bread by hand, add the remaining water to the yeast/flour mixture and then stir in the dry ingredients. Turn out onto a floured surface and knead for 10-12 minutes. Continue with the directions as follows.) Place the dough in a lightly oiled bowl, cover tightly with plastic wrap and let rise until doubled, about 1-1½ hours, depending on the temperature.

Punch the dough down and turn it out onto a floured board. Flatten the dough into a large rectangular shape and spread the olives over it. Fold the dough in over the olives, sprinkle with ½-¾ cup of the remaining flour and knead for 5 minutes to distribute the olives evenly. (The extra flour is needed because of the moisture in the olives.) Cut the dough into 2 pieces and shape each half into round loaves. Dust a large cookie sheet with a little of the semolina flour and lay the loaves on top. Cover with a cloth and let the loaves rise to about 2½ times their size, about 45 minutes to 1 hour.

Preheat the oven to 375° F (190° C). Just before baking, score the top of each loaf in a tic-tac-toe pattern, using a sharp, thin-bladed knife or a razor blade. Place in the preheated oven and bake for 35-40 minutes, until the bottom sounds hollow when tapped. Cool completely on racks.

Cook's Tip

This recipe can be used to make wonderful bread sticks. Simply make a ½ recipe of Olive Bread. Knead the dough for 8-9 minutes, then cover and let rise for 45 minutes to 1 hour. Punch the dough down and knead for 2-3 minutes. Divide the dough into 48 pieces, roll out into rope shapes approximately 6 inches (15 cm) long and place on greased cookie sheets. Cover and let rise for 30 minutes. Bake in a preheated 400° F (200° C) oven for 13-15 minutes and they're ready to serve.

"The taste of an olive is older than meat, older than wine."

Laurence Durrell

Zuppe e Insalate

Soups & Salads

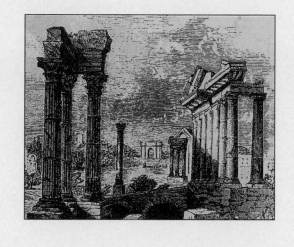

Brodo di Tacchino

TURKEY BROTH WITH PUMPKIN GNOCCHI

Thanksgiving at the Stellino household in California always brings my wife home with her arms full of shopping bags. Her eyes sparkle as she shows me the new decorations: little turkey salt and pepper shakers, paper-mâché pilgrims, a turkey made of straw and bags full of colorful autumn leaves.

As I sit surrounded by an ocean of tissue paper watching my wife string plastic pumpkins, turkeys, autumn leaves and pilgrims across the dining room, I thank my lucky star for bringing her into my life. This is my idea of Thanksgiving, a moment to stop and be thankful for things that make life worth living.

I hope this recipe helps you and your loved ones enjoy a fabulous holiday dinner — even if it isn't Thanksgiving!

SERVES 6 TO 8

1 turkey carcass
1 carrot, quartered
1 rib celery, quartered
1 white onion, peeled and quartered
1 teaspoon dried thyme
1 teaspoon dried sage
½ cup white wine
3 quarts (3 l) Chicken Stock (see page 228)
2 eggs beaten well, shells reserved
1 recipe Pumpkin Gnocchi (see page 86)

The day before serving, place all the ingredients, including the egg shells, in a large stock pot and bring to a boil. Reduce the heat and simmer, with the lid slightly ajar, for 1½ hours. Skim any foam that rises to the top every 30 minutes.

Remove the carcass and vegetables from the stock and discard. Strain the stock through a fine sieve lined with cheesecloth. Place in the refrigerator until the next day. All the fat will rise to the top, harden and become solid white. Skim it off and discard.

The day of serving, bring 1½-2 quarts (1½-2 l) of the stock to a boil. Carefully drop in the gnocchi, stirring gently with a spoon to prevent them from sticking to the bottom of the pan. After the gnocchi have risen to the top of the stock, cook them for 2 minutes longer and serve the soup immediately.

COOK'S TIP

If you are not going to use the turkey stock within 2-3 days of making it, cool it in the refrigerator and remove any fat that has risen to the top. Place in freezer containers or sealable plastic bags and freeze for up to 3 months.

Pasta in Brodo con la Cupola
PASTA SOUP TOPPED WITH PUFF PASTRY

SERVES 6

6 cups Chicken Stock (see page 228)
¾ cup finely diced carrots
¾ cup finely diced celery
4 garlic cloves, finely chopped
1 (9-ounce) (250-g) package refrigerated tortellini pasta
¾ cup frozen peas, thawed
2 tablespoons chopped fresh Italian parsley
½ teaspoon salt
¼ teaspoon black pepper
1 (17-ounce) (480-g) package puff pastry sheets, thawed
1 egg, lightly beaten

Top your favorite soup with this simple puff pastry crust and you'll always add a touch of elegance to delight your guests.

Pour the chicken stock, carrots, celery and garlic into a large saucepan and bring to a boil. Stir in the tortellini, peas and parsley. Reduce the heat, add the salt and pepper and simmer for 5 minutes.

Preheat the oven to 400° F (200° C). While the soup is simmering, roll out the puff pastry sheets to flatten the creases. Cut 6 circles to fit the circumference of the six ovenproof soup bowls. Pour the soup into the soup bowls and top with a round of puff pastry. Press the pastry around the edges of the bowl to make it stick and brush with the beaten egg. Put the bowls of soup on a baking sheet and place in the oven. Bake for 8-10 minutes, until the tops are puffed and golden brown. Serve immediately.

Minestra Impanata
Vegetable and Bread Soup

Serves 4

7 tablespoons olive oil

4 garlic cloves, thickly sliced

¼ teaspoon red pepper flakes

2 leeks, white part only, sliced

¼ cup red wine

½ teaspoon salt

¼ teaspoon black pepper

1 teaspoon chopped fresh rosemary

¼ beef bouillon cube or ½ teaspoon Worcestershire sauce

1 teaspoon sugar

4 cups Chicken Stock or Enhanced Chicken Stock (see page 228 or 229)

1 (28-ounce) (800-g) can peeled Italian tomatoes,
drained, chopped and juices reserved

3 tablespoons chopped fresh basil

½ pound mushrooms, quartered

1 cup frozen peas, thawed

1½ cups Italian seasoned croutons

4 tablespoons freshly grated Pecorino Romano cheese

During my sophomore year in high school, a classmate asked me to come to his country house and help do a bit of work. What can I say? I had been eyeing some really cool American-made suede basketball sneakers and needed extra funds. So, I signed up for what I thought would be a weekend of fun-filled field activities.

As soon as I saw the dilapidated villa, I feared I had made a grave miscalculation. We arose at 5:30 a.m. to go into the vineyard and picked grapes straight through the morning. I could barely walk to the stables where the table was set for lunch. It was quite a simple affair, fresh baked bread, this soup and a salad, washed down by strong local wine; but I swear to you, that soup tasted like paradise. It soared through my tired muscles and brought a smile to my very sullen face.

In a large saucepan set on medium-high heat, cook 3 tablespoons of the oil, the garlic, red pepper flakes and leeks for 3 minutes. Pour in the red wine and cook 3 more minutes. Stir in the salt, pepper, rosemary, the beef bouillon cube or Worcestershire sauce and the sugar and cook for 3 minutes. Pour in the chicken stock, tomatoes and reserved juices and bring to a boil. Reduce the heat and simmer, uncovered, for 15-20 minutes.

Remove 1 cup of the soup and purée it in a blender or food processor. Return it to the pot and add the basil, mushrooms and peas. Bring to a boil, reduce the heat and simmer, uncovered, for 15-20 minutes. Add the croutons, stirring well, and cook 3-5 minutes. The soup should look like a chunky porridge.

Ladle into bowls and garnish with the remaining olive oil, if you wish, and the cheese.

Minestra di Cipolle e Gorgonzola con Prosciutto

Onion Soup with Gorgonzola and Prosciutto

Serves 6

4 tablespoons olive oil
3 pounds (1.4 kg) onions, thinly sliced
6 garlic cloves, thickly sliced
1 tablespoon chopped fresh thyme
1 tablespoon chopped fresh Italian parsley
1 tablespoon chopped fresh basil
1 tablespoon chopped fresh sage
¼ teaspoon red pepper flakes
1½ cups diced prosciutto, loosely packed
1 tablespoon flour
1 cup dry Marsala wine
1½ cups crumbled Gorgonzola cheese
5 cups Chicken Stock (see page 228)
½ teaspoon salt
¼ teaspoon black pepper
1 cup croutons

Heat the olive oil in a large stock pot or Dutch oven set on medium-high heat until sizzling, about 2 minutes. Add the onions, garlic, thyme, parsley, basil, sage, red pepper flakes and ½ of the prosciutto. Cook for 12 minutes, until the juices released by the onions have almost cooked away and they are beginning to brown. Stir in the flour and cook for 5 minutes to continue browning the onions. Pour in the Marsala and ½ of the Gorgonzola and cook for 2 minutes. Add the stock, salt and pepper and bring to a boil. Reduce the heat and simmer, uncovered, for 30 minutes.

To serve, spoon the soup into bowls and top with the remaining prosciutto, Gorgonzola and croutons.

Trentino Alto Adige is the northernmost region in Italy, bordering with Austria. Its people often speak better German than Italian!

On a trip with my wife, we spent an evening in a small village (the population was less than 200) just 15 miles from the Austrian border. The dinner in our small "pensione" (hotel) was shared around a large table with the few other guests and the proprietor's family. I can honestly say that I barely understood a word of my host's Germanic Italian. But by mixing some sign language, English, Italian and German, we managed to have a fun evening together.

Despite the language barrier, we all agreed that the following recipe, our main course for the evening, was absolutely delicious: proof that the appreciation of good food is not restricted by linguistic boundaries.

Zuppa di Patate e Aglio

POTATO AND GARLIC SOUP

I guarantee that the next recipe will prove that old Italian proverb, "il mangiar povero e il piu gustoso" (humble food is always the tastiest).

Maybe it's just the Italian in me, but how can you go wrong with potatoes and garlic? Nanci and I enjoy sharing this soup on chilly winter nights with a nice green salad and a glass of robust red wine. And I will tell you that we even give a bowl to our cat, Felix, who we have nicknamed Filippo, since he looks so Italian. (Sometimes I think he meows with an accent.) Yes, and he enjoys it very much.

Call me crazy, but as I look at Nanci smiling through the candlelight, and Filippo purring contentedly, I think I'm the luckiest man in the world.

Try this dish soon. I believe that of all your culinary experiments, it will be one of the simplest and most satisfying.

SERVES 6

4 tablespoons olive oil

2 heads garlic, separated into cloves and peeled (approximately 20 cloves)

1 onion, halved lengthwise and thinly sliced

¼ teaspoon red pepper flakes

1 tablespoon chopped fresh thyme

1 tablespoon chopped fresh rosemary

1 tablespoon chopped fresh sage

½ teaspoon salt

½ teaspoon black pepper

2 pounds (900 g) thin-skinned white potatoes,
peeled and cut into ½-inch (1.5-cm) dice

6½ cups Chicken Stock (see page 228)

¼ cup chopped fresh Italian parsley

Heat the oil in a small stockpot or Dutch oven set on medium-high heat, until sizzling, about 2 minutes. Add the whole garlic cloves and sauté until well browned, about 1½ minutes. Reduce the heat to medium and add the onion, red pepper flakes, thyme, rosemary, sage, salt and pepper. Cook for 10 minutes, until the onion is soft. Stir in the potatoes and chicken stock and bring to a boil. Reduce the heat to low and simmer for 45 minutes with the lid slightly ajar, until the potatoes are falling apart.

Scoop the soup into a food processor or blender and process in several batches, until the consistency of cream. Return the soup to the Dutch oven and just heat through.

Ladle the soup into individual bowls and garnish with the chopped parsley.

COOK'S TIP

This soup can also be made with Roasted Garlic (see page 224). Simply roast 2 heads of garlic. Add the peeled, roasted garlic cloves to the onions after they've cooked for 10 minutes and then proceed with the rest of the recipe.

Zuppa di Zucca con le Salsiccie

PUMPKIN SOUP WITH SAUSAGES

SERVES 4

2 tablespoons olive oil

1 pound (450 g) sweet Italian sausages, cut into ½-inch (1.5-cm) pieces

4 garlic cloves, thickly sliced

1 red onion, chopped

8 ounces (225 g) button mushrooms, quartered

2 tablespoons chopped fresh sage

½ cup finely diced celery

½ teaspoon dried thyme

½ cup dry Marsala wine

4 cups Chicken Stock (see page 228)

2 cups canned pumpkin

¾ teaspoon salt

¼ teaspoon black pepper

1 cup uncooked small shell pasta or broken spaghetti or fettuccine

4 tablespoons freshly grated
Parmigiano Reggiano cheese (optional)

Heat the oil in a large nonstick sauté pan set on high heat. Add the sausage and brown for 3 minutes. Using a slotted spoon, remove the sausage to a 3-quart saucepan and set aside. Add the garlic, onion, mushrooms, sage, celery and thyme to the same sauté pan and cook on medium-high heat for 3-5 minutes, stirring occasionally. Stir in the Marsala wine and cook 2 more minutes.

Pour the contents of the sauté pan into the saucepan with the cooked sausage. Add the chicken stock, pumpkin, salt and pepper and bring to a boil over medium heat, stirring often. Reduce the heat to a simmer and cook for 40 minutes, stirring every 10 minutes.

Add the pasta, increase the heat to a soft boil and cook, stirring often to make sure the pasta is not sticking to the bottom of the pan, for 5 more minutes. Reduce the heat to a simmer and cook 3 minutes longer. This recipe will produce a very thick soup. If you prefer it thinner, just add more stock.

Serve in deep pasta bowls garnished with the grated cheese, if you wish.

My cousins and I always visited my grandmother, Nonna Adele, in the summer. The dining table was the center of social interaction, with my aunts and uncles begging Nonna shamelessly for their favorite childhood dishes — like our present, past and future all meeting before our eyes.

Nonna Adele contributed to the blurring of time, by telling stories of our parents' past. We'd gather around her huge wooden table and our moms and dads were transformed into family legends.

I'm sure this isn't the only reason Nonna's food was magical, but undeniably, those times left an unbreakable bond of kinship. I only hope that a taste of this beautiful dish from my Nonna's repertoire will unleash magic inside of you and bring you and your dear ones close together.

Zuppa di Carote

Carrot Soup

I first tried this soup in a French restaurant discovered while traveling through the Black Forest region of Germany, go figure!

The chef/owner, Herbert, had trained in Paris to start his German restaurant, and also had a little house on the Italian coast where he and his wife spent summer vacations. As he shared his passions about food, his eyes flashed like warm sunlight sneaking through the cloudy sky. Then he grabbed a couple of bottles of wine, sat down at our table and literally showered Nanci and me with stories and anecdotes.

As I reflect on that night, I marvel how passion and friendship are pure emotions unchecked by political boundaries. This soup reminds me how the simplicity of good food can break barriers between strangers.

Serves 6

4 tablespoons olive oil
1 onion, chopped
4 garlic cloves, thickly sliced
2 pounds (900 g) carrots, peeled and cut into ½-inch (1.5-cm) slices
2 tablespoons chopped fresh thyme
¼ teaspoon red pepper flakes
6 cups Chicken Stock (see page 228)
½ teaspoon salt
¼ teaspoon black pepper
1 teaspoon ground cumin
½ teaspoon nutmeg
6 tablespoons drained plain yogurt (see Cook's Tip)
6 tablespoons chopped fresh chives

Heat the olive oil in a medium stockpot or Dutch oven set on medium-high heat until sizzling, about 2 minutes. Add the onion, garlic, carrots, thyme and red pepper flakes and cook for 5 minutes, stirring occasionally, until the onion becomes translucent and the carrots begin to release their juices. Stir in the chicken stock, salt and pepper and bring to a boil. Reduce the heat and simmer for 30 minutes, with the lid ajar.

Spoon the soup into a food processor or blender and purée in several batches. Return to the same pot, stir in the cumin and nutmeg and heat through.

To serve, ladle the hot soup into bowls and top with a dollop of the strained yogurt and a tablespoon of the chopped chives.

Cook's Tip

Draining yogurt removes the whey, giving it a thicker consistency, which works well for cooking. To drain, simply place lightly salted, plain yogurt (be sure it has no gelatin added) in a cheesecloth-lined strainer set over a bowl. Let it drain for several to 24 hours. The longer it drains, the thicker it will become. After several hours it will be the thickness of sour cream.

Zuppa di Broccoli Patate e Aglio

BROCCOLI, POTATO AND GARLIC SOUP

SERVES 6

4 tablespoons olive oil

15 garlic cloves, peeled

½ pound (225 g) Russet potatoes, peeled and quartered

1½ pounds (750 g) broccoli, cut into pieces, stems included

¼ teaspoon red pepper flakes

6½ cups Chicken Stock (see page 228)

4 tablespoons freshly grated Pecorino Romano cheese

Heat the oil in a large pot set on high heat until sizzling, about 2 minutes. Add the garlic cloves and cook for 2-3 minutes, until the garlic begins to brown. Add the potatoes, broccoli and red pepper flakes and continue to cook, stirring, for 2-3 minutes. Pour in the chicken stock and bring to a boil. Reduce the heat to low and simmer, with the lid ajar, for 45-50 minutes.

Purée the soup in a blender or food processor. Return to the pot just to heat through. The soup can be eaten now or reheated the next day.

To serve, ladle into large bowls and top with the cheese.

COOK'S TIP

When you cut up the broccoli, discard the bottom ½ inch (1.5 cm) of the stem. They tend to be dried out and too fibrous.

Instead of using grated cheese to top the soup, use a vegetable peeler to shave off thin slices of cheese and sprinkle on top of the soup.

One day, my friend, Fabrizio, and I took a long car ride to the coastal town of Sciacca, where his family had some country property. While Fabrizio took a tour of the fields with their estate manager, I took a nap inside their 200-year-old baroque villa.

Once Fabrizio's work was done, we hopped back in the car to ride home. Suddenly, the car ground to a halt — completely out of gas, about two miles from Fabrizio's home!

It's funny but looking back on that day, my main impression is not of grumbling about the car, but of the enchanting walk home, savoring a breeze that carried the perfume of warm grass and meadow flowers.

When we arrived at the villa, I volunteered to cook and, using whatever was available, created this great soup. Savoring the fine wine that Fabrizio dug up from the cellar, I was almost happy the car had run out of gas.

Insalata a Sorpresa
Apple, Green Bean and Bell Pepper Salad

"*Che confusione!*" (*What a mix-up of ingredients!*) That's what my mother said when I first described this recipe to her. However, you should have seen the beautiful expression of happiness that beamed from her face with each bite she took.

You know, even though I'm in my late thirties now, I still often feel like "Nicolino" (Little Nick) around my mother. Maybe that's why every little, apparently insignificant, compliment she gives me, fills my heart with beaming pride. I guess I'll always be my mother's little boy...and proud of it!

Serves 6

¾ cup toasted walnut pieces
4 tablespoons honey
Pinch + ¼ teaspoon salt
¼ cup apple cider vinegar
⅓ cup vegetable oil or light olive oil
⅛ teaspoon black pepper
1 red bell pepper, cut into matchsticks
4 ounces (115 g) thin green beans, ends trimmed
or regular green beans, ends trimmed and cut in half lengthwise,
parboiled for 3 minutes
2 apples, unpeeled, cut into matchsticks
2 heads Belgian endive, cut into matchsticks

Preheat the oven to 400° F (200° C). In a small bowl, mix together the walnuts, 2 tablespoons of the honey and the pinch of salt. Spread the walnuts on a greased baking sheet and cook for 5 minutes in the preheated oven. Remove and set aside.

In a food processor or blender, combine the vinegar, oil, the remaining honey, the remaining salt and the pepper. Process until the mixture is creamy and well blended.

In a large bowl, toss the bell pepper, green beans, apples and Belgian endive with the dressing. Sprinkle each serving with the honey-roasted walnuts.

Cook's Tip
The honey roasted walnuts are wonderful as a snack on their own. Make extra to have on hand for garnishing tossed salads, soups or even desserts.

Insalata di Pomodori e Cipolle

TOMATO AND ONION SALAD

SERVES 4

2 tablespoons balsamic vinegar

½ teaspoon anchovy paste

3 tablespoons olive oil

1 pound (450 g) Roma tomatoes, cut into 1½- to 2-inch (4- to 5-cm) dice

½ large red onion, thinly sliced, soaked in 1 cup ice water

and 2 tablespoons white wine vinegar for 30 minutes and patted dry

¼ teaspoon salt

¼ teaspoon black pepper

¾ cup Italian seasoned croutons

2 tablespoons chopped fresh basil

½ cup crumbled feta cheese

In a large bowl, combine the vinegar and anchovy paste. Slowly whisk in the oil until completely mixed. Add the tomatoes, onions, salt and pepper and stir until well coated. Mix in the croutons, basil and feta cheese. Let rest for 10 minutes.

Just before serving, re-toss the salad and place in individual serving bowls.

COOK'S TIP

Marinating the onions for 30 minutes softens their taste and texture. If you enjoy the taste of onions in their natural state or are using sweet onions such as Walla Wallas or Vidalias, omit this step.

The summer of 1975 was my last season in Sicily before coming to America on a student exchange. A group of friends got together at Franco's country house, a rustic two bedroom building perched atop the hills overlooking the city of Cefalú.

We had gone fishing early that morning and got back to the house about 11 o'clock to prepare our lunch. We gathered around the table on a shaded terrace with a view over the ocean and town far below. The menu that day was this Tomato and Onion Salad with grilled fish from the morning's catch.

As we sat eating and laughing, I realized America was far away and I would probably not be back for a long time. With the weight of time pressing heavily, I don't think I could have asked for a more pleasing picture to save in my memory.

Insalata Caprese
Fresh Mozzarella, Tomato and Basil Salad

So many people have asked me for this recipe, that I felt compelled to include it in this book.

First I must warn you, if the mozzarella cheese, tomatoes and basil are not fresh, you will not experience the essence of this salad's success. I know that I always encourage you in my television show to improvise and use canned goods that are readily available, but this dish is an exception. I also must urge you to use the best grade of extra virgin olive oil.

I apologize for my madness in insisting on these details. But I know you'll forgive me once you have taken your first bite, which will seduce you into taking another, and another...and you'll understand why, when it comes to this dish, fresh is best!

Serves 4

10 ounces (300 g) water-packed fresh mozzarella cheese
4 large Roma tomatoes
¾ teaspoon salt
¼ teaspoon black pepper
8 medium leaves fresh basil
3 tablespoons extra virgin olive oil

Cut the cheese and tomatoes into ¼-inch (6-mm) slices. The slices of cheese should be approximately the same size as the tomato slices. (When you buy the mozzarella, look for balls that are about the same size as the tomatoes.) Sprinkle the tomatoes with ½ teaspoon of the salt and ⅛ teaspoon of the pepper.

Lay the basil leaves one on top of the other and roll them up tightly. Cut across the roll in thin slices — don't cut them too thin.

Fan ¼ of the tomato and cheese slices on each serving dish, alternating the cheese and tomato. Drizzle with the olive oil and sprinkle with the remaining salt and pepper. Top with the sliced basil.

Cook's Tip

Instead of cutting the basil into thin strips, put whole leaves of basil between the tomato and cheese slices — you'll love it!

Insalata d'Asparagi

Asparagus Salad with Honey Mustard Dressing

Serves 4

SALAD:

20-32 spears fresh asparagus
(5 per person if the spears are large, 8 if they are skinny)
2 ounces (60 g) "lox" style salmon, cut into thin strips
1 hard boiled egg, finely grated or chopped
2 tablespoons drained capers
½ small red bell pepper, cut into ¼-inch (6-mm) dice

HONEY MUSTARD DRESSING:

¼ cup low-fat mayonnaise
2 tablespoons honey mustard
1 tablespoon lemon juice
¼ cup extra virgin olive oil
1 tablespoon chopped fresh Italian parsley

FOR THE SALAD

Cook the asparagus in boiling water until just tender. Remove the spears and immediately run under cold water to stop the cooking process. Pat dry and set aside.

FOR THE DRESSING

Combine the mayonnaise, mustard, lemon juice and olive oil in a food processor, blending well. Stir in the parsley.

To assemble the salad, arrange the cooked asparagus spears on serving plates. Sprinkle the lox, egg and capers over the top. Drizzle with the dressing and sprinkle with the red pepper. Serve immediately.

COOK'S TIP

Toss the Honey Mustard Dressing with 1 pound diced, cooked potatoes, the asparagus cut into bite-size pieces and the remaining salad ingredients for a salad that's out-of-this-world.

Every time I make this recipe I can still see the trembling hands of a young waiter, assembling it under the stern supervision of a stone-faced maître d'hôtel.

Nanci and I were the only guests at a very formal restaurant in the French Alsatian countryside. As the young waiter trembled, I remembered the way I felt every time I prepared one of my father's recipes for the first time and presented it for his approval.

Well, I'm happy to report that the end result brought a beaming smile from the stern maître d'hôtel, and an urgent request from me for the recipe.

Condimenti per Insalate
ASSORTED VINAIGRETTES TOSSED WITH MIXED GREENS

Simple green salads with a flavorful vinaigrette are a wonderful addition to a meal of pasta and bread. Here are three of my favorite dressings. Toss them with mixed baby salad greens and enjoy!

Insalatina Verde
GREEN SALAD WITH BALSAMIC VINAIGRETTE

SERVES 4

1 tablespoon balsamic vinegar
⅛ teaspoon salt
⅛ teaspoon black pepper
3 tablespoons extra virgin olive oil
4-5 ounces (115-150 g) mixed baby salad greens

Combine the vinegar, salt and pepper in a medium bowl. Whisk in the olive oil. Place the salad greens in a bowl large enough for tossing and pour the vinaigrette over them. Toss until well coated.

COOK'S TIP
Feel free to experiment with various fresh herbs in this dressing for an exciting change in flavor. Use herbs such as oregano, basil, thyme or sage.

Insalata Condita con Miele e Succo D'Arancia
MIXED SALAD WITH HONEY ORANGE VINAIGRETTE

SERVES 4

¼ cup freshly squeezed orange juice
2 tablespoons white wine vinegar
2 tablespoons olive oil
1 tablespoon grated orange zest
2 teaspoons honey
¼ teaspoon cumin
¼ teaspoon black pepper
4-5 ounces (115-150 g) mixed baby salad greens

Whisk together the orange juice, vinegar, oil, orange zest, honey, cumin and pepper. Place the greens in a large bowl and toss with the vinaigrette. Serve immediately.

Insalata Condita con Pepe Verde e Miele

MIXED GREEN SALAD WITH GREEN PEPPERCORN HONEY VINAIGRETTE

SERVES 4

2 teaspoons green peppercorns
⅛ teaspoon salt
½ teaspoon black pepper
1 tablespoon white wine vinegar
2 teaspoons lemon juice
½ tablespoon honey
½ teaspoon Dijon mustard
3 tablespoons extra virgin olive oil
4-5 ounces (115-150 g) mixed baby salad greens

Put the green peppercorns, salt and pepper in the bowl of a food processor or blender and pulse to coarsely chop the peppercorns. Add the white wine vinegar, lemon juice, honey and mustard and process until well blended. With the machine running, slowly pour in the oil and process until the vinaigrette is creamy.

Place the greens in a large bowl, pour over the vinaigrette and toss until well coated.

COOK'S TIP

This dressing is marvelous poured over hot cooked vegetables such as green beans, broccoli, artichokes or whatever you like. Let the vegetables marinate in the dressing for 15-30 minutes and serve at room temperature.

*"Cooking is like love —
it should be entered into
with abandon
or not at all."*

SYDNEY SMITH

Insalata d'Arance e Cipolle e Finocchi

Mixed Salad with Oranges, Onion and Fennel

It was an hour's drive to the little town of Bagheria from our home in Palermo, where we bought oranges from Carmelo and his wife, Guiseppina. To this date, I must tell you that I've never had an orange as sweet and juicy! This is my personal adaptation of Guiseppina's Orange Salad.

Serves 4

¼ teaspoon salt
⅛ teaspoon black pepper
¼ cup freshly squeezed orange juice
¼ cup olive oil
1 tablespoon balsamic vinegar
4 ounces (115 g) mixed baby salad greens
(include some of the bitter greens, such as arugula or endive)
½ red onion, peeled, halved and thinly sliced, soaked in 1 cup ice water
and 2 tablespoons white wine vinegar for 30 minutes, drained and patted dry
1 large fennel bulb (about 8-10 ounces) (225-300 g), large outer leaves
removed and discarded, cut in half and thinly sliced lengthwise
4 large oranges, peeled, sliced into ¼-inch (6-mm) thick rounds
and rounds cut in half
16 large shaved strips Parmigiano Reggiano cheese or 4 tablespoons freshly grated

In a large salad bowl, whisk the salt, pepper, orange juice, olive oil and balsamic vinegar until completely mixed. Add the salad greens to the bowl and toss until well coated. Gently mix in the onion, fennel and oranges.

Spoon into serving bowls and top each one with 4 shavings of the cheese or 1 tablespoon of grated cheese.

Cook's Tip

I think shaving the cheese in this salad gives you more tang and presence. An easy way to go about it is using a vegetable peeler. Just start at the top of the piece of cheese and move down with a quick but firm motion.

Insalata Du Zú Tano

Uncle Gaetano's Caesar Salad

Serves 4

2 anchovy fillets

3 whole garlic cloves, peeled

3 tablespoons low-fat mayonnaise

2 tablespoons white wine vinegar

⅛ teaspoon salt

⅛ teaspoon black pepper

2 tablespoons olive oil

2 hearts of romaine lettuce (a head of romaine with the
two outer layers removed), cut crosswise into 2-inch pieces

2 Roma tomatoes, seeded and diced

2 tablespoons freshly grated Pecorino Romano cheese

Process the anchovy fillets, garlic, mayonnaise, vinegar, salt and pepper in a food processor to a smooth consistency. Add the oil slowly, to form a dressing which will be slightly thickened and creamy.

In a large bowl, toss the romaine leaves with the dressing until well coated. Divide the leaves on four serving dishes and top with the diced tomatoes and grated cheese.

"Zú Tano" was a small eating establishment in the heart of Palermo's historic district. The host, Uncle Gaetano, was bald, short and quite round, his vast pants hugging him right below a huge pot belly. Nevertheless, he moved from table to table with the grace and agility of a ballerina, charming his patrons with a quick wit and inspired rendition of the Sicilian dialect, as beautiful as if it was his mother tongue.

Because I pestered him with so many questions about his food, Zú Tano predicted that I'd be a chef one day. Let me share with you the first recipe he taught me, my favorite salad.

Insalata Condita con Pancetta e Gorgonzola

Romaine Salad with Pancetta and Gorgonzola Dressing

I discovered this irresistible combination while traveling in Switzerland at a little restaurant near Lucerne.

The proprietor, Marie Beignet, a French citizen, said she first tasted it while dining in Belgium at an Italian restaurant. Here she met her future husband, Jean-Louis. He said he learned this recipe while visiting Italy, in a little town near Palermo, where I grew up!

I wonder what great cosmic design made me travel so far in order to discover a recipe which came from a restaurant next door to my birthplace!

Anyway, these thoughts always make me chuckle as I savor each bite of this delicious salad. The truth of why I stumble onto great recipes is beyond the mysterious intricacies of culinary destiny. Simply put, I'm a lucky man and I love to share my culinary findings with all my readers.

Serves 4

Pancetta and Gorgonzola Dressing:
2 tablespoons olive oil
2 garlic cloves, thickly sliced
½ cup chopped onion
½ cup diced pancetta or bacon
⅔ cup crumbled Gorgonzola cheese
¼ teaspoon black pepper
4 tablespoons sherry vinegar or red wine vinegar

Salad:
2 hearts of romaine lettuce, cut into 2-inch (5-cm) pieces
1 cup croutons

For the Dressing

Heat the oil in a medium sauté pan set on medium-high heat until sizzling, about 2 minutes. Add the garlic, onion and pancetta and cook until the pancetta is crispy-brown, about 7 minutes. Transfer to a food processor or blender and process until coarsely chopped. Add ⅓ cup of the cheese, the pepper and vinegar and process until smooth.

For the Salad

Put the romaine into a large salad bowl, pour the dressing over and mix well. Add the croutons and toss again.

To serve, place on salad plates and sprinkle with the remaining cheese.

Cook's Tip

For a more formal presentation, leave the romaine leaves whole and toss with the dressing. Serve on larger plates.

Insalata Mista

Mixed Salad with Italian Cheese Dressing

Serves 4
Italian Cheese Dressing:

2 ounces (60 g) freshly grated Parmigiano Reggiano cheese
2 ounces (60 g) freshly grated Pecorino Romano cheese
2 garlic cloves, thickly sliced
2 teaspoons chopped fresh Italian parsley
¼ teaspoon salt
¼ teaspoon black pepper
2 tablespoons freshly squeezed lemon juice
2 tablespoons white wine vinegar
2 tablespoons water
1½ teaspoons honey

Salad:

½ onion, thinly sliced and soaked in 1 cup cold water
and 2 tablespoons white wine vinegar for 20 minutes, drained and patted dry
6 romaine lettuce leaves, torn into small pieces
4-5 ounces (115-150 g) mixed baby salad greens
5 radishes, thinly sliced
½ cucumber, halved, seeded and thinly sliced
4 ounces (115 g) sugar snap peas, ends trimmed

For the Dressing

Put the cheeses, garlic, parsley, salt and pepper into a food processor or blender and process for 10 seconds. Add the lemon juice, vinegar, water and honey and process until the mixture is creamy, about 30 seconds.

For the Salad

Put the onion, romaine, mixed greens, radishes, cucumber and sugar snap peas in a large bowl and toss with the dressing until the greens are well coated. Serve immediately.

As fate would have it, the very good carpenter who built my bathroom, Dave Hyeronimus, is also a very good chef. It was Dave who gave me this recipe: a deceptively simple salad that is the perfect addition to a satisfying meal.

So the next time you're looking for a finely crafted piece of furniture, call Dave, and if you're really lucky — I mean really lucky — maybe he'll even cook for you!

Insalata di Pollo

WARM CHICKEN SALAD

Sundays were my father's and my opportunity to spend quality time together and indulge in our favorite activities: wandering around the Sicilian countryside and eating. One time, we ventured into the mountain range between Palermo and Trapani. My father had spent a great deal of his youth in this area, tending a small herd of sheep.

The foundation for this recipe was the result of an inventive young Vincenzo, who was simply trying to improvise with the few supplies left him in the small wooden shack where he tended his sheep. I added the chicken in later versions.

So, what started out of the necessity of the moment, became in my father's hands, a small culinary masterpiece.

SERVES 4

1 pound (450 g) boneless, skinless chicken breasts,
cut into ½-inch (1.5-cm) cubes
½ teaspoon salt
¼ teaspoon black pepper
⅓ cup balsamic vinegar
2 tablespoons coarsely ground mustard
1 tablespoon sugar
4 tablespoons olive oil
4 cloves garlic, finely chopped
1 tablespoon chopped fresh thyme
6 ounces (175 g) of arugula or spinach, washed
1 cup grapes, preferably red, washed and cut in half
½ cup crumbled feta cheese or goat cheese

Sprinkle the chicken pieces with the salt and pepper. Mix the balsamic vinegar, mustard and sugar together. Set aside.

Heat the olive oil in a large sauté pan set on high heat until it starts to sizzle, about 2 minutes. Cook the prepared chicken until it starts to brown, about 1 minute. Add the garlic and thyme and cook 1 minute. Pour in the vinegar mixture and cook until thick and glossy, about 1 more minute.

Arrange the greens on a platter or individual serving plates. Top with the chicken and the warm sauce. Sprinkle with the grapes and the cheese and serve.

Insalata di Capesante
Scallop Salad with Orange Vinaigrette

Serves 4
Scallop Salad:
½ onion, thinly sliced and soaked in 1 cup cold water
and 2 tablespoons white wine vinegar for 20 minutes, drained and patted dry
4-5 ounces (115-150 g) mixed baby salad greens
4 tablespoons extra virgin olive oil
1 tablespoon olive oil
12 large sea scallops (approximately ¾ pound) (350 g), cut in half horizontally
¼ teaspoon salt
⅛ teaspoon black pepper

Orange Vinaigrette:
1 tablespoon honey
1 tablespoon Dijon mustard
½ cup fresh orange juice
2 tablespoons white wine vinegar
¼ teaspoon salt
¼ teaspoon black pepper

For the Salad

Put the onions, salad greens and the 4 tablespoons of extra virgin olive oil into a large bowl and toss well. Arrange the greens on 4 small serving plates.

For the Vinaigrette

Whisk together the honey, mustard, orange juice, vinegar, salt and pepper. Set aside.

To finish the salad, pour the olive oil into a large sauté pan set on high heat. Season the scallops with the salt and pepper. When the pan is almost smoking, add the seasoned scallops and cook for 1 minute on each side. Remove the scallops from the pan and arrange around the greens on each serving plate. Pour the vinaigrette into the pan, stir to scrape up any pan residues and cook for 1-2 minutes, until reduced to a syrup-like consistency. Spoon the vinaigrette over the scallops and greens and serve.

I get really exasperated when my restaurant waiter is someone with a turned-up nose who endures taking my food order like it was poison. But it's even worse when the food they bring turns out to be the best thing I've ever had, and I suddenly realize that the only way I can get the beautiful recipe is to ask the same haughty waiter.

That's exactly how this recipe came about. I was faced with a French waiter who pointed out with cutting precision all the many small ways in which I managed to butcher the French pronunciation of each dish I ordered.

Well, revenge is sweet. I resolved to figure out the recipe myself without asking that waiter. The restaurant eventually went out of business. And may I just add that my dish is better than the original.

Insalata di Tonno
Tuna Salad with Caper Vinaigrette

It was quite common for my brother, Mario, and me to show up at the dinner table with one or two uninvited guests. But Mother almost seemed to have a sixth sense to warn her when this was going to happen, because she always seemed prepared.

I thought I had her the day I brought home half of my basketball team unannounced. She graciously welcomed all of them then retreated to the kitchen, where she attacked the cupboards like a tornado. For a moment I thought that this time she would concede defeat and take us out for pizza. But suddenly, she opened the last cupboard and turned around holding two large cans of tuna. With a gleam in her eyes, she whipped up the recipe before you. Next time you don't know what to make for dinner, before you give up and go for "takeout," try this quick salad. You'll be happy you did!

Serves 4
Caper Vinaigrette:
1 tablespoon drained capers, finely chopped
1 tablespoon finely chopped fresh oregano
2 tablespoons freshly squeezed lemon juice
2 tablespoons white wine vinegar
1 teaspoon sugar
¼ teaspoon salt
½ teaspoon black pepper
¼ cup olive oil
Dash cayenne pepper

Salad:
1 pound (450 g) green beans, ends trimmed, cut in half
2 large (approximately 1½ pounds) (750 g) potatoes, cooked, cut into ½-inch (12-mm) dice
1 (12-ounce) (350-g) can water-packed white tuna, drained and flaked
½ red onion, thinly sliced, soaked in 1 cup ice water and 2 tablespoons white wine vinegar for 30 minutes, drained and patted dry
5 ounces (150 g) mixed baby salad greens
2 ounces (½ cup) (60 g) chopped oil-packed sun-dried tomatoes
½ cup toasted pine nuts

For the Vinaigrette
Whisk together the capers, oregano, lemon juice, vinegar, sugar, salt, pepper, oil and cayenne in a large bowl. Set aside until ready to use.

For the Salad
Cook the green beans in a pot of boiling water for 3 minutes. Drain the beans, pat dry and place in the bowl with the dressing, stirring gently. Cover the bowl and put the beans in the refrigerator to cool.

When the beans are cooled, gently stir in the potatoes, tuna, onion, salad greens, sun-dried tomatoes and pine nuts.

Insalata di Bistecca

Steak Salad

Serves 4

2 garlic cloves, chopped

2 tablespoons chopped oil-packed sun-dried tomatoes

2 tablespoons chopped shallots

1 tablespoon chopped fresh Italian parsley

1 tablespoon chopped fresh basil

1 tablespoon chopped fresh thyme

¾ cup dry red wine

⅓ cup balsamic vinegar

¾ teaspoon salt

¼ teaspoon black pepper

1 (1- to 1¼-pound) (450- to 575-g) flank steak

¼ cup olive oil

6 ounces (175 g) mixed baby salad greens

2 diced Roma tomatoes

The day before serving, combine the garlic, sun-dried tomatoes, shallots, parsley, basil, thyme, red wine, balsamic vinegar, salt and pepper in a large bowl. Lay the flank steak on a cutting board, poke holes in both sides with a fork, place in the bowl and turn to coat with the marinade. Cover and refrigerate overnight, turning the steak once.

The day of serving, remove the steak from the marinade, scraping off the excess bits of herbs and pour the leftover marinade into a medium saucepan. Place the steak on a broiler pan and let it sit at room temperature for 20 minutes. Cook the steak under the broiler for 4-5 minutes per side for medium-rare steak. Let it rest for 10 minutes, then cut into thin slices.

While the steak is resting, boil the reserved marinade over high heat for 5 minutes. Remove from the heat and pour into a blender. Add the olive oil and process for about 2 minutes. Place the salad greens and diced tomatoes in a large bowl and toss with ⅓ of the dressing. Toss the meat with as much of the remaining dressing as needed to coat it well. To serve, place the greens on a large platter and put the meat on top. Spoon any remaining dressing around the meat slices.

This recipe holds a soft spot in my heart. It represents the first time I cooked for someone without any family assistance.

The lucky person that ate this dish was my brother, Mario. I believe that even in my early teens, this salad proved that I had signs of culinary greatness. But Mario is much more tempered in his recollection of the event. He maintains that after a day at the beach, he was so hungry that he would have gulped down stale bread.

Well, may I just state for the record, that today when I serve this dish to Mario, he always asks for seconds. According to him, all these years of practice are starting to pay off!

Paste e Risotti

Pasta & Risotto

Pasta alla Beccafico
PASTA WITH RAISINS AND PINE NUTS

The "beccafico" name belongs to a Sicilian dish, particularly famous in my hometown of Palermo, that has nothing to do with pasta. The original beccafico dish consists of fresh sardine fillets stuffed with a flavorful mixture of garlic, pine nuts, lemon peel, parsley, onions and raisins. The stuffed sardines are then breaded and deep fried in oil — not exactly what I'd call a light lunch!

Yet, I was still fascinated by the combination of raisins and pine nuts and eventually developed this pasta dish. It quickly became a favorite with my restaurant patrons and I'm sure will be one of your favorites, too.

SERVES 4 TO 6
3 quarts (2.75 l) water
1 pound (450 g) pasta — penne rigate or spaghetti
8 tablespoons olive oil
6 garlic cloves, thickly sliced
¼ teaspoon red pepper flakes
1 cup raisins, soaked in 1 cup hot water for 20 minutes, drained, water discarded
½ cup pine nuts
4 tablespoons chopped fresh Italian parsley
4 tablespoons chopped fresh basil
½ teaspoon salt
½ teaspoon black pepper
4 tablespoons Italian Bread Crumbs (see page 218), toasted (see below)
4 tablespoons freshly grated Pecorino Romano cheese

Bring the water for the pasta to a boil in a large pot. Add the pasta and cook until just tender.

While the pasta is cooking, heat the oil in a large sauté pan set on medium-high heat until sizzling, about 2 minutes. Stir in the garlic, red pepper flakes, raisins and pine nuts. Cook for 1-2 minutes until the pine nuts are brown and the raisins have puffed up like balloons. Remove from the heat and stir in the parsley, basil, salt and pepper.

When the pasta is cooked, drain and return it to the pot. Pour the sauce over the pasta and stir well. Sprinkle with the bread crumbs and cheese, toss and serve.

COOK'S TIP

To toast bread crumbs, place them in a nonstick sauté pan set on high heat for 2-3 minutes. They'll change color in front of your eyes to a toasty brown color. Be careful not to overcook them. They can be done several days ahead, placed in a container and stored until you need them.

Menu Suggestion
STUFFED MUSHROOMS
PASTA WITH RAISINS AND PINE NUTS
BREAD
CHERRY ALMOND RICE PUDDING

Wine Suggestion
SAUVIGNON BLANC

Pasta alla Pikkio Pakkio

PASTA WITH COLD TOMATO SAUCE

SERVES 4 TO 6

*1 (28-ounce) (790-g) can peeled Italian tomatoes,
drained and chopped, ½ cup juices reserved
¼ teaspoon sugar
¾ teaspoon salt
¼ teaspoon black pepper
½ teaspoon red pepper flakes
1 tablespoon chopped fresh basil
2 garlic cloves, finely chopped
4 tablespoons extra virgin olive oil
3 quarts (2.75 l) water
1 pound (450 g) pasta – spaghetti or penne
4 tablespoons freshly grated Pecorino Romano cheese*

"*Pikkio pakkio*" is a Sicilian expression that signifies "thrown together." This is exactly what my mother, Massimiliana, did the night before our summertime trips to the beach. Simply throwing the ingredients together and letting them marinate overnight creates a perfectly flavored sauce to enjoy by lunchtime. It represents a basic "no fuss" approach to cooking that also yields great results.

In a large bowl, mix together the tomatoes, reserved juice, sugar, salt, pepper, red pepper flakes, basil, garlic and olive oil. Cover and let sit for at least 4 hours at room temperature or overnight in the refrigerator for the flavor to mature. If refrigerated, bring back to room temperature before serving.

Bring the water for the pasta to a boil in a large pot. Cook the pasta in the boiling water until just tender, drain well and transfer to a large bowl. Pour the sauce over the pasta and toss until well coated. Stir in the cheese and the pasta is now ready to be enjoyed!

COOK'S TIP

A variation on this recipe is to return the pasta to the cooking pot after draining. Pour the sauce over the pasta and cook over medium heat for 3-4 minutes, stirring. Stir in the cheese and serve.

Menu Suggestion
PASTA WITH COLD TOMATO SAUCE
BREAD
MARINATED FRUIT SALAD

Wine Suggestion
FRASCATI

Pasta alla Checca

Pasta with Fresh Tomatoes and Basil

Nobody knows for sure what "checca" (pronounced kek-ka) really means. Where I grew up in Palermo, it was the endearing nickname for someone named Francesca.

So, if you ask my opinion, I believe that this dish was named after a certain Lady Francesca, by her lover. This nameless young chef wanted to immortalize his beloved by creating the perfect pasta dish, something that imitated the ruby red of her pouty lips with tomatoes, the sweetness of her smile with basil and the excitement of her kisses with red pepper flakes. What more could a woman ask for than to be forever remembered by this culinary masterpiece?

Menu Suggestion

ROMAINE SALAD WITH PANCETTA AND GORGONZOLA DRESSING
PASTA WITH FRESH TOMATOES AND BASIL
CANTELOUPE WITH APPLE ROSEMARY SYRUP

Wine Suggestion
ZINFANDEL

SERVES 4 TO 6

3 quarts (2.75 l) water
4 tablespoons olive oil
4 garlic cloves, thickly sliced
½ teaspoon red pepper flakes
2 pounds (900 g) fresh Roma tomatoes, peeled, seeded and quartered
¾ teaspoon salt
½ teaspoon black pepper
½ teaspoon dried oregano
15 fresh basil leaves, whole
1 teaspoon sugar
¾ cup Chicken Stock (see page 228)
¾ cup Tomato Sauce (see page 225)
1 pound (450 g) pasta — spaghettini or angel hair
4 tablespoons freshly grated Pecorino Romano cheese

Bring the water for the pasta to a boil in a large pot.

Heat the oil and garlic in a large sauté pan set on medium-high heat until the oil starts to sizzle, about 2 minutes. Stir in the red pepper flakes, tomatoes, salt, pepper, oregano, basil and sugar and cook for 2 minutes. Add the chicken stock and tomato sauce and bring to a boil. Reduce the heat to low and simmer, uncovered, for 8-10 minutes. You want the tomatoes to cook through but not fall apart.

Cook the spaghetti in the boiling water until just tender. Drain well and return to the pot. Pour the sauce over the pasta and cook over medium heat for 3 minutes, stirring constantly, until the pasta is well coated. Top with the cheese and toss well.

COOK'S TIP

The technique of tossing the pasta with the sauce in a pan set on medium heat is an old restaurant trick. The pasta and the sauce finish cooking together, causing the sauce to thicken and coat the pasta perfectly.

Pasta con l'Arrugola

PASTA WITH ARUGULA

SERVES 4 TO 6

3 quarts (2.75 l) water

4 tablespoons olive oil

4 garlic cloves, thickly sliced

1 (1-pound) (450-g) can peeled Italian tomatoes,
drained, chopped and juices reserved separately

3 ounces (90 g) chopped anchovy fillets or 1 ½ tablespoons anchovy paste

½ teaspoon red pepper flakes

½ teaspoon salt

¼ teaspoon black pepper

1 ½ cups clam juice

4 cups loosely chopped arugula leaves

1 pound (450 g) pasta — spaghetti or spaghettini

4 tablespoons freshly grated Pecorino Romano cheese

Bring the water for the pasta to a boil in a large pot.

In a large sauté pan, heat the oil and garlic over medium-high heat until the oil begins to sizzle, about 2 minutes. Add the tomatoes, anchovies, red pepper flakes, salt and pepper and cook for 3-5 minutes, tossing once. Stir in the clam juice and the reserved tomato juices, bring to a boil and simmer, uncovered, for 10 minutes. Add the chopped arugula, stir well and cook 5 minutes longer.

Cook the pasta in the boiling water until just tender. Drain well and return to the pot. Pour the sauce over the pasta and mix well. Cook over medium heat, stirring constantly, for 3 minutes, until the pasta is well coated. Sprinkle with the cheese and serve.

COOK'S TIP

Often, when using canned anchovy fillets, I find that I have half the can left. For the best storage of my leftover anchovies, I drain them well and place the fillets in a single layer on a sheet of plastic wrap, with space between each one. Wrap tightly and place in a freezer bag. Next time I need anchovies, I just pull what I need from the bag and return the remaining to the freezer.

Unfortunately, the culinary world mourns my dear friend, Dave Hyeronimus's loss, since a few years ago this talented young chef abandoned the professional cooks' ranks.

Dave decided to follow another dream, diving head first into the world of carpentry, specializing in crafting fine furniture.

I was lucky enough to sample the following recipe at Dave's house, something I assure you felt like a mystic experience. Once you try it, you'll wish that Dave would overcome his passion for carpentry and return to the restaurant trade.

Menu Suggestion

PASTA WITH ARUGULA
BREAD
COFFEE ICE

Wine Suggestion

ORVIETO

Pasta con Gli Asparagi e Funghi

PASTA WITH ASPARAGUS AND MUSHROOMS

When Mario and I lived together in college, it was an unspoken agreement that I always handled the cooking. You see, Mario had always shown a general sense of uneasiness around anything that dealt with the kitchen.

However, to my great surprise and satisfaction, the day came when Mario prepared an absolutely fantastic dinner for a group of intimate friends. I was beaming inside as he brought this dish to the table, so moved that I even wrote my Mom and Dad to give them an account of that special event.

I guess this recipe will always live in the Stellino family folklore as the symbol of the return of the prodigal son.

SERVES 4 TO 6

3 quarts (2.75 l) water
4 tablespoons olive oil
1 pound (450 g) asparagus, cut into 2-inch (5-cm) pieces
¾ pound (450 g) shiitake mushrooms, sliced (see Cook's Tip)
¼ cup chopped shallots
4 garlic cloves, chopped
¾ cup white wine
½ cup chopped oil-packed sun-dried tomatoes
4 tablespoons chopped fresh basil
2 cups Chicken Stock (see page 228)
1 pound (450 g) pasta — penne or farfalle
½ teaspoon salt
¼ teaspoon black pepper
4 tablespoons freshly grated Parmigiano Reggiano cheese

Bring the water for the pasta to a boil in a large pot.

While the water is heating, heat the oil in a large sauté pan set on high heat until sizzling, about 2 minutes. Add the asparagus and mushrooms and cook until they begin to brown, about 3-4 minutes. Stir in the shallots and garlic and cook for 1 minute. Add the wine and reduce by half, about 5 minutes, stirring up any brown bits from the bottom of the pan. Add the tomatoes and half the basil and cook for 1-2 minutes. Pour in the chicken stock, bring to a boil, reduce the heat and simmer, uncovered, for 7-8 minutes.

Cook the pasta in the boiling water until just tender. Drain it well and return to the pot. Season the sauce with the salt and pepper and pour over the pasta. Cook over medium heat for 2-3 minutes, stirring, until well coated. Add the remaining basil and the cheese and toss.

COOK'S TIP

If you don't have access to fresh shiitake mushrooms, you can use the same amount of fresh button mushrooms or 1 ounce (30 g) of dried shiitake mushrooms soaked in ½ cup of hot chicken stock for 30 minutes. Drain and chop well.

Menu Suggestion
GREEN SALAD
WITH BALSAMIC VINAIGRETTE
PASTA WITH ASPARAGUS
AND MUSHROOMS

Wine Suggestion
PINOT GRIGIO

Pasta Siragusana

PASTA WITH EGGPLANT AND BELL PEPPERS

SERVES 4 TO 6

½ pound (225 g) eggplant, cut into 1-inch (2.5-cm) cubes
¼ teaspoon salt
3 quarts (2.75 l) water
5 tablespoons olive oil
3 bell peppers, 1 each of red, yellow and green, cut into 1-inch (2.5-cm) squares
5 garlic cloves, thickly sliced
¼ cup pitted Greek or Sicilian black olives, halved
1 tablespoon drained capers
⅛ teaspoon red pepper flakes
4 tablespoons chopped fresh basil
1 cup Tomato Sauce (see page 225)
1 cup Chicken Stock (see page 228)
1 pound (450 g) pasta — penne, rigatoni or tortiglioni
4 tablespoons freshly grated Pecorino Romano cheese (optional)

Sprinkle the eggplant cubes with the salt and place them in a colander to drain. Cover with a dish and place a heavy weight on top. Let the eggplant drain for 15 minutes to remove the bitter juices, pat dry with a towel and set aside.

Bring the water for the pasta to a boil in a large pot.

Heat the oil in a large nonstick sauté pan set on high heat until sizzling, about 2 minutes. Cook the eggplant cubes and bell pepper for 5 minutes, tossing twice. The eggplant should be nicely browned and the peppers slightly charred. Add the garlic, olives, capers, red pepper flakes and basil, mix well and cook for 3 minutes, stirring once. Pour in the tomato sauce and chicken stock, bring to a boil, reduce the heat and simmer, uncovered, for 10 minutes.

While the sauce is simmering, cook the pasta in the boiling water until just tender. Drain well and return it to the pot. Pour the sauce over the pasta and cook for 3 minutes, stirring continuously, until most of the sauce has been absorbed and the pasta shines with a beautiful, deep red gloss. Stir in the optional cheese, if you wish. The pasta is now ready to be served.

Siragusa is one of the most beautiful towns in Sicily, with a glorious historic past. It started as the capital of the Greek colonies in Sicily, when many temples and monuments were built, some of which survive today. Legend has it that the Greek people exposed the Sicilians to the finer things in life. I had this dish at a small restaurant in an old part of town. The owner was gracious enough to share this recipe with me. That afternoon exploring the ruins of Dionysius' palace, I kept thinking how much we Sicilians owe to the Greeks and their culture. But no matter what the historical implications, this is still a dish to be enjoyed today with your friends.

Menu Suggestion
PASTA WITH EGGPLANT
AND BELL PEPPERS
BREAD
UPSIDE-DOWN APPLE PIE

Wine Suggestion
ROSSO DI MONTALCINO

Pasta con i Carciofi i Porri e l'Olive

PASTA WITH ARTICHOKES, LEEKS AND OLIVES

This dish finds its origin in the tradition of "cucina povera" (poor man's cooking): humble and readily available ingredients tossed with pasta. However, be prepared for an explosion of rich and subtle flavors, culminating in a rush of culinary delight, that cannot in any fashion or form be defined as "poor." I think it's the artichokes' mysterious and subtle taste that seduces the palate into a dance of gourmand ecstasy. But you don't need to get so philosophical. Keep an open mind and let this recipe work its magic on you.

SERVES 4 TO 6

3 quarts (2.75 l) water
5 tablespoons olive oil
5 garlic cloves, thickly sliced
¼ teaspoon red pepper flakes
2 leeks, white part only, sliced
½ cup pitted Greek or Sicilian black olives, coarsely chopped
5 artichoke hearts, diced (see page 14 for cleaning instructions)
or 1 (9-ounce) (250-g) package frozen artichoke hearts,
cut into 1-inch (2.5-cm) pieces
1 (14½-ounce) (415-g) can stewed tomatoes,
drained and chopped, juices reserved separately
½ teaspoon salt
⅛ teaspoon black pepper
2 cups Chicken or Enhanced Stock (see page 228 or 229)
1 pound (450 g) pasta — tortiglioni or penne rigate
2 tablespoons chopped fresh basil
3 tablespoon freshly grated Parmigiano Reggiano cheese (optional)

Bring the water for the pasta to a boil in a large pot.

In a large sauté pan set on medium-high heat, cook the olive oil, garlic and red pepper flakes for 2 minutes. Add the leeks, olives, diced artichoke hearts and stewed tomatoes and cook, tossing, for 3 minutes. Stir in the salt and pepper and cook 2 minutes longer. Pour in the stock and reserved tomato juices, bring to a boil, reduce the heat and simmer, uncovered, for 15 minutes.

Cook the pasta in the boiling water until just tender. Drain the pasta and return it to the pot. Stir in the sauce and chopped basil and cook over medium heat for 3 minutes, until the pasta is well coated. Remove from the heat, add the optional cheese, if you wish, and stir well. The pasta is now ready.

Menu Suggestion
PASTA WITH ARTICHOKES,
LEEKS AND OLIVES
BREAD
ORANGES WITH CARAMEL SAUCE
AND VANILLA ICE CREAM

Wine Suggestion
CHARDONNAY

Pasta alla Carbonara

PASTA WITH EGGS, PANCETTA AND CHEESE

SERVES 4 TO 6

3 quarts (2.75 l) water
4 tablespoons olive oil
5 tablespoons diced pancetta or bacon
4 garlic cloves, thickly sliced
¼ teaspoon red pepper flakes
4 tablespoons chopped fresh Italian parsley
¾ cup white wine
¾ cup Chicken Stock (see page 228)
2 egg yolks
5 tablespoons freshly grated Pecorino Romano cheese
½ teaspoon black pepper
¼ cup pasta cooking water (from above)
1 pound (450 g) pasta — tortellini or tortiglioni

The name of this dish translates literally into "pasta of the coal miner." I think that's because its full-bodied flavor is the perfect restorative following a long and exhausting day. It's been popular throughout Italy for centuries, especially with a glass of good wine.

Just one word of warning: after eating this meal for lunch, don't even think about going back to work immediately. Save it for savoring as the perfect ending to a hard day or as lunch for a lazy afternoon on your day off.

Bring the water for the pasta to a boil in a large pot.

In a large sauté pan, heat the oil over medium-high heat until sizzling, about 2 minutes. Add the pancetta and cook for 1 minute. Stir in the garlic, red pepper flakes and 2 tablespoons of the parsley. Cook for 2 minutes. Pour in the wine and boil until reduced by half, about 4-5 minutes. Add the chicken stock and bring to a boil. Reduce the heat to medium and cook, uncovered, for 10 minutes. The consistency should be thick enough to coat the pasta.

Cook the pasta in the boiling water until just tender.

Mix the egg yolks in a medium bowl with the Romano cheese, black pepper and the remaining parsley. Just before the pasta is finished cooking, slowly whisk ¼ cup of the hot pasta water into the egg yolk mixture, beating vigorously to prevent scrambled eggs. Set aside.

Drain the pasta well and return to the pot. Pour the cooked sauce over the pasta, tossing well over medium heat until well coated. Add the egg mixture and quickly toss — don't keep on the heat more than 1 minute. Remove from the heat and keep tossing until the egg yolks are cooked and the pasta is well coated.

Menu Suggestion
PASTA CARBONARA
SCALLOPS WITH SPINACH
BREAD
STRAWBERRY GRANITA

Wine Suggestion
CHARDONNAY

Pasta alla Vodka
PASTA WITH VODKA

Legend has it that a merchant ship once smuggled a few cases of Russian vodka into the seaport city of Genoa. Inspired by this zesty foreign liquor, the local chefs created many recipes, with this pasta being one of the greatest successes. Indeed, Pasta with Vodka has almost become a staple recipe.

I wonder what the captain of that merchant ship would think if he could see how his little cargo of smuggled goods influenced a whole new generation of pasta recipes?

SERVES 4 TO 6
3 quarts (2.75 l) water
3 tablespoons olive oil
4 garlic cloves, thickly sliced
½ cup chopped pancetta or bacon
¼ teaspoon salt
¼ teaspoon black pepper
¼ teaspoon red pepper flakes
1 ½ teaspoons chopped fresh rosemary
1 tablespoon chopped fresh sage
½ cup vodka
1 ½ cups Tomato Sauce (see page 225)
1 ½ cups Chicken Stock (see page 228)
1 pound (450 g) pasta — penne or tortellini
4 tablespoons freshly grated Pecorino Romano cheese

Bring the water for the pasta to a boil in a large pot.

Heat the oil in a large sauté pan set on medium-high heat until sizzling, about 2 minutes. Sauté the garlic, pancetta, salt, pepper, red pepper flakes, rosemary and sage for 2-3 minutes, until the pancetta is beginning to brown. Stir in the vodka, scraping up any brown bits from the bottom of the pan. Cook for 2-3 minutes. Add the tomato sauce and chicken stock, stirring well. Bring to a boil, reduce the heat to medium-low and cook, uncovered, for 15-20 minutes.

Cook the pasta in the boiling water until just tender. Drain well and return it to the pot. Pour the sauce over the pasta and cook, stirring, over medium heat for 3 minutes, until the sauce has been absorbed. Sprinkle the cheese over the pasta and mix well. The pasta is now ready to be enjoyed!

COOK'S TIP
The addition of fresh rosemary and sage adds a new dimension to this dish. Feel free to experiment with your favorite fresh herbs or eliminate them altogether.

Menu Suggestion
ASPARAGUS SALAD
WITH HONEY MUSTARD DRESSING
PASTA WITH VODKA
BREAD

Wine Suggestion
CHENIN BLANC

Pasta alla Matriciana

PASTA WITH PANCETTA, TOMATOES AND ONIONS

SERVES 4 TO 6

3 quarts (2.75 l) water
3 tablespoons olive oil
4 garlic cloves, thickly sliced
1 cup (5 ounces) (150 g) diced pancetta or bacon
¼ teaspoon red pepper flakes
½ cup white wine
1 (28-ounce) (790-g) can peeled Italian tomatoes,
drained and chopped, juices reserved separately
½ cup Onion Purée (see page 219)
4 tablespoons chopped fresh basil
1 pound (450 g) pasta — spaghetti, ziti or penne rigate
4 tablespoons freshly grated Pecorino Romano cheese

Bring the water for the pasta to a boil in a large pot.

Heat the olive oil in a large sauté pan set on medium-high heat until sizzling, about 2 minutes. Add the garlic, pancetta and red pepper flakes. Sauté for 3-4 minutes, until the pancetta begins to brown. Pour in the wine and stir up any brown bits that might be clinging to the bottom of the pan. Boil until reduced by half, about 3-5 minutes. Add the chopped tomatoes and cook for 3 minutes. Stir in the onion purée, reserved tomato juices and basil and bring to a boil. Reduce the heat to medium-low and cook, uncovered, for 10-15 minutes.

Cook the pasta in the boiling water until just tender. Drain well and return it to the pot. Pour the sauce over the pasta and cook, stirring, over medium heat for 3 minutes, until the sauce is absorbed. Add the cheese, toss well and serve.

COOK'S TIP

As a substitute for the Onion Purée, sauté a thinly sliced white or red onion in 3 tablespoons of olive oil over medium heat for 12-15 minutes. Add to the recipe at the same time that the Onion Purée would be added.

The hills of the Lazio region hold many pleasant memories from my childhood. They were my father's favorite route on our yearly pilgrimage north to spend the summer with my maternal grandmother.

A few years ago, I found myself retracing the same route while vacationing in Italy with my wife. The countryside was as lush and soft as green velvet, its aroma of fertile earth mixed with rain on the cool breeze.

We stopped in a trattoria my family had often visited, where Nanci and I shared this pasta dish.

I present you with this recipe, savoring the warmth of the past, and assuring you of the comfort it will always bring to the present.

Menu Suggestion
CAULIFLOWER AU GRATIN
PASTA WITH PANCETTA,
TOMATOES AND ONIONS
BREAD
MARINATED FRUIT SALAD

Wine Suggestion
CHIANTI

Pasta con i Rapini

PASTA WITH BROCCOLI RAPINI

One of my mother's favorite places to buy high quality produce was a small stand run by an older couple, Santo and Concetta.

Santo was short, bald and fat with large calloused hands that never stopped moving. He wore his battered work clothes with the elegance of an English lord. Concetta, his wife, was a plump woman whose hair exploded in undulating silver curls, and her wrinkled face sparkled with hazel eyes that shone like diamonds on velvet.

Santo had been taught operatic singing by a priest in his village who recognized his natural talent. Occasionally in the middle of helping a customer, he would break into an aria of operatic rapture. Songs of love flew into the air with the power of a passion belied by his diminutive body. Customers would stand enchanted by these mellifluous melodies. Cars driving by

SERVES 4 TO 6

3 quarts (2.75 l) water
1 bunch (12-16 ounces) (350-450 g) broccoli rapini, cut across in 1-inch (2.5-cm) pieces (mustard greens may be substituted)
1 pound (450 g) pasta — penne rigate or rigatoni
6 tablespoons olive oil
8 tablespoons diced pancetta or bacon
4 garlic cloves, thickly sliced
¼ teaspoon red pepper flakes
1 cup pasta cooking water (from above)
½ chicken bouillon cube, crumbled
¼ teaspoon salt
¼ teaspoon black pepper
4 tablespoons freshly grated Pecorino Romano cheese

Bring the water to a boil in a large pot and parboil the rapini for 1 minute. Drain, reserving the water and broccoli separately. Return the water to the large pot and return to a boil. Add the pasta to the boiling water and cook until just tender.

While the pasta is cooking, begin preparing the sauce right away. Heat the olive oil in a large sauté pan set on medium-high heat until sizzling, about 2 minutes. Add the pancetta and cook for 1 minute. Stir in the garlic and red pepper flakes and cook for 2 minutes. Raise the heat to high, add the cooked rapini and cook for 3-4 minutes. The rapini and garlic will begin to brown. Stir in 1 cup of water from the cooking pasta, the bouillon cube, salt and pepper. Cook for 2-3 minutes, until thickened.

When the pasta is cooked just tender, drain and return to the pot. Pour the sauce over the pasta and cook over medium heat for 3 minutes, stirring well. Toss with the cheese for the perfect finishing touch.

In recipes using pasta water in the sauce, make sure that you take the water from the pan after the pasta has been cooking for awhile. The pasta adds starch to the water, which helps to thicken the sauce a bit as you cook it down.

would stop and park. Then Santo would move through the crowd as an actor on the stage, making his way toward Concetta. Then, while holding her hand, he would finish his aria by sealing it with a kiss on Concetta's blushing cheeks.

By now the crowd would be applauding and wiping away small tears, especially my mom. Then business would pick up again at a booming rate.

I always envied Santo and his ability to sing out his love to his wife with such musicality. What follows might not appear to be a recipe for a romantic meal, but picture yourself buying the produce from Santo and Concetta, and even this prosaic broccoli could become the inspiration for a haunting melody of love.

Menu Suggestion
PASTA WITH BROCCOLI RAPINI
BREAD
LITTLE PURSES WITH PEARS
AND RICOTTA

Wine Suggestion
ZINFANDEL

Pasta con Pancetta e Peperoni

PASTA WITH PANCETTA AND BELL PEPPERS

Early in life, my father, Vincenzo, taught me how he dealt with "the blues." "Nicolino," he would say, "aggiusta il compasso." (Nick, you've got to box the compass within.)

You see, my father taught me to think about the blues as if they were a blanket of fog, obscuring the view ahead. By adjusting or boxing the compass within, one could rediscover their sense of lost direction. The key to boxing the compass was to immerse oneself in a pleasure-filled activity. To both my father and myself, that activity was cooking.

Today, as my life presents new challenges, the following recipe has always been my foolproof tool for boxing my compass and curing the blues.

SERVES 4 TO 6

3 quarts (2.75 l) water
4 tablespoons olive oil
8 tablespoons diced pancetta or bacon
4 garlic cloves, thickly sliced
¼ teaspoon red pepper flakes
½ cup chopped onion
3 bell peppers, preferably 1 each red, green and yellow, quartered lengthwise, each quarter sliced crosswise into ¼-inch (6-mm) slices
2 tablespoons chopped fresh thyme
2 tablespoons chopped fresh basil
½ cup white wine
¾ cup Tomato Sauce (see page 225)
¾ cup Chicken Stock (see page 228)
¼ teaspoon salt
¼ teaspoon black pepper
1 pound (450 g) pasta — penne rigate, rigatoni or tortellini
4 tablespoons freshly grated Parmigiano Reggiano cheese

Bring the water for the pasta to a boil in a large pot.

While the water is heating, heat the olive oil in a large sauté pan set on medium-high heat until sizzling, about 2 minutes. Cook the pancetta for 1 minute. Add the garlic, red pepper flakes, onion, bell peppers, thyme and basil. Cook for 7-8 minutes. Pour the wine into the pan, stirring up any brown bits from the bottom. Cook until reduced by half, about 2-3 minutes. Stir in the tomato sauce, chicken stock, salt and pepper. Reduce the heat and simmer, uncovered, for 5-7 minutes until the consistency is thick.

Cook the pasta in the boiling water until just tender, drain and return to the pot. Pour the sauce over the pasta and cook for 3 minutes over medium heat, tossing to coat the pasta. Stir in the cheese and serve.

Menu Suggestion
TOMATO AND ONION SALAD
PASTA WITH PANCETTA
AND BELL PEPPERS
APPLE CUSTARD TART

Wine Suggestion
MERLOT

Pasta con le Salsicce, Zucchine e Peperoni

PASTA WITH SAUSAGE, ZUCCHINI AND BELL PEPPERS

SERVES 4 TO 6

3 quarts (2.75 l) water

2 tablespoons olive oil

8 ounces (225 g) hot Italian sausage, removed from the casing

2 bell peppers, 1 red and 1 yellow, cut into ½-inch (1.5-cm) squares

2 zucchini, cut into ½-inch (1.5-cm) pieces

½ red onion, diced

4 garlic cloves, thickly sliced

¼ teaspoon salt

⅛ teaspoon black pepper

⅛ teaspoon red pepper flakes

¼ teaspoon dried oregano

¼ cup dry Marsala wine

2 cups Chicken Stock (see page 228)

1 pound (450 g) pasta — penne rigate, tortiglioni or rigatoni

1 tablespoon butter (optional)

3 tablespoons freshly grated Pecorino Romano or Parmigiano Reggiano cheese

Bring the water to a boil in a large pot.

Heat the oil over high heat in a large sauté pan, until sizzling about 2 minutes. Add the sausage meat to the pan, stirring to prevent sticking. Cook until browned, about 3 minutes. With a slotted spoon, remove the meat from the pan and set aside.

In the same pan, cook the peppers, zucchini, red onion, garlic, salt, pepper, red pepper flakes and oregano over medium heat for 3 minutes, stirring well. Add the cooked sausage with any juices that have accumulated and the Marsala wine and cook for 3 minutes, stirring to dislodge any brown bits from the bottom of the pan. Add the chicken stock, bring to a boil, reduce the heat and simmer, uncovered, for 15 minutes.

While the sauce is simmering, cook the pasta in the boiling water until just tender. Drain well and return to the pot. Add the sauce and the butter, if you wish, and cook for 3 minutes over medium heat, stirring continuously, until most of the sauce has been absorbed. Remove from the heat, spoon onto serving plates and sprinkle with the cheese.

While I have always passionately appreciated sausage in my pasta sauce, vegetables were always completely optional. I credit my favorite aunt, Buliti, for changing my mind. She lived with us when I was small and was my best pal for the first sixteen years of my life. When I was very young, I thought she was my big sister. I can still remember how sorry I was when at the tender age of four I was kindly informed otherwise.

Aunt Buliti's true name was "Alfredina" and I have no clue how she became Buliti; however, it should be noted that my mother's family was particularly creative in the art of nicknames. For example, my mother's name is Massimiliana, but her nickname is Maria!

Menu Suggestion

ROASTED ARTICHOKE HEARTS
WITH MUSHROOM CAVIAR
PASTA WITH SAUSAGE, ZUCCHINI
AND BELL PEPPERS
STRAWBERRY SAUCE
OVER VANILLA ICE CREAM

Wine Suggestion

BARBERA

Pasta al Sugo Stracotto di Broccoli, Salsiccie e Pomodori Secchi

PASTA WITH BROCCOLI, SAUSAGE AND SUN-DRIED TOMATOES

The name of this dish translates as "pasta in love," and there's a story that explains why.

A long time ago there was a handsome young broccoli farmer called Rosario "Il Broccolaio," who had fallen in love with an irresistibly beautiful young maiden, Rosalia. Her parents had rejected all her suitors. Fired to passion by her shimmering black curls and blushing porcelain cheeks, Rosario came to Rosalia's house to court her love.

Under the watchful eyes of Rosalia's mother and father, Rosario presented four gifts: a broccoli, a sausage, a dried tomato and a pot wrapped in a red checked cloth. Then, with his piercing blue eyes (very rare among Sicilians) flashing with emotion, he told them this story:

"The broccoli, tomatoes and sausage are the symbol of my daily passion, work and love. By themselves they are

SERVES 4 TO 6

2 tablespoons olive oil

1 pound (450 g) hot Italian sausage, removed from the casing

4 garlic cloves, thickly sliced

1 pound (450 g) broccoli, cut into florets, stems peeled and cut into ½-inch (1.5-cm) dice

2 tablespoons chopped sun-dried tomatoes (not oil-packed)

¼ teaspoon salt

⅛ teaspoon black pepper

⅛ teaspoon red pepper flakes

¼ cup white wine

2 cups Chicken Stock (see page 228)

3 quarts (2.75 l) water

1 pound (450 g) pasta — penne, tortiglioni or rigatoni

3 tablespoons freshly grated Pecorino Romano or Parmigiano Reggiano cheese

1 tablespoon butter (optional)

Heat the oil in a large sauté pan set on medium heat, until almost sizzling, about 2 minutes. Cook the sausage meat for 3 minutes or until lightly browned. Transfer the sausage to a bowl with a slotted spoon and set aside.

Add the garlic, broccoli, tomatoes, salt, pepper and red pepper flakes to the same pan and cook over medium heat for 3 minutes, stirring to mix well. Add the cooked sausage and the wine and cook 3 more minutes, stirring to scrape up any brown bits from the bottom of the pan. Add the chicken stock and bring to a boil. Reduce the heat, cover the pan, with the lid slightly ajar, and simmer for 30 minutes.

Just before the sauce is done, bring the water for the pasta to a boil in a large pot. Add the pasta and cook until just tender. Drain well and return to the pot. Add the sauce and cook over medium heat for 3 minutes until most of the sauce is absorbed by the pasta. Remove from the heat, add the cheese and the butter, if you wish, and mix well.

The pasta is ready to be served.

Cook's Tip

When buying wine to use in recipes, don't use anything you wouldn't drink. And most importantly, don't buy the wines labeled "cooking" wines that you might find in your grocery store. They have salt added and are normally made with inferior wines.

humble things, but when these earthy ingredients are cooked by the passion within, simmered by the love I feel for your daughter, spiked by the image of the happiness I want to bring her, they become the meal inside this pot. This dish is the tangible vision of the future I aspire to, the love I wish to share, the talent that I possess and the drive of my ambition."

Well, legend has it that Rosalia's parents were so impressed by this pasta dish that they agreed to let Rosario court Rosalia and they were soon married and lived happily ever after.

Okay, maybe it's just a story. But when I met my wife's parents, I cooked for them. And just like Rosario, I married my dream.

Menu Suggestion
MIXED SALAD WITH ORANGES, ONION AND FENNEL
PASTA WITH BROCCOLI, SAUSAGES AND SUN-DRIED TOMATOES
CINNAMON SUGAR COOKIES

Wine Suggestion
SAN GIOVESE DI ROMAGNA

Pasta Incaciata
Baked Pasta Wrapped in Eggplant Slices

This dish is one of the most spectacular in the book, a "celebratory meal" to make for a truly special event.

Legend has it that it was originally conceived as a poor man's dinner, prepared very simply with pasta, cheese and tomato sauce wrapped in fried eggplant slices. But it assumed a whole new personality in the hands of 14th century professional chefs employed by Sicilian royal families who added the different sauces and its elegant eggplant wrap.

I assure that you will feel ecstatic when you bring this dish to the dinner table. Your friends will be taken aback with wonderment and surprise. You'll quickly become the hot story, talked about all over town. People will soon start stopping you on the street asking you to autograph this recipe.

All right, I'm exaggerating a little bit...or am I?

Serves 10 to 12
2 (1½-pound) (750-g) eggplants
1½ teaspoons salt
3 tablespoons olive oil

Béchamel Sauce:
3 cups milk
3 tablespoons butter
3 tablespoons flour
⅛ teaspoon nutmeg

Filling:
3 quarts (2.75 l) water
1 pound (450 g) pasta — penne or ziti
2 tablespoons olive oil
⅓ cup Italian Bread Crumbs (see page 218)
4 cups Ragú Sauce (see page 227)
¾ cup freshly grated Parmigiano Reggiano cheese
¾ cup freshly grated Pecorino Romano cheese
¾ cup grated sharp provolone cheese
1 pound (450 g) honey-baked ham, cut into thin strips

The day before serving, slice the eggplants lengthwise into ¼-inch (6-mm) slices. Sprinkle with the salt and lay the slices on top of one another in 1 large colander or in 2 small colanders. Place a dish on top and weight it down (a large can of tomatoes works well). Drain for 20 minutes. Dry the eggplant slices with paper towels.

Preheat the oven to 425° F (220° C). Line a baking sheet with parchment paper if you're not using a nonstick pan. Brush the paper and eggplant slices with the olive oil and cook in the oven for 25 minutes, until lightly brown. Set aside.

For the Béchamel Sauce

Bring the milk to a soft boil in a large saucepan. In another large saucepan, make a roux by stirring the butter and flour over medium heat until they form a thick paste. Add the nutmeg to the boiling milk, then pour it, a little at a time, into the warm roux, whisking vigorously to prevent lumps. When all the milk has been added, continue whisking over medium heat until the sauce thickens, about 3-5 minutes. Set aside.

For the Filling

Bring the water to a boil and cook the pasta until just tender. Drain well, return to the pot and toss with the 2 tablespoons of olive oil. Set aside.

To assemble, grease a deep 9 x 17-inch (23 x 43-cm) baking dish and coat with the bread crumbs. Line the pan with the cooked eggplant slices, edge-to-edge, and hanging over the sides of the pan. (It's okay if there are spaces showing between the slices.) About 9 slices should be enough to cover the dish.

Mix the cooked pasta with 3 cups of the ragú sauce, 1 cup of the béchamel sauce and half of each of the cheeses. Stir well. Pour half the pasta mixture into the prepared dish. Top with the ham, the remaining cheeses, ragú sauce, béchamel sauce and pasta mixture.

Fold the eggplant slices over the top and cover with approximately 5 more slices. Cover the dish with plastic wrap and place a baking sheet on top with 3 large cans to weight it down. Place in the refrigerator overnight.

The day of serving, preheat the oven to 400° F (200° C). Remove the plastic wrap, re-cover the dish of pasta with aluminum foil and bake for 1 hour. Remove the foil and bake for another 30 minutes. Remove from the oven and let rest for 15 minutes.

To serve, invert onto a large serving dish and cut into wedges or thick slices.

"I like a cook who smiles out loud when he tastes his own work. Let God worry about your modesty; I want to see your enthusiasm."

Robert Farrar Capon

Menu Suggestion
Crostini
Baked Pasta Wrapped
in Eggplant Slices
Bread
Pears with Chocolate Sauce

Wine Suggestion
Barbaresco

Insalata cà Pasta

Pasta with Ham, Leeks, Lettuce and Mushrooms

At the age of 14, I went with some friends to visit the town of Petralia Sohana, a two hour bus ride from Palermo. We were going the see the famous "Targa Florio," one of the oldest race car Grand Prix events in Europe.

That evening, we ate at a very small trattoria where the five to ten dinner guests shared a meal with the chef's own family. That night I tasted this dish with a group of strangers. Maybe it was the food, maybe the magic of the sunset before, maybe the warmth of the hostess, Signora Mirta's, smile, but for a while I felt like I was at home dining with friends.

This is my version of La Signora Mirta's recipe and I'm sure it will evoke the same magic for you as it did for me so many years ago.

Menu Suggestion
PASTA WITH HAM, LEEKS, LETTUCE AND MUSHROOMS
ORANGES WITH
WHITE CHOCOLATE AND MINT

Wine Suggestion
CHENIN BLANC

SERVES 4 TO 6

3 quarts (2.75 l) water
3 tablespoons olive oil
4 ounces (115 g) ham, finely diced
8 ounces (225 g) mixed mushrooms, preferably shiitake and portobello
or white button mushrooms
1½ cups thinly sliced leeks, white part only
4 garlic cloves, thickly sliced
2 cups chopped iceberg lettuce
2 cups Chicken Stock (see page 228)
¼ teaspoon salt
¼ teaspoon black pepper
1 pound (450 g) pasta — penne rigate, tortiglioni or rigatoni
1 tablespoon butter (optional)
2 tablespoons freshly grated Pecorino Romano cheese

Bring the water for the pasta to a boil in a large pot.

Heat the olive oil over high heat in a large nonstick sauté pan until sizzling, about 2 minutes. Cook the diced ham until brown, about 2 minutes. Add the mushrooms, leeks, garlic and lettuce and cook for 5 minutes. Stir in the stock, salt and pepper, bring to a boil and simmer, uncovered, for 20 minutes.

Cook the pasta in the boiling water until just tender. Drain the pasta and return it to the pot. Add the sauce and cook over medium heat, stirring continuously, until most of the sauce is absorbed by the pasta — about 3 minutes. Remove from the heat, add the butter, if you wish, and the cheese and mix well.

The pasta is ready to be served.

COOK'S TIP

For a more traditional taste, use roughly chopped curly endive or a mix of baby salad greens instead of the iceberg lettuce, which is milder in flavor.

Pasta di Ferruccio

Pasta with Shrimp and Green Onions

Serves 4 to 6

3 quarts (2.75 l) water

4 tablespoons olive oil

4 garlic cloves, thickly sliced

2 bunches green onions, white part
and 2 inches (5 cm) of the green tops, cut into ¼-inch (6-mm) pieces

½ pound (225 g) shrimp (16-20 count),
peeled, deveined and tail cut off, cut into 3 pieces

¼ teaspoon red pepper flakes

¼ cup brandy

½ cup Tomato Sauce (see page 225)

¼ cup Chicken Stock (see page 228)

2 tablespoons whipping cream

4 tablespoons chopped fresh Italian parsley

¼ teaspoon salt

¼ teaspoon black pepper

1 pound (450 g) pasta — tortellini, penne or linguine

4 tablespoons freshly grated Parmigiano Reggiano cheese

Ferruccio was an old friend of my father's who was a gifted storyteller. He was often invited to hold court at our house to entertain a selected group of friends with a meal and a story.

As I grew older, I enjoyed the privilege of being invited to one of Ferruccio's storytelling events. It was a night of enchantment, that culminated for me in Ferruccio honoring me by asking my help in assembling this pasta dish.

While my memory of Ferruccio's stories has grown dim, I'll never forget this dish that he taught me that night.

Bring the water for the pasta to a boil in a large pot.

Heat the oil in a large sauté pan set on medium-high heat until sizzling, about 2 minutes. Add the garlic and onions and cook for 2-3 minutes. Stir in the shrimp and red pepper flakes and cook until the shrimp starts to turn pink, but is not fully cooked, about 2 minutes. Carefully pour the brandy into the pan, stirring up any brown bits from the bottom. Cook for 1 minute. Remove the shrimp from the pan with a slotted spoon. (Be careful not to overcook the shrimp up to this point — remember, it will continue to cook when tossed with the pasta.) Pour in the tomato sauce, chicken stock, cream, parsley, salt and pepper and cook for 5 minutes on medium-low heat.

Cook the pasta in the boiling water until just tender, drain and return to the pot. Pour the sauce and shrimp over the pasta, stir well and cook over medium heat for 3 minutes. Stir in the cheese and serve.

Menu Suggestion
PASTA WITH SHRIMP
AND GREEN ONIONS
FRIED TOMATOES
BREAD

Wine Suggestion
CHARDONNAY

Pasta con i Gamberi e Gli Asparagi

PASTA WITH SHRIMP AND ASPARAGUS

SERVES 4 TO 6

3 quarts (2.75 l) water

4 tablespoons olive oil

4 garlic cloves, thickly sliced

1 pound (450 g) asparagus (peeled from 1 inch (2.5 cm)
below the tips if the spears are large), cut into 1-inch (2.5-cm) pieces

2 tablespoons chopped shallots

3 tablespoons chopped fresh Italian parsley

2 tablespoons chopped oil-packed sun-dried tomatoes

½ teaspoon curry powder

¼ teaspoon red pepper flakes

1 pound (450 g) shrimp (20-25 count), peeled and deveined

¼ cup brandy

¾ cup clam juice

¾ cup Tomato Sauce (see page 225)

½ teaspoon salt

¼ teaspoon black pepper

1 pound (450 g) pasta — linguine or spaghetti

4 tablespoons freshly grated Parmigiano Reggiano cheese

Many years ago when Nanci and I were traveling through the Tuscany countryside, we became completely lost. After a series of frustrating dead ends, where I may have insulted her map reading skills and she may have said some disagreeable things about my refusal to ask directions, the only thing we could agree upon was the fact that we were lost!

So, stuck in the middle of nowhere, we finally decided to follow a dirt road and find a farmer to ask for directions. Wouldn't you know that inauspicious looking road led us right to a crowded parking lot next to a rustic farmhouse restaurant called "La Rughetta."

Since both of us were very hungry, we went in and asked for a table. Our host seated us outside on a terrace shadowed by a thickly overgrown trellis. I was so tired, I declined to look at a menu, asking the host to

Bring the water for the pasta to a boil in a large pot.

Heat the olive oil and garlic in a large sauté pan set on medium-high heat until the oil is sizzling, about 2 minutes. Add the asparagus, shallots, 1½ tablespoons of the parsley, the sun-dried tomatoes, curry powder and red pepper flakes and cook for 3 minutes. Stir in the shrimp and cook until it changes color, about 2 minutes. Slowly pour the brandy over the shrimp, being careful to avoid small flare-ups. Boil until the pan juices are reduced by half, about 2 minutes. Remove the shrimp from the pan and set aside. Stir in the clam juice, tomato sauce, the remaining parsley, the salt and pepper and bring to a boil. Reduce the heat and simmer for 5-7 minutes. Just before tossing with the pasta, return the shrimp to the sauce to heat through.

Cook the pasta in the boiling water until just tender. Drain well and return to the pot. Pour the sauce over the pasta and cook over medium heat for 3-4 minutes, stirring, until well coated. Top with the cheese.

Cook's Tip

The best way to cut asparagus is on the diagonal, which is commonly called the "Chinese cut." If you cut the pieces about ¼-inch (6-mm) thick, you do not have to peel the stalks, even the larger ones.

bring the pasta of his choice and a bottle of local wine.

Nanci and I were still a bit upset, but as we sat motionless, looking at the world around us, we were captivated by the spell of the moment. I found myself holding her hand, pressing gently, hoping it told her what I couldn't say, I was sorry.

When the waiter brought our food and wine, we savored every bite. What follows is my version of a dish that has come to symbolize the chance to stop and appreciate the simple details of our daily life. I can't promise you it will patch up things the next time you're in a disagreement, but count on it for a special moment.

Menu Suggestion
MIXED SALAD
WITH ITALIAN CHEESE DRESSING
PASTA WITH SHRIMP
AND ASPARAGUS
BREAD
LITTLE PURSES
WITH PEARS AND RICOTTA

Wine Suggestion
FUMÉ BLANC

Pasta con le Capesante
PASTA WITH SCALLOPS AND ARTICHOKES

My father, Don Vincenzo, could tell incredible stories, embellishing the details like a weaver choosing the strands for a beautiful tapestry.

One time he told me the story of Orlando, a fierce Sicilian dragonslayer whose strength and courage were due to a magic potion made with artichokes. While the belief still shone from my young eyes, he proceeded to cut a few artichokes from my grandmother's garden and went into the kitchen to prepare this recipe.

I later discovered that Orlando was really a French hero and nobody else had ever heard of this special artichoke magic potion. However, every time I prepare this dish, I think of my father's cooking and stories, that become more dear with the patina of time.

SERVES 4 TO 6

3 quarts (2.75 l) water

1 pound (450 g) large sea scallops, cut in half

¼ teaspoon salt

¼ teaspoon black pepper

4 tablespoons olive oil

4-5 fresh artichoke hearts, parboiled (see page 14 for cleaning instructions) or 1 (9-ounce) (250-g) package frozen artichoke hearts, cut into 1-inch (2.5-cm) pieces

¾ cup pitted Greek or Sicilian black olives, halved

¼ cup drained capers

4 garlic cloves, thickly sliced

¼ teaspoon red pepper flakes

½ cup white wine

½ cup oil-packed sun-dried tomatoes, thinly sliced

2 cups Chicken Stock (see page 228)

3 tablespoons chopped fresh Italian parsley

1 pound (450 g) pasta — linguine or spaghetti

4 tablespoons freshly grated Parmigiano Reggiano cheese (optional)

Bring the water for the pasta to a boil in a large pot.

Season the scallops with ⅛ teaspoon each of the salt and pepper. Heat 2 tablespoons of the olive oil until sizzling in a large sauté pan set on medium-high heat, about 2 minutes. Add the scallops in a single layer and cook for 1 minute on each side, to brown. Transfer to a bowl and set aside.

Add the remaining oil to the same pan and heat until sizzling. Add the artichoke hearts, olives, capers, garlic and red pepper flakes and cook for 2-3 minutes, until the artichokes begin to brown. Stir the wine into the pan, scraping up any brown bits from the bottom. Cook for 2-3 minutes, until reduced by half. Add the sun-dried tomatoes, chicken stock, half of the parsley and the remaining salt and pepper. Bring to a boil, reduce the heat and simmer for 5-7 minutes.

Cook the pasta in the boiling water until just tender, drain and return to the pot. Return the scallops and any accumulated juices to the sauce, pour over the pasta and cook over medium heat for 2 minutes, stirring and tossing, until the pasta is well coated. Add the remaining parsley and the cheese, if you wish, and toss. The pasta is ready to serve!

Cook's Tip

Capers are the unopened flower bud of a trailing shrub, capparis spinosa, that grows all over the Mediterranean and have been in use for many centuries. After the buds are picked, they are preserved by packing in salt or pickling in brine. Brine-cured capers are readily available in most areas and add a wonderful touch to sauces, pasta dishes, salads and appetizers.

Most Italian chefs frown upon the idea of adding cheese to fish dishes. I must be crazy, but I like it over this pasta.

"Dining is and always was a great artistic opportunity."
Frank Lloyd Wright

Menu Suggestion
Canteloupe with Prosciutto and Gorgonzola
Pasta with Scallops and Artichokes
Bread
Molded Chocolate Pudding

Wine Suggestion
Pinot Grigio

Pasta al Sugo di Tonno e Pomodori

PASTA WITH TUNA AND TOMATOES

My Aunt Buliti lived with my family in Palermo for 15 years and created many of my favorite childhood dishes. What made this really fun to watch is that she would cook while dancing to blaring music, all the while swinging her hand in the air as if playing the guitar or holding a tomato sauce-soaked spoon like a microphone. Even my mother and father would stop and join Mario and I to watch Aunt Buliti as she cooked, shaking their heads and smiling.

This is my version of one of her many great dishes. Even now that she is married, with children of her own, deep in my heart, I think of her as the sister I never had.

SERVES 4 TO 6

3 quarts (2.75 l) water
4 tablespoons olive oil
½ onion, chopped
4 garlic cloves, thickly sliced
¼ teaspoon red pepper flakes
½ teaspoon salt
¼ teaspoon black pepper
1 tablespoon sugar
¼ cup drained capers
4 ounces (115 g) chopped oil-packed sun-dried tomatoes
1½ cups Chicken Stock (see page 228)
1½ cups Tomato Sauce (see page 225)
3 tablespoons chopped fresh Italian parsley
1 (8-ounce) (225-g) can water packed white tuna, drained and flaked
1 pound (450 g) pasta — penne, farfelle, or shell
3 tablespoons freshly grated Parmigiano Reggiano cheese

In a large pot, bring the water for the pasta to a boil.

Heat the oil in a large sauté pan set on medium-high heat until sizzling, about 2 minutes. Cook the onion and garlic for 3 minutes. Add the red pepper flakes, salt, pepper, sugar, capers and sun-dried tomatoes and cook for 2 minutes. Stir in the chicken stock, tomato sauce and 1½ tablespoons of the parsley and bring to a boil. Reduce the heat and simmer for 5-8 minutes. Add the tuna to the simmering sauce, mix well and remove from the heat.

Add the pasta to the boiling water and cook until just tender. Drain well and return to the pot. Add the sauce and cook over medium heat for 2-3 minutes, stirring, until well coated. Stir in the cheese and the remaining parsley and serve to your guests.

COOK'S TIP

To add a different dimension, combine 5 tablespoons of balsamic vinegar and 5 tablespoons of sugar in a nonstick sauté pan. Bring to a boil and reduce by half, about 5 minutes. Stir into the sauce to give it a sweet and sour finish.

Menu Suggestion

PASTA WITH TUNA AND TOMATOES
STEAK SALAD
FRIED TOMATOES
BREAD
LEMON ICE

Wine Suggestion
ROSSO DI MONTALCINO

Pasta al Sugo di Tonno e Limone

PASTA WITH TUNA AND LEMON

SERVES 4

3 quarts (2.75 l) water

1 pound (450 g) penne pasta

¼ cup olive oil

3 garlic cloves, thickly sliced

¼ teaspoon red pepper flakes

1 (6½-ounce) (190-g) can water packed tuna, drained and flaked

¼ cup fresh lemon juice

Zest of 1 lemon, grated

½ teaspoon salt

¼ teaspoon black pepper

3 tablespoons chopped fresh Italian parsley

¼ cup pasta cooking water

¼ cup freshly grated Parmigiano Reggiano cheese (optional)

Bring the water for the pasta to a boil in a large pot. Add the pasta and cook until just tender.

While the pasta is cooking, heat the oil, garlic and red pepper flakes in a large sauté pan set on medium heat until sizzling, about 3 minutes. Remove the pan from the heat and carefully add the tuna (if it hasn't been well-drained, you will get excessive spattering from the oil), lemon juice, lemon zest, salt, pepper, 2 tablespoons of the chopped parsley and the pasta cooking water. Return the pan to low heat and stir well. Cook for 2-3 minutes and remove from the heat.

Drain the cooked pasta and return it to the pot. Pour the sauce over the pasta, add the remaining parsley and cook on medium heat for 3 minutes, tossing until well coated. Remove from the heat and stir in the cheese. The pasta is now ready to serve.

COOK'S TIP

After you've added pasta to boiling water, always stir gently with a wooden spoon to prevent the pasta from sticking to the bottom of the pan and from clumping together. Stir again when the water comes back to the boil.

On the annual Festival of the Village Saint, it was customary for all the unmarried women to prepare a dish for a contest. This year, it was to be judged by a handsome fisherman, Turiddu. Each of the young ladies stood behind her creation while Turiddu tasted. When he came to Nunziata's pasta, Turiddu felt an explosion of flavor.

Turning to Nunziata, her eyes seemed to reflect ocean waves breaking onto a sandy shore into a million tiny diamond flecks, each reflecting the orange glow of the setting sun.

What follows is the recipe of the dish that legend reports to have brought Turiddu and Nunziata together.

Menu Suggestion

EGGPLANT WITH TOMATOES
PASTA WITH TUNA AND LEMON
CINNAMON SUGAR COOKIES
DIPPED IN CHOCOLATE

Wine Suggestion

CHARDONNAY

Pasta con il Pollo e il Rosmarino

PASTA WITH ROSEMARY CHICKEN

Roasted chicken with garlic and rosemary stuffed under the skin, infusing their irresistible flavors into the juicy meat, was part of the Stellino family culinary heritage. This recipe combines the rich taste tradition of the original ingredients in a sauce that will marry well with your favorite pasta. I can safely say that my mother, father and brother have all passed their seal of approval on the changes — now it's time for yours.

So bring this fabulous pasta dish to your table and then stand back and watch. Under the spell of its fabulous combination of basic ingredients, you will soon hear a chatter of happy voices, a little slice of life blooming around your table. I think there is nothing more satisfying than this simple enjoyment of the fruits of your loving labor in the kitchen.

SERVES 4 TO 6

½ cup olive oil

3 tablespoons balsamic vinegar

1 teaspoon salt

½ teaspoon black pepper

4 tablespoons finely chopped fresh rosemary or 2 tablespoons dried (see Cook's Tip)

4 (6- to 8-ounce) (175- to 225-g) skinless, boneless chicken breasts

3 quarts (2.75 l) water

4 garlic cloves, thickly sliced

2 tablespoons chopped shallots

½ cup white wine

1½ cups Chicken Stock (see page 228)

½ cup whipping cream

1 pound (450 g) pasta — penne, rigatoni or tortiglioni

3 tablespoons freshly grated Pecorino Romano cheese

The night before serving, combine 4 tablespoons of the olive oil, the balsamic vinegar, ½ teaspoon of the salt, ¼ teaspoon of the pepper and 2 tablespoons of the chopped rosemary. Toss the chicken breasts in the marinade and refrigerate, covered, overnight.

The day of serving, preheat the oven to 425° F (220° C). Remove the chicken from the marinade and place on a rack in a roasting pan. Discard the marinade. Bake for 20 minutes. Remove the chicken from the oven and set aside until cool enough to handle. Cut into ½-inch (1.5-cm) cubes and sprinkle with the remaining salt and pepper. Set aside.

Bring the water for the pasta to a boil in a large pot.

Heat the remaining olive oil and the garlic in a large sauté pan set on medium-high heat until the garlic begins to sizzle, about 2 minutes. Add the shallots and the remaining rosemary and cook for 2-3 minutes. Pour in the wine and boil until reduced by half, about 2 minutes. Add the chicken stock and cream, bring to a boil and cook on medium heat for 10-15 minutes, until the sauce has thickened slightly. Add the reserved cooked chicken and cook for 5 minutes longer.

While the sauce is cooking, add the pasta to the boiling water and cook until just tender. Drain the pasta well and return to the pot. Pour the sauce over the pasta and cook, stirring, over medium heat for 3-5 minutes, until the pasta is well coated. Add the cheese and mix well. The pasta is ready to be served.

COOK'S TIP

Rosemary, an aromatic, evergreen shrub with green leaves like curved pine needles, is an herb native to the Mediterranean. When substituting fresh rosemary for dried in a recipe, use just twice as much fresh for dried, instead of the normal three times as much. This is because of rosemary's strong flavor.

If you find yourself completely out of rosemary, try substituting thyme or tarragon. As a general rule when substituting herbs in a recipe, start with half the amount called for and then add more if necessary, to your taste.

"There is no love sincerer than the love of food."

GEORGE BERNARD SHAW

Menu Suggestion
PASTA WITH ROSEMARY CHICKEN
BREAD
PEAR AND WALNUT TART

Wine Suggestion
CHARDONNAY

Gnocchi[1]
POTATO DUMPLINGS

"Ridi bambino
che la mamma
ha fatto gli gnocchi."
(Laugh child,
mother has
made you gnocchi.)

ITALIAN SAYING

LET'S TALK ABOUT GNOCCHI

Gnocchi is one of the most beloved Italian dishes, equally common from the North to the South. Once you master the following basic recipes, the variations are only limited by your imagination. But before I let you roam freely into the fabulous gnocchi territory, let me give you a few hints.

THE POTATO

Dry baking potatoes, like the Russet, are the best choice for this dish. They have a higher starch content and less moisture and make gnocchi that are light and tender.

I've opted to peel and quarter the potatoes to cook them more quickly. This is a step abhorred by traditional pasta chefs, since it is believed that potatoes cooked this way tend to absorb more water which requires using more flour and produces a tough and dense gnocchi. I feel that with careful handling, it is possible to create light gnocchi using this method.

An alternate method is to cook the potatoes in their skins. Use 2 pounds (900 g) of unpeeled Russets in place of the 1¾ pounds (790 g) of peeled potatoes listed in the master recipe. Place the unpeeled potatoes in a large pot filled with cold water to cover by 2 inches (5 cm). Cover the pan and bring the water to a boil. Remove the cover, reduce the heat to medium-low and cook for 40-45 minutes, until the potatoes are pierced easily with a fork. Place them in cold water until they are easy to handle and then peel. Put the potatoes through a potato ricer at once. Continue with the same amount of ingredients as per the master recipe.

EQUIPMENT

The best tool you can use to mash the potatoes is a top-of-the-line potato ricer with small holes. This tool will create a fine, silk-like texture. A potato masher should only be used as a last resort as it tends to leave lumps in the potato mixture which make a coarser texture.

Help Me! It's Sticking

No matter what tools you use, nothing prepares you for the sense of complete panic you feel the first time you mix the ingredients and try to form the gnocchi dough while everything seems to stick to your hands. Here are a couple of tricks that work for me.

Mix all the ingredients in a large bowl with a rubber spatula, using only 1 cup of the flour in this step. Pour ¼ cup of the remaining flour on the working surface and knead the dough with your hands, using the pastry scraper to gather any dough that sticks to the top of the working surface. Once you've gotten good at this, it will take you only a few minutes to incorporate the flour and shape the kneaded dough into a ball. If you feel the dough sticking to your fingers, don't worry, a few more turns and it will be okay. Remember that the amount of flour needed will change depending on the humidity and other conditions in your kitchen. Yes, making gnocchi is not an exact science — it is a tactile journey.

What Is The Correct Gnocchi Texture?

Tender cooked gnocchi run the risk of breaking when tossed with the sauce. As the gnocchi cool off after they're cooked, they tend to toughen. Leftover gnocchi are never as soft as when you have just made them. Once you feel you've reached a texture to your liking when kneading the dough, pull off a couple of small pieces of the dough, shape them, cook in boiling water and taste to test for consistency. My advice is to look for a texture that will produce a soft, delicate, yet resilient gnocchi which will maintain its shape as you toss them with the sauce. Keep adding cheese or flour until you get your desired consistency.

A Few Last Words

Remember, the first time is always the toughest. It will only take you a couple of tries and just like my grandmother, you'll be adding a pinch of this and a bunch of that, a couple of turns of the dough and the gnocchi are ready.

Have fun, life is an adventure!

"What I say is that, if a fellow really likes potatoes, he must be a pretty decent sort of fellow."

A. A. Milne

Gnocchi al Sugo di Pomodoro

POTATO GNOCCHI WITH TOMATO SAUCE

As children, my brother, Mario, and I couldn't wait until Mother made gnocchi. It started the day before serving when Mother hand selected the proper potatoes. She would hold them carefully, squeeze and smell, then it was either into her shopping bag or tossed aside. I asked her, what are you looking for? At the time I dismissed this as one of my mother's many eccentricities. But I've slowly grown to appreciate her passion for food and eating.

Well, there was hardly a word exchanged as Mario and I dove into our bowls filled with gnocchi. The only sounds were the clicking of forks and the soft hums of pleasure. My mother would watch us, smiling and beaming with pride, softly shaking her head as if listening to music, that soft sound of love that only a mother would know.

SERVES 4 TO 6
GNOCCHI:

1 ¾ pounds (790 g) baking potatoes, preferably Russet, peeled and quartered
2 cups all-purpose flour
½ teaspoon salt
¼ teaspoon nutmeg
1 cup + 4 tablespoons (optional) freshly grated Parmigiano Reggiano cheese

TOMATO SAUCE:

3 tablespoons olive oil
4 garlic cloves, thickly sliced
¼ teaspoon red pepper flakes
1 (28-ounce) (790-g) can peeled Italian tomatoes, drained, chopped and juices reserved separately
1 teaspoon sugar
¼ teaspoon salt
⅛ teaspoon black pepper
½ teaspoon dried oregano
2 tablespoons chopped fresh basil
3 quarts (2.75 l) water

FOR THE POTATO GNOCCHI

Put the potatoes into a large pot with enough cold water to cover by 2 inches (5 cm), cover and bring to a boil. Remove the cover, reduce the heat to medium-low and cook for 15-20 minutes, until the potatoes are so soft they will break with pressure from the back of a spoon. Drain well, return to the pan and shake them over moderate heat, uncovered, to dry them out, about 1-2 minutes. Force the dried potatoes through a potato ricer. (Don't use a food processor for mashing potatoes — it will make the potatoes gummy.)

In large bowl, mix 1½ cups of the flour, the salt, nutmeg and cheese. Stir in the mashed potatoes. Turn the mixture out onto a lightly floured board and knead lightly until it is soft, pliable and just a bit sticky. Don't over-knead the dough. Put the dough into a bowl, cover and refrigerate for about 1 hour.

For the Tomato Sauce

Cook the olive oil, garlic and red pepper flakes for 2 minutes in a large sauté pan set on medium heat. Stir in the drained tomatoes and cook for 3 minutes. Add the sugar, salt, pepper, oregano and basil and cook for 3 more minutes, stirring once. Stir in the reserved tomato juices, bring to a boil and simmer for 10 minutes. Keep warm until the gnocchi are cooked.

To Shape the Gnocchi

Cut the chilled gnocchi dough into 5 pieces. Dust each piece and the work surface with the remaining flour. Roll each piece of dough into a ¾-inch (2-cm) thick rope and cut each rope into ½-inch (1.5-cm) pieces. On the fine grating side of a cheese grater, hold the pieces of dough against the grater with the tip of your thumb. Gently roll the dough down the grater for a distance of about 3 inches (8 cm). As you do this, the gnocchi will curl around your thumb and the grater will leave a series of decorative indentations on the back side. (An alternate method is to press the dough against the tines of a dinner fork to create a ribbed impression.) Place each finished gnocchi on a lightly floured baking sheet, making sure they don't touch. Refrigerate the gnocchi until you're ready to cook them.

To Cook the Gnocchi

Bring the water for the gnocchi to a boil in a large pot. Put ¼ of the warm sauce in a large, warmed serving bowl. Cook the gnocchi ¼ at a time. The gnocchi will fall to the bottom of the pan when dropped into the water. As they begin to cook they will rise to the top, about 2 minutes. Cook for 2 more minutes and remove them with a slotted spoon to the bowl with the tomato sauce. Stir until coated, using a rubber spatula to prevent breaking the gnocchi. Stir gently, as if you are folding beaten egg whites into a mixture. Continue cooking the gnocchi, ¼ at a time, and adding them to the other cooked gnocchi with another quarter of the warm tomato sauce. Garnish with the remaining cheese.

"There is an emanation from the heart in genuine hospitality which can not be described but is immediately felt, and puts the stranger at once at his ease."

Washington Irving

Menu Suggestion
Uncle Gaetano's
Caesar Salad
Gnocchi with Tomato Sauce
Bread

Wine Suggestion
Merlot

Gnocchi con i Due Pomodori
Potato Gnocchi with Sun-dried Tomato Sauce

The Sicilian summer was often the occasion for a visit to my paternal grandmother, Maria. I remember the large terrace behind her home, filled with large tables on which rows and rows of tomatoes were laid upon straw beds to dry in the sun. The straw allowed air to circulate underneath and prevented the tomatoes from rotting. Grandma then packed the tomatoes in olive oil, preserving their flavor for our family all winter long.

The following dish combines Grandmother Maria's sun-dried tomatoes with my other grandmother, Adele's, gnocchi recipe. I always feel my two grandmothers smiling at me as I bring their favorites back to life through my cooking.

Menu Suggestion
SAVORY MEAT PIE
GNOCCHI
WITH SUN-DRIED TOMATO SAUCE
BAKED PEARS
WITH SWEETENED RICOTTA

Wine Suggestion
SAUVIGNON BLANC

SERVES 4 TO 6
3 tablespoons olive oil
½ onion, chopped
4 garlic cloves, chopped
1 (1-pound) (450-g) can peeled Italian tomatoes,
drained, chopped and juices reserved separately
4 ounces (115 g) (⅔ cup) finely chopped oil-packed sun-dried tomatoes
¾ cup Chicken Stock (see page 228)
¼ teaspoon salt
¼ teaspoon black pepper
2 tablespoons chopped fresh basil
1 recipe Potato Gnocchi (see pages 82-83)
¾ cup toasted pine nuts
4 tablespoons freshly grated Parmigiano Reggiano cheese

Heat the olive oil in a large sauté pan set on medium-high heat until sizzling, about 2 minutes. Add the onion and garlic and cook for 2 minutes. Stir in the tomatoes and sun-dried tomatoes and cook for 3 minutes. Add the chicken stock, salt, pepper, basil and reserved tomato juices. Bring to a boil and simmer for 5-8 minutes.

Cook the gnocchi as directed on page 83, tossing them with the sauce. Sprinkle with the pine nuts and cheese and gently stir.

COOK'S TIP
Toasting pine nuts can be easily done on the stove top, in the oven or in the microwave. On the stovetop, place the nuts in a single layer in an ungreased sauté pan and cook over medium heat for 5-8 minutes, stirring or shaking the pan to keep them from scorching. Remove from the pan as soon as they are toasted to your liking. If left in the pan they will continue cooking and may burn. For oven toasting, place them on a baking sheet and cook in a 350° F (180° C) oven for 7-8 minutes, stirring occasionally. In the microwave, cook on a paper plate at 100 percent power for 1 minute. Stir and let stand for a minute, then cook for another 1½ minutes.

Gnocchi con il Sugo di Noci e Gorgonzola

POTATO GNOCCHI WITH WALNUTS AND GORGONZOLA

SERVES 4 TO 6

8 ounces (225 g) Gorgonzola cheese, crumbled
¾ cup Chicken Stock (see page 228)
¼ teaspoon salt
¼ teaspoon black pepper
1 recipe Potato Gnocchi (see pages 82-83)
1 cup roughly chopped toasted walnuts

In a small saucepan set on medium heat, heat the Gorgonzola cheese, chicken stock and walnuts until the cheese melts, about 3-5 minutes. Simmer for about 2 minutes, until the sauce has thickened slightly. Stir in the salt and pepper and keep warm.

Cook the gnocchi as directed on page 83, drain and transfer to a large, heated serving bowl. Pour the sauce over the gnocchi and stir until well coated. Serve immediately.

COOK'S TIP

If you would like to make the gnocchi ahead of time, place the baking trays of uncooked gnocchi in the freezer. Once frozen, transfer them to freezer bags for up to 1 month. When ready to use, simply cook the frozen gnocchi as directed above. The frozen gnocchi will not float to the top of the water until they have thawed.

I first had this gnocchi combination in a little pensione around the town of Bergamo while traveling with my wife, Nanci. It was late fall, cold and snowing outside, and the room was almost empty.

A carafe of local red wine left us completely relaxed and then the gnocchi arrived. As the wind roared outside in the snow covered fields, we were completely happy and comfortable.

You don't have to wait for the cold winter nights to enjoy this recipe. Nanci and I enjoy this on summer nights at our home, while the candles' flickering light, glowing in the summer breeze, reminds us of the warming fireplace on that cold winter night in Bergamo.

Menu Suggestion
GNOCCHI WITH WALNUTS
AND GORGONZOLA
SCALLOP SALAD
WITH ORANGE VINAIGRETTE
MOCHA CREME CARAMEL

Wine Suggestion
CHARDONNAY

Gnocchi di Zucca e Salvia
PUMPKIN GNOCCHI WITH SAGE

I think pumpkin is quite a pleasing variation from the traditional potato gnocchi dough. I was first exposed to this dish during one of my family's trips in northern Italy. My mother was so enthused that she started consulting her culinary texts to find the perfect recipe.

I continued this search on my own, trying to find the best combination that would also ease the preparation. I think you'll be surprised how simple this dish can be. The most important part of this recipe is the mixing of the dough. The secret lies in handling the dough quickly, but gently. The dough will be slightly sticky, but with proper handling, will produce fabulously light and tasty gnocchi.

While I present the traditional sauce for this dish, you can use any pasta sauce to make up your favorite combination. Oh, and forget about counting calories on this one.

SERVES 6 TO 8
PUMPKIN GNOCCHI:
2 cups canned pumpkin
1 ¾ cups all-purpose flour
1 cup freshly grated Parmigiano Reggiano cheese
1 teaspoon chopped fresh sage (optional)
¼ teaspoon nutmeg

SAGE SAUCE:
6 tablespoons butter
4 garlic cloves, thickly sliced
3 tablespoons coarsely chopped fresh sage
¼ teaspoon nutmeg
⅛ teaspoon salt
⅛ teaspoon black pepper
4 tablespoons freshly grated Parmigiano Reggiano cheese

FOR THE PUMPKIN GNOCCHI

Mix the pumpkin, 1½ cups of the flour, the cheese, sage and nutmeg in a large bowl with a spatula or wooden spoon. Spread the remaining ¼ cup of flour on a flat work surface and knead the dough, using a pressing and folding motion, until well mixed, as if you were making bread. The dough should not be kneaded too long. The longer the dough is kneaded the more flour it will absorb, resulting in heavier gnocchi. Move quickly and lightly, as the dough will stick to your hands if you press too hard.

Cut the dough into 4 equal pieces and roll them on the floured surface to form a ¾-inch (2-cm) thick rope. With a sharp knife, cut the dough ropes into ½-inch (1.5-cm) pieces.

Place the finished gnocchi on a lightly floured baking sheet and refrigerate until you're ready to cook them. If you are preparing the gnocchi to be served at a later date, they can be frozen. Simply place the baking sheet of gnocchi in the freezer. Once they are frozen solid, transfer them to freezer bags for up to 1 month. (Follow the same steps for cooking as you would if they were unfrozen.)

To cook the gnocchi, drop them into a large pot (the wider the pot the better) of boiling water. Stir them gently with a spoon, as they will initially fall to the bottom of the pan and may stick. After the gnocchi float to the top of the water, cook them for 2 minutes longer and then remove to a large bowl filled with warm water. Cook all the gnocchi before beginning the sauce.

For the Sage Sauce
Place all the sauce ingredients except the cheese in a large (12-inch) (30-cm), nonstick sauté pan set on medium-low heat. Stir well and cook for 5 minutes.

Add the gnocchi to the sauce in the pan, using a slotted spoon to lift them from the bowl of warm water. Toss the gnocchi in the sauce over medium heat for 3 minutes.

Spoon the gnocchi into serving dishes and top each with 1 tablespoon of the grated cheese. Pour any sage butter remaining in the sauté pan over the gnocchi.

Cook's Tip
All of the gnocchi sauces are equally good for tossing with your favorite pasta.

"Memory is the diary that we all carry about with us."
Oscar Wilde

Menu Suggestion
Roasted Bell Peppers with Balsamic Vinegar
Pumpkin Gnocchi with Sage
Bread

Wine Suggestion
Rosso di Montalcino

Gnocchi con Zucchero e Cannella
GNOCCHI WITH SUGAR AND CINNAMON

Although it sounds quite sweet, this pasta is not a dessert. I discovered this on a rainy day in September when I was visiting one of my favorite restaurants, called La Vecchia (The Old Lady), with my wife, Nanci.

Our waiter, Roberto, persuaded us to order a house specialty that was, in his words, imperative. He returned to our table with this recipe: bowls of potato gnocchi, over which he poured butter, sugar, cheese and cinnamon! I was convinced he was joking, but at my wife's insistence, I took a bite. What followed was an array of delicate flavors dancing around the aromas of fine exotic spices. I was wrong with my preconceived ideas and I was happy to admit it.

SERVES 4 TO 6

1 recipe Potato Gnocchi (see pages 82-83)
8 tablespoons freshly grated Parmigiano Reggiano cheese
1 teaspoon cinnamon
4 teaspoons sugar
8 tablespoons melted butter

Cook the gnocchi as directed on page 83, drain and place in 6 individual serving bowls. Sprinkle each dish equally with the cheese, cinnamon and sugar. Pour the melted butter over the top.

Menu Suggestion
GREEN SALAD
WITH BALSAMIC VINAIGRETTE
GNOCCHI WITH
CINNAMON AND SUGAR
BREAD

Wine Suggestion
CHENIN BLANC

Risotto Quattro Formaggi
Risotto with Four Cheeses

Serves 6
6 cups Chicken Stock (see page 228)
2 tablespoons butter
2 tablespoons olive oil
1 onion, preferably white, finely chopped
2 garlic cloves, chopped
3 cups arborio rice
1 cup white wine
½ teaspoon salt
¼ teaspoon black pepper
6 tablespoons freshly grated Parmigiano Reggiano cheese
2 ounces (60 g) Italian Fontina cheese, grated
6 tablespoons freshly grated Asiago cheese
1 ounce (30 g) Gorgonzola cheese, crumbled
3 tablespoons chopped fresh Italian parsley

In a large covered stockpot, bring the chicken stock to a boil, reduce the heat to low and keep warm. In a 4-quart (3.75 l) saucepan set on medium heat, cook the butter and the olive oil until sizzling, about 2 minutes. Add the onion and cook 2 minutes. Reduce the heat to low, add the garlic and cook for 4 minutes. Add the rice and stir well. Raise the heat to medium-high and stir in the wine, salt and pepper, cooking until the wine is evaporated, about 2 minutes.

Pour in 3 cups of the simmering stock, stir well and bring to a boil for 2 minutes. Reduce the heat to low, cover the saucepan and let the rice cook undisturbed for 15 minutes. Uncover the saucepan and stir the risotto. Don't worry if it's dry. Raise the heat to medium and add ½ cup of the simmering stock, stirring well until it's all incorporated. Continue adding the simmering stock ½ cup at a time and stirring well until the risotto is cooked. This process will take about 5-8 minutes. Taste the rice with each addition of the stock. The rice is perfectly cooked when it is tender to the bite. Don't worry if there is additional stock left. Turn off the heat, add a final ½ cup of the stock, all four cheeses and the parsley. Mix well and let it rest for 3 minutes. Serve immediately.

In my family, we always made our own holiday traditions when it came to food. I loved this dish's creamy, cheesy texture for Easter. I'm almost afraid to admit its simple culinary appeal. But maybe it's important for you to see that even inside the body of this adult chef and author, still beats the giddy heart of an enthusiastic child. I still make this dish around Easter and share it with my friends. As I sit back and watch their enjoyment, I laugh softly thinking about their inner child coming out.

This recipe is a real "diet buster." Save it for special occasions when you can throw caution to the wind. Prepare it for the special times of your family and start a tradition of your own.

Menu Suggestion
Mixed Salad
with Honey Orange Vinaigrette
Risotto with Four Cheeses
Bread

Wine Suggestion
Orvieto

Risotto Primavera
Risotto with Vegetables

Nobody can surpass the subtle cunning of a mother. Let me explain. I'm sure you know by now that as a child I was a sworn enemy to any kind of vegetable. But my mother was not about to back down on this battle and declare defeat. She was determined to incorporate vegetables in my daily diet and to top it all off, I was going to like it!

The list of her successes is too long to mention here. But I feel I should point out this very recipe embodies her greatest triumph. By mixing risotto with a medley of pretty colored, diced vegetables, all nestled in a bed of flavorful herbs, I was conquered. I dedicate this dish to all the mothers that have to deal with the challenging palates of their offspring. I hope this will help in their efforts. However, if nothing else, I know you'll love it for its own merits.

SERVES 6

6 cups Chicken Stock (see page 228)
2 tablespoons butter
2 tablespoons olive oil
1 onion, preferably white, finely chopped
2 garlic cloves, chopped
2 teaspoons chopped fresh sage
2 teaspoons chopped fresh thyme
3 cups arborio rice
1 cup white wine
½ teaspoon salt
¼ teaspoon black pepper
1 cup carrots, cut into ¼-inch (6-mm) dice
1 cup yellow zucchini, cut into ¼-inch (6-mm) dice
1 cup green zucchini, cut into ¼-inch (6-mm) dice
1 cup frozen peas, thawed
6 tablespoons freshly grated Parmigiano Reggiano cheese
3 tablespoons chopped fresh Italian parsley

In a large covered stockpot, bring the chicken stock to a boil, then reduce the heat to low and simmer until needed.

In a 4-quart (3.75 l) saucepan set on medium heat, cook the butter and olive oil until sizzling, about 2 minutes. Add the onion and cook 2 minutes. Reduce the heat to low, add the garlic and herbs and cook for 4 minutes. Stir in the rice and mix well. Raise the heat to medium-high and add the wine, salt and pepper, cooking until the wine is completely absorbed, about 2 minutes.

Add 3 cups of the simmering stock and the carrots, stir well, bring to a boil and cook for 2 minutes. Reduce the heat to low, cover and let the rice cook undisturbed for 15 minutes. Uncover the saucepan and stir the risotto. Don't worry if it's dry. Raise the heat to medium, add both the zucchini, peas and ½ cup of simmering stock, stirring well until it's all incorporated. Continue adding

the simmering stock ½ cup at a time, stirring well, until the risotto is cooked. This process will take about 5-8 minutes. Taste the rice with each addition of the stock. The rice is perfectly cooked when it is tender to the bite. Don't worry if there is additional stock left.

Turn off the heat, add a final ½ cup of the stock, the grated cheese and parsley, mix well and let it rest for 3 minutes. Stir well and serve while still piping hot.

COOK'S TIP

The success of risotto lies in using the right rice. In Italy rices are graded superfino, fino, semifino and ordinario. For risottos be sure to use rices only from the first two grades. My favorite, Arborio, is a superfino. Arborio is a medium-grain white rice that is very fat and contains a high proportion of starch, which contributes to the creaminess of the risotto. Other superfino varieties are Roma, Maratelli and Carnaroli. A good rice of the fino grade is Vialone.

"Rice is born in water and must die in wine."

BRILLAT-SAVARIN

Menu Suggestion
TOMATO AND ONION SALAD
RISOTTO WITH VEGETABLES
BREAD

Wine Suggestion
CHIANTI

Risotto con i Gamberi, Curry e Piselli

Risotto with Shrimp, Curry and Peas

Serves 6

3 cups Chicken Stock (see page 228)

3 cups Shrimp Stock (see page 231), (see Cook's Tip)

2 tablespoons butter

2 tablespoons olive oil

1 onion, preferably white, finely chopped

2 teaspoons curry powder

2 garlic cloves, chopped

3 cups arborio rice

1 cup white wine

½ teaspoon salt

¼ teaspoon black pepper

1 pound (450 g) large shrimp (13/15 count),
shelled and each shrimp cut into 4 pieces

1½ cups frozen peas, thawed

6 tablespoon freshly grated Parmigiano Reggiano cheese

4 tablespoons whipping cream

3 tablespoons chopped fresh Italian parsley

Just like my mother did when she first came to Sicily as a bride, my wife, Nanci, set about mastering the fine nuances of Italian cooking after we were wed. My Grandmother Adele was particularly fond of my American wife. She welcomed Nanci to the family and into her heart, spending hours with her in the kitchen, passing on the cooking secrets she had shared with her own daughters.

So one day there came a night when Nanci ordered me to sit down at the table while she took culinary charge of the food for the evening. Just as I had seduced her many years before with my cooking, she concocted for me the most delicious of all love potions. I was delighted to see how the culinary traditions of my family were now filtering through her own passion with such spectacular results.

In a large covered pot, bring the chicken and shrimp stocks to a boil, then reduce the heat to low and simmer until needed.

In a 4-quart (3.75 l) saucepan set on medium heat, cook the butter and olive oil until sizzling, about 2 minutes. Add the onion and curry powder and cook 2 minutes. Reduce the heat to low, add the garlic and cook for 4 minutes. Stir in the rice and mix well. Raise the heat to medium-high and add the wine, salt and pepper, cooking until the wine is evaporated, about 2 minutes.

Add 3 cups of the simmering stock, stir well, bring to a boil and cook for 2 minutes. Reduce the heat to low, cover the saucepan and let the rice cook, undisturbed, for 15 minutes. Uncover the saucepan and stir the risotto. Don't worry if it's dry. Raise the heat to medium and add ½ cup of the simmering stock, stirring well

until it's all incorporated. Continue adding the simmering stock ½ cup at a time and stirring well until the risotto is cooked. This process will take about 5-8 minutes. During the last 2-3 minutes, add the shrimp and peas. The rice is perfectly cooked when tender to the bite. Don't worry if there is additional stock left.

Turn off the heat, add a final ½ cup of the stock, the cheese, cream and parsley. Mix well and let it rest, covered, for 3 minutes. Stir well and serve while still piping hot.

COOK'S TIP

If you don't have time to make shrimp stock, you can make an acceptable substitute by mixing 4 cups of Chicken Stock (see page 228) with 2 cups of clam juice.

"A recipe is only a theme which an intelligent cook can play each time with a variation."

MADAME BENOIT

Menu Suggestion
UNCLE GAETANO'S CAESAR SALAD
RISOTTO WITH SHRIMP,
CURRY AND PEAS
BREAD
ZABAGLIONE WITH SPARKLING WINE

Wine Suggestion
CHARDONNAY

I Secondi

Entrees

Pollo Arrosto con la Salsa Verde

WHOLE ROASTED CHICKEN WITH SALSA VERDE

Who said roasted chickens are all the same? As you've come to discover by now, Italians are experts in the many ways of preparing chicken. It is also true that the versatile personality of this delectable meat responds well to the creative urges of any chef. It's like a tango dance under the moonlight where the chef leads and the chicken follows, creating a melodic symphony of a culinary orchestra.

Yes, food cooked to perfection, like this simple yet unique chicken, is like music that seduces your feelings as well as your palate. Go with the flow and enjoy the culinary dance.

SERVES 4

ROASTED CHICKEN:

2 tablespoons chopped garlic
¾ teaspoon salt
¾ teaspoon black pepper
Zest of 1 lemon, finely chopped
1 (4-pound) (1.8-kg) chicken, washed and patted dry
8 lemon slices, ¼ inch (6 mm) thick
2 tablespoons olive oil

SALSA VERDE:

1 slice white bread
½ cup extra virgin olive oil
2 tablespoons red wine vinegar
2 tablespoons drained capers
2 garlic cloves, peeled
1 cup loosely packed Italian parsley leaves
1 cup loosely packed oregano leaves
1 teaspoon anchovy paste
2 tablespoons freshly grated Parmigiano Reggiano cheese
2 teaspoons hearty mustard

FOR THE ROASTED CHICKEN

Preheat the oven to 425° F (220° C). Place the garlic, salt, pepper and lemon zest on a cutting board and chop to a fine consistency, blending all the ingredients well.

Pat the chicken, inside and out, with a paper towel until dry. Loosen the skin, pushing with your fingers around the breast, thighs and back. Stuff 2 of the lemon slices under the skin on each breast and on the back. Rub the inside of the chicken with ⅓ of the garlic mixture. Place the chicken on a vertical roaster, brush it with the olive oil and rub the remaining garlic mixture over the outside.

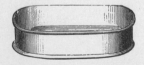

Place the chicken in the oven, reduce the temperature to 350° F (180° C) and roast for 30 minutes. Remove the chicken from the oven, baste it well with the juices that have accumulated in the pan and rotate a ¼ turn clockwise. Cover the top part of the chicken with a tent of foil to keep it from getting too brown. Roast for 1 more hour, repeating the ¼ turn clockwise and basting every 30 minutes. Test the chicken to see if it's fully cooked by inserting the tip of a sharp knife in the thickest part of the thigh. When fully cooked, the juices that run out will be clear. If the juices are not clear, cook 10 minutes longer. Remove the chicken from the oven and let it rest for 10 minutes.

For the Salsa Verde

Put the bread, oil and vinegar into a food processor or blender. Add the capers, garlic, parsley, oregano, anchovy paste, cheese and mustard and pulse the machine on and off until everything is just finely chopped, but not a paste. The salsa should have a somewhat loose consistency, resembling a soft pesto sauce. Taste for seasoning and add additional salt if necessary.

Cut the chicken into serving pieces and serve with the salsa on the side.

"Poultry is for the cook, what canvas is for the painter."

Brillat-Savarin

Menu Suggestion
Whole Roasted Chicken
with Salsa Verde
Herbed Mashed Potatoes
Bread
Three Nut Tart

Wine Suggestion
Chianti

Fricassea di Pollo
CHICKEN FRICASSEE

La Signora Musumeci lived upstairs from my family. She was particularly fond of my mother and her two diavoletti (little devils) and she'd always make a big fuss about Mario and me every time we ran into her. I remember her jewelry-laden hands and her lips saturated with red lipstick. She always wanted to hug and kiss our rosy cheeks. No matter how much Mario and I squirmed, she'd manage to land big smackers all over our forehead and cheeks, leaving a trail of lip marks and the scent of Chanel No. 5 perfume.

Little did I know that in the years to come I would actually be pursuing such encounters with members of the opposite sex instead of running away, but at that tender age, who knew?

SERVES 4

2 tablespoons flour
1 teaspoon ground sage
1 teaspoon ground rosemary
1 teaspoon ground thyme
½ teaspoon salt
½ teaspoon black pepper
4 (6-ounce) (175-g) boneless, skinless chicken breasts
5 tablespoons olive oil
1 pound (450 g) mixed wild mushrooms, quartered
or 1 pound (450 g) button mushrooms, quartered,
mixed with ½ ounce (15 g) dried porcini mushroom pieces
2 tablespoons chopped pancetta or bacon
2 tablespoons chopped fresh Italian parsley
1 tablespoon chopped garlic
½ cup white wine
1 cup Chicken Stock (see page 228)
¾ cup whipping cream
4 slices prosciutto
4 slices provolone or ½ cup shredded sharp imported provolone
½ cup peas, fresh or frozen
½ cup diced carrot
Chopped fresh parsley, for garnish

In a small bowl, mix the flour, sage, rosemary, thyme, ¼ teaspoon of the salt and ⅛ teaspoon of the pepper. Roll the chicken breasts in the flour mixture until well coated. Set aside 1 tablespoon of the leftover coating.

Heat 3 tablespoons of the oil in a large sauté pan set on high heat until sizzling, about 2 minutes. Brown the breasts, about 2 minutes on each side. Remove the chicken to a plate and set aside.

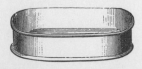

Add the remaining 2 tablespoons of oil to the same pan, and heat until it sizzles, about 2 minutes. Add the mushrooms, pancetta and parsley and cook for 3 minutes. Lower the heat to medium-high, stir in the reserved 1 tablespoon of chicken coating and the garlic and cook 2 minutes more. Pour in the wine, stir well and boil until reduced by half, about 3 minutes. Add the stock, cream and the remaining salt and pepper, reduce the heat and simmer for 10 minutes.

Meanwhile, cut a pocket in the thickest side of each browned chicken breast and stuff with a slice of the prosciutto and a slice of the provolone. Place the stuffed chicken breasts in the pan along with the peas and carrots and simmer for 10 more minutes, turning the breasts once. The sauce should be thick enough to coat the breasts. If it isn't, remove the breasts to a serving plate and cook the sauce on high heat until thickened.

To serve, place the chicken breasts on a serving plate and spoon the sauce over them. Garnish with the chopped fresh parsley.

Cook's Tip

If you are unable to find the dried herbs in the ground form, you can use 1 tablespoon of dried whole herbs and grind in a mortar and pestle or spice mill to make 1 teaspoon of ground herbs.

The fact remains that La Signora Musumeci was a great cook and my mom loved to spend time with her to learn new dishes. The following recipe is my adaptation of one of her dishes which became quite a hit in our family. It is the perfect "all-in-one" dish.

Menu Suggestion
PASTA WITH EGGPLANT
AND BELL PEPPERS
CHICKEN FRICASSEE
GREEN BEANS
WITH GARLIC AND TOMATOES
BREAD
CINNAMON SUGAR COOKIES
DIPPED IN CHOCOLATE

Wine Suggestion
CABERNET SAUVIGNON

Pollo alla Zagara
Chicken with Orange Cream Sauce

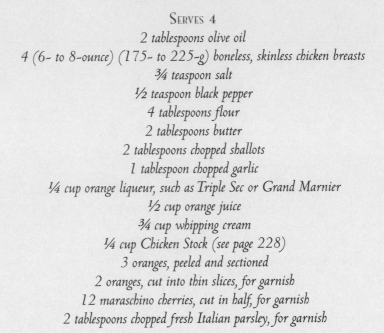

There are moments that remain frozen in time for me, like a photo that never fades: the first time I held a girl's hand, my first kiss. The aroma of the "zagara" (orange blossom), always evokes these romantic images of Sicily, and also reminds me of one of the most important decisions in my life.

Toward the end of my sophomore year in college in the United States, my father and I were traveling through the Arizona desert. The first night we spent at a beautiful old resort called "The Palms," halfway between Scottsdale and Phoenix. Our cottage was located in the middle of an orange grove.

That night I couldn't sleep. Sitting beside my bed, I kept watching the perfect night sky, while the scent of the orange blossoms slowly pervaded the room.

Serves 4

2 tablespoons olive oil
4 (6- to 8-ounce) (175- to 225-g) boneless, skinless chicken breasts
¾ teaspoon salt
½ teaspoon black pepper
4 tablespoons flour
2 tablespoons butter
2 tablespoons chopped shallots
1 tablespoon chopped garlic
¼ cup orange liqueur, such as Triple Sec or Grand Marnier
½ cup orange juice
¾ cup whipping cream
¼ cup Chicken Stock (see page 228)
3 oranges, peeled and sectioned
2 oranges, cut into thin slices, for garnish
12 maraschino cherries, cut in half, for garnish
2 tablespoons chopped fresh Italian parsley, for garnish

Heat the olive oil in a large sauté pan set on high heat until sizzling, about 2 minutes. Season the chicken breasts with ½ teaspoon of the salt and ¼ teaspoon of the pepper and roll in the flour. Cook the breasts until browned, about 2 minutes on each side. Remove the chicken to a plate and set aside. Discard the oil in the pan.

Cook the butter in the same pan over medium-high heat until sizzling, about 2 minutes. Add the shallots and garlic and cook for 3 minutes. Pour in the orange liqueur, stirring well to dislodge the pan residues and cook for 2 minutes. Add the orange juice, cream and chicken stock and bring back to a boil. Stir in the remaining salt and pepper, reduce the heat to low and simmer for 5 minutes. Add the browned chicken and any accumulated juices and simmer for 8 to 10 minutes. Just before serving, gently stir in the orange sections.

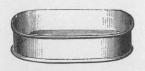

To serve, place a chicken breast in the middle of each serving dish and cover with sauce. Garnish each with the orange slices, maraschino cherry halves and parsley.

Cook's Tip

To easily section oranges, cut a slice off each end of the orange. Stand the orange on a cutting board and remove the peel and white pith by cutting down the sides with a thin knife. Cut alongside the membrane to separate the sections.

A sense of familiarity, longing and hope attacked my heart, and suddenly I felt in my heart like this was home. The next morning I applied over the phone to Arizona State University in Tempe, Arizona, without even visiting the campus.

My application was accepted and I reported to Arizona State for my next semester. The following two years will always be in my mind as two of the best years of my life.

I dedicate this dish to the magic spell of the aromatic orange blossom, and the adventurous spirit inside all of us.

Menu Suggestion
GREEN BEANS WITH
GARLIC, LEMON AND MINT
CHICKEN WITH
ORANGE CREAM SAUCE
RICE PILAF
RASPBERRY TIRAMISU

Wine Suggestion
RIESLING

Pollo della Signora Leila

APRICOT CHICKEN

Growing up in Italy, I never experienced other ethnic cuisines, like Chinese, Mexican, Thai or even other Mediterranean countries! But I had one friend, Karim, who had been raised in Libya. His family had been forced to leave for political reasons.

An invitation to Karim's house for lunch was an adventure, one that carried my thoughts and senses into new culinary worlds. Karim's mother, Signora Leila, mixed spices and ingredients together in ways I had never imagined.

What follows is my version of Signora Leila's fabulous Libyan cooking, my first exposure to other Mediterranean cuisines.

Menu Suggestion

MIXED SALAD WITH ORANGES, ONION AND FENNEL
APRICOT CHICKEN
RICE PILAF
HAZELNUT CAKE

Wine Suggestion

RIESLING

SERVES 6 TO 8

5 garlic cloves, chopped
2 tablespoons dried oregano leaves
1 teaspoon salt
1 teaspoon black pepper
1 cup white wine vinegar
½ cup olive oil
1 cup dried apricots, chopped
½ cup green olives (Spanish), chopped
½ cup drained capers, lightly chopped
3 bay leaves
1 cup dry white wine
¼ cup chopped fresh Italian parsley
¼ cup Dijon mustard
1 red bell pepper, chopped
2 (3-pound) (1.4-kg) cut-up fryer chickens

Mix together all the ingredients, except the chicken, in a medium bowl. Place the chicken in a large glass, ceramic or stainless steel bowl, pour over the marinade, cover and refrigerate for 6 hours or overnight.

Preheat the oven to 350° F (180° C). Arrange the chicken pieces in 2 (9 x 13-inch) (23 x 33-cm) baking dishes. Pour in the marinade and bake for 50-60 minutes or until the juices in the thigh pieces run clear. Remove the chicken pieces to a serving platter, pour the juices on top and let cool for 15 minutes before serving.

COOK'S TIP

If you would like the sauce to be thicker, pour the pan juices into a medium saucepan and bring to a boil over medium-high heat. Remove the pan from the heat and stir in a slurry of 2 tablespoons cornstarch mixed with 2 tablespoons of water. Return to the heat to thicken and clear, stirring constantly, about 1 minute.

Pollo all'Ungherese

Chicken Paprikash

Serves 4

½ teaspoon salt

¼ teaspoon black pepper

3 tablespoons paprika

¼ teaspoon cayenne pepper

¼ cup flour

1 (3- to 4-pound) (1.4- to 1.8-kg) chicken, cut into pieces

3 tablespoons olive oil

1 small onion, thinly sliced

4 cloves garlic, thickly sliced

1 red bell pepper, thinly sliced

1 green bell pepper, thinly sliced

½ cup white wine

1 (1-pound) (450-g) can peeled Italian tomatoes

1 cup Chicken Stock (see page 228)

3 tablespoons chopped fresh Italian parsley

Mix together the salt, pepper, paprika and cayenne pepper. Coat the chicken pieces with the mixture then dust with the flour, shaking off the excess.

Heat 3 tablespoon of the olive oil in a nonstick high-sided fry pan on high heat. Add the seasoned chicken pieces and cook until quite brown, about 2 minutes per side. Transfer the chicken to a plate and set aside.

Save the oil left in the pan. Reduce the heat to medium-high and cook the onion, garlic and peppers for 5-8 minutes, until soft. Pour in the wine and boil until reduced by half, stirring, about 2-3 minutes. Add the tomatoes, their juice and the chicken stock. Break up the tomatoes with the back of a spoon and stir well. Return the cooked chicken to the pan, bring to a boil, reduce the heat medium-low and simmer, with the lid ajar, for 15-20 minutes, turning the chicken once.

Remove the chicken to a serving dish with a slotted spoon. Cook the sauce 5 more minutes. Taste and adjust the salt and pepper to your liking. Pour the sauce over the chicken and sprinkle with the chopped parsley.

I'll never forget the shy Hungarian, named Franz, who fell in love with my Aunt Titi. He had gone to great lengths to take Italian lessons, but still found it difficult to communicate. Still, however, love can enable a man to walk through fire, and Frantz was determined to make Aunt Titi proud; so he offered to cook dinner for the whole family and served this dish.

I am happy to report that love worked its magic that night. Not only were we all impressed with this recipe, but we all fell in love with Frantz's charming personality. That night, Frantz asked, and was granted, Grandma's permission to marry Aunt Titi.

Menu Suggestion

Tomato and Onion Salad
Chicken Paprikash
Mashed Potatoes
Grapefruit Custard Tart

Wine Suggestion

Zinfandel

Bocconcini di Pollo con le Mandorle
Chicken Nuggets with Almonds

"*Please, no more chicken!*" It was this decree from my father that inspired my mother to create this spectacular recipe. In fact, she told me that she actually resolved to create something that would make my father apologize!

So, in an evening that has become a Stellino family legend, my mother fixed this dish and arranged for Mario and I to be over at a friend's house to spend the night. When we returned home the next evening, both my brother and I noticed an extravagant amount of flowers around the house.

Then, two days later, there was a new addition to our kitchen: a sparkling new dishwasher! And I'll never forget what my mother told the dishwasher delivery men: "*Never underestimate the power of a well-cooked chicken.*"

Serves 4

4 (6-ounce) (175-g) skinless boneless chicken breasts,
cut into ¾-inch (2-cm) cubes
¼ teaspoon salt
⅛ teaspoon black pepper
¾ cup Italian Bread Crumbs (see page 218)
4 tablespoons vegetable oil
4½ tablespoons olive oil
1 white onion, thinly sliced
1 stalk celery, sliced
4 tablespoons chopped oil-packed sun-dried tomatoes
4 garlic cloves, thickly sliced
½ teaspoon red pepper flakes
1 tablespoon tomato paste
¾ cup white wine
1 (1-pound) (450-g) can stewed tomatoes, drained, chopped
and juices reserved separately
1 cup Chicken Stock (see page 228)
3 tablespoons chopped fresh Italian parsley (optional)
⅓ cup slivered almonds
¼ teaspoon sugar

Sprinkle the chicken pieces with salt and pepper and then coat with the bread crumbs, shaking off the excess.

Heat the vegetable oil in a large sauté pan set on high heat until it begins to sizzle, about 2 minutes. Add the seasoned chicken pieces and brown for 2 minutes on each side. Remove from the pan with a slotted spoon and set aside. Discard any oil left in the pan.

Heat 4 tablespoons of the olive oil in the same pan set on high heat until it sizzles, about 2 minutes. Add the onion, celery, sun-dried tomatoes, garlic and red pepper flakes. Cook for 2-3 minutes, stirring well. Stir in the tomato paste, reduce the heat to medium-low and cook, with the lid slightly ajar, for 8-10 minutes.

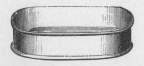

Increase the heat to high, pour in the wine and cook for 2-3 minutes, until the wine has reduced by half. Add the chopped tomatoes, stir well and cook for 2 minutes. Stir in the reserved tomato juices and the chicken stock and bring to a boil. Reduce the heat to a simmer and cook for 5 minutes. Return the browned chicken pieces and the parsley to the pan, stir well and cook for 5-8 minutes.

While the chicken is cooking, toast the almonds. Heat the remaining ½ tablespoon olive in a small nonstick pan set on high heat. Add the almonds and sugar and cook for 1-2 minutes, stirring well to keep the almonds from burning. Transfer the almonds to a small bowl and set aside.

When the chicken is ready, transfer it to a serving bowl and top with the toasted almonds.

Cook's Tip
This dish tastes better reheated the next day. Just add a little bit of chicken stock as you reheat it over medium heat in a sauté pan.

You can create a thicker sauce by simmering it for a longer time. If you want more sauce, increase the amount of tomato paste to 2 tablespoons and the chicken stock to 1½ cups.

"One cannot think well, love well, sleep well, if one has not dined well."

Virginia Woolf

Menu Suggestion
Onion Soup with
Gorgonzola and Prosciutto
Chicken Nuggets with Almonds
Mixed Salad with
Honey Orange Vinaigrette
Bread

Wine Suggestion
Dolcetto d'Alba

Scaloppine di Pollo

Chicken Scallopine with Porcini Rosemary Sauce

This dish is ultimate proof of the saying, "necessity is the mother of invention." The word "scallopine" is most often associated with veal, but veal meat comes with a high price tag. My recipe for chicken scallopine is perfect for the home cook who wants to provide the best for their family within a restricted budget.

But I must confess that I don't feel frugal when I eat this dish: it's a fabulous flavor combination of unique ingredients that brings out a surprising new character in simple chicken breasts.

Don't feel that your creativity is confined to this scallopine recipe. Feel free to substitute chicken for veal in all your favorite recipes. Ah, just think of the possibilities!

Serves 4

4 (6- to 8-ounce) (175- to 225-g) boneless, skinless chicken breasts
¼ teaspoon salt
¼ teaspoon black pepper
4 tablespoons flour
3 tablespoons olive oil
4 tablespoons butter
1 tablespoon porcini mushroom powder (see Cook's Tip)
1 tablespoon chopped fresh rosemary
4 tablespoons toasted pine nuts (optional)
(For toasting directions see Cook's Tip, page 84)
½ cup white wine
½ cup Chicken Stock (see page 228)

Remove the chicken tenderloin, the thin, tapering piece of meat on the lower edge of the breast, from each breast half and freeze for another use. Slice each chicken breast into 3 pieces, across the grain. Pound the slices lightly between plastic wrap to a thickness of ¼ inch (6 mm). Sprinkle with the salt, pepper and flour and set aside.

Pour the oil and 1 tablespoon of the butter into a large sauté pan and cook over high heat until the oil starts to sizzle, about 2 minutes. Add the prepared chicken scallops and cook 1 minute on each side until lightly brown. You may need to brown in 2 batches depending on the size of the pan. Remove the chicken from the pan and set aside. Pour off any excess oil.

Return the pan to high heat and stir in the porcini powder, rosemary and pine nuts, if you wish. The pan will start to smoke quickly. Immediately pour in the wine and boil until reduced by half, about 2-3 minutes. Add the chicken stock, bring to a boil and boil for 1 minute. Return the reserved chicken to the pan and reheat it in the sauce for 1 minute. Transfer the chicken to a serving platter. Add the remaining butter to the sauce, turn off the heat, and mix well. Pour the hot sauce over the chicken and serve.

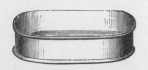

Cook's Tip

Porcini mushrooms are named after "little pigs" in Italian and called *boletus* in Latin. They can be expensive, but are generally considered to be the finest tasting wild mushroom.

When buying fresh porcini, look for firm, rounded caps with white undersides. The caps of fresh mushrooms vary in color from ivory to brown, but in general, the darker the cap, the more intense the flavor. When buying dried porcini, look for the primarily light-colored part of the mushroom, not the dark gnarled pieces, which are not as good.

Porcini, like any dried mushroom, need to be soaked before using. Use one cup of hot water or chicken stock for each ½ ounce (15 g) of dried porcini and soak for ½ hour. Remove them from the liquid, reserving the liquid, and squeeze dry. Strain the soaking liquid through a paper towel or coffee filter and use it to flavor sauces and soups. If you're not going to use the liquid right away, freeze and use later.

Porcini Mushroom Powder

Grind ¼- to ½-ounce (7- to 15-g) dried porcini mushrooms in a small processor or coffee mill to a powder consistency. Don't make large quantities of porcini powder at one time because the flavor can become unpleasantly strong when the powder is exposed to air for long periods.

As a substitute for the porcini mushroom powder, use dried shiitake mushroom powder or ½ of a beef bouillon cube, crumbled. The flavor of the sauce will be different with the bouillon cube, but still very tasty.

"When a happy moment, complete and rounded as a pearl, falls into the tossing ocean of life, it is never wholly lost."

Agnes Repplier

Menu Suggestion
ASPARAGUS SALAD
WITH HONEY MUSTARD DRESSING
CHICKEN SCALLOPINE
WITH PORCINI ROSEMARY SAUCE
GREEN BEANS WITH ALMONDS
BREAD
ORANGES WITH
WHITE CHOCOLATE AND MINT

Wine Suggestion
PETIT SYRAH

Pollo del Cacciatore
Hunter's Chicken

Every Italian family has a recipe for this classic dish. You will find many factions arguing over the inclusion of tomato paste, the exclusion of tomato sauce, or the merits of white versus red wine.

My mother didn't bother arguing about these things. She just went ahead and made it the way she knew best. I must tell you that I don't recall ever having a better Hunter's Chicken than my mother's. Maybe it's the romance of youth or the longing memories of my past in Sicily. I'll let you be the judge, but I believe this dish will reward you with culinary delight.

Serves 4

1 (3- to 4-pound) (1.4- to 1.8-kg) chicken, cut into pieces
¼ teaspoon salt
¼ teaspoon black pepper
½ cup flour
7 tablespoons olive oil
1 small white onion, diced
2 bay leaves
¾ pound (350 g) mushrooms, quartered (mixed wild or white button)
4 garlic cloves, thickly sliced
4 tablespoons chopped pancetta or bacon
½ teaspoon red pepper flakes
3 tablespoons chopped fresh Italian parsley
½ cup red wine
1 (1-pound) (450-g) can peeled Italian tomatoes
1 cup Chicken Stock (see page 228)
½ cup Tomato Sauce (see page 225)

Sprinkle the chicken with the salt and pepper and flour, shaking to remove the excess flour. Heat 4 tablespoons of the olive oil in a large nonstick high-sided fry pan set on high heat. Add the chicken to the pan and cook until well browned, about 3 minutes per side. Transfer the chicken to a plate and set aside.

Save the chicken fat left in the pan, adding enough of the oil to make 4 tablespoons. Cook the onion, bay leaves and mushrooms over medium heat, for 5 minutes. Add the garlic, pancetta, red pepper flakes and half of the parsley and cook for 3 minutes. Pour in the wine and cook for 3 minutes, stirring and scraping the bottom of the pan to mix in the flavorful pan residues. Add the tomatoes and their juice, the chicken stock, tomato sauce and browned chicken pieces. Break the tomatoes into smaller pieces with the back of a spoon. Bring to a boil, reduce the heat and simmer, uncovered, for 15-20 minutes.

Transfer the chicken to a serving dish. Cook the sauce 5 more minutes. Taste for salt and pepper. Pour the sauce over the chicken, sprinkle with the remaining chopped parsley and serve.

Menu Suggestion
Artichoke Sauté
Hunter's Chicken
Sour Cream and
Chive Mashed Potatoes
Bread
Baked Pears
with Sweetened Ricotta

Wine Suggestion
Chianti

Tacchino Arrosto
Roast Turkey with Herbs

Serves 10 to 12
8 tablespoons chopped garlic
3 teaspoons salt
3 teaspoons black pepper
4 tablespoons chopped fresh rosemary
4 tablespoons chopped fresh sage
1 (12- to 14-pound) (5.4- to 6.3-kg) turkey
3 recipes Vegetarian Stuffing (see page 214)
4 tablespoons olive oil

Preheat the oven to 325° F (170° C).

Place the garlic, salt, pepper, rosemary and sage on a cutting board and chop and blend them together with a knife. Loosen the skin on the turkey, pushing with your fingers around the breast, thighs and back. Stuff ⅔'s of the chopped seasoning mixture underneath the skin over the thighs, legs, breast and back. Use the handle of a plastic spatula to run under the skin and help distribute the seasoning. Stuff the turkey with the vegetarian stuffing, being careful not to pack it too tightly. (If you have leftover stuffing, cook it in a greased baking dish, covered with foil, for 45 minutes, alongside the turkey.) Brush the turkey skin with the olive oil and rub with the remaining seasoning mixture.

Place the turkey in a roasting pan and cook for 3½-4 hours, basting every ½ hour with the pan juices, until the internal temperature of the thigh reaches 165-170° F (74-77° C) and the juices run clear. If the turkey begins to get too brown, cover it loosely with a sheet of aluminum foil, shiny-side-up. Remove the turkey from the oven and let it rest, loosely covered with foil, for 10-15 minutes before carving.

As a young boy in Italy, I can remember watching old American movies showing Thanksgiving dinner starring a roasted turkey. It felt like a culinary call coming to me over the screen and I wondered if I'd ever get to taste such a marvelous roast!

This might explain why I was almost giggling with anticipation for my first Thanksgiving dinner in America. Over the years I have come to appreciate the care it takes to roast a turkey to flavorful perfection. I took this on as a personal challenge and finally developed this recipe. I'm proud to present it to you as a gift and encourage you to use it at your next family gathering.

Menu Suggestion
Roast Turkey with Herbs
and Stuffing
Sweet Potato Souffle
Green Beans with Almonds
Pumpkin Cheesecake
Three Nut Tart

Wine Suggestion
Pinot Noir

Brasato al Barolo
POT ROAST BRAISED IN RED WINE

SERVES 4 TO 6

2 onions, 1 coarsely chopped and 1 finely chopped

2 carrots, 1 coarsely chopped and 1 finely chopped

2 stalks celery, 1 coarsely chopped and 1 finely chopped

8 garlic cloves, 2 crushed and 6 thickly sliced

1 bottle (750 ml) dry red wine, preferably Barolo

1 (2½- to 3-pound) (1.2- to 1.4-kg) chuck roast, tied

1 teaspoon salt

¾ teaspoon black pepper

4 tablespoons flour

4 tablespoons olive oil

¼ teaspoon red pepper flakes

⅓ cup diced pancetta or bacon

3 bay leaves

1 teaspoon dried thyme

1 teaspoon dried rosemary

1 tablespoon chopped fresh Italian parsley

2 tablespoons tomato paste

3 cups Chicken or Beef Stock (see page 228 or 230)

This dish was a favorite of my father, but only occasionally graced the Stellino family dinner table. You see, my mother used this fabulous meal as a negotiating tool with Macchiavellian undertones. In other words, it was a deliberate and effective technique to soften my father's defenses before she launched an attack in support of some major acquisition, like a new television or bicycle for Mario. There were even those unfortunate occasions when we needed unexpected upholstery work on my father's favorite chair and who could forget the fateful night when I asked my father for permission to come to America?

I knew I could rely on this pot roast to work its magic. You would have to be blind not to notice the tenderness of my father as he looked at my mother across the table. I hope it will bring you the same happiness that it brought my family.

The night before serving, in a large bowl, combine the coarsely chopped onion, carrot and celery with the crushed garlic cloves and the red wine. Put the chuck roast in the marinade, cover and refrigerate overnight, turning once.

The day of serving, remove the roast from the marinade and pat dry. Strain the vegetables from the marinade, reserving the liquid. Discard the vegetables. Season the meat with the salt and pepper and dust with 2 tablespoons of the flour, shaking off the excess. Heat 1½ tablespoons of the oil in a large Dutch oven set on medium-high heat until sizzling, about 2 minutes. Brown the meat on both sides in the hot oil, about 3 minutes. Transfer the meat to a bowl and set aside.

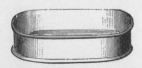

Add the remaining olive oil to the pan and heat on medium-high heat until sizzling, about 2 minutes. Add the thickly sliced garlic, red pepper flakes and pancetta and cook for 1 minute. Add the finely chopped onion, carrot and celery along with the bay leaves, thyme, rosemary and parsley. Cook for 3-4 minutes, until almost dry. Stir in the tomato paste and cook for 1-2 minutes. Add the remaining flour and cook for 1-2 minutes longer. At this point the mixture will be very thick and pasty.

Pour in the reserved marinade liquid and the beef or chicken stock and bring to a boil, stirring to dislodge any brown bits from the bottom of the pan. Return the cooked meat and any accumulated juices to the pan, reduce the heat and simmer, covered, for 2 hours, turning every half hour. Transfer the meat to a cutting board to rest, covering it with a tent of foil to keep warm.

While the meat is resting, bring the cooking liquid to a boil and cook, stirring frequently, until reduced by half, about 30-40 minutes. Cut the meat into thin slices and reheat in the sauce, if necessary.

To serve, arrange the meat slices on a serving platter with the sauce served on the side.

Cook's Tip

In this recipe I use a soffritto — finely chopped aromatic vegetables, herbs and sometimes pork fat, such as pancetta — which is sautéed in oil, to create a flavorful base for the pot roast sauce. It is a useful technique to use for all kinds of soups, sauces and sauced preparations. To speed the preparation of the soffritto ingredients, use the food processor to chop the vegetables.

For a smoother sauce, remove the pot roast from the pan, place the vegetables and part of the juices into a food processor and purée until smooth. Return to the pan to reheat.

"When love and skill work together, expect a masterpiece."
John Ruskin

Menu Suggestion
MIXED GREEN SALAD
WITH GREEN PEPPERCORN
HONEY VINAIGRETTE
POT ROAST BRAISED IN RED WINE
GARLIC MASHED POTATOES
BREAD
UPSIDE-DOWN APPLE PIE

Wine Suggestion
BAROLO

Spezzatino Marocchino
MOROCCAN VEAL STEW

Legend has it that a young Spanish fisherman was navigating his boat through the Straits of Gibraltar when he found himself caught in the midst of a sudden storm. Even though he fought valiantly against the raging waves, his small vessel was overpowered and he was thrown overboard. Just as he thought he was about to drown, a wave threw him to safety on the shores of a foreign land, Morocco.

The young man crawled to safety, and as he thanked his lucky stars, he passed out. The next morning, a local family found his barely breathing body and took him to their shack. Over the next few days, they nurtured him back to health. He attributed his recovery to a "magic potion" that he was fed daily by his kind caretakers, a mysterious concoction of seductive flavors. The Moroccan family was more than happy to share their secret with the young fisherman.

SERVES 4 TO 5

1½ pounds (750 g) eggplant, cut into 1-inch (2.5-cm) cubes

1¼ teaspoons salt

1½ pounds (750 g) veal stew meat

½ teaspoon pepper

1½ tablespoons flour

6 tablespoons olive oil

1 onion, quartered and sliced

4 garlic cloves, thickly sliced

½ cup toasted pine nuts (see Cook's Tip, page 84)

1 cup dark raisins

1 teaspoon curry powder

1 cup white wine

5 cups Chicken Stock (see page 228)

2 tablespoons chopped fresh Italian parsley

4 cups hot cooked white rice

or Rice Pilaf with Lemon Zest (see Cook's Tip, page 171)

Put the eggplant into a colander, sprinkle with 1 teaspoon of the salt, cover with a dish, put a heavy weight on top and let drain for 15 minutes. Remove from the colander and pat dry.

Season the meat with ¼ teaspoon of the salt and the pepper. Place the flour in a bowl, add the meat and toss until well coated, shaking off the excess.

Heat 2 tablespoons of the oil in a large high-sided fry pan set on medium-high heat, until sizzling, about 2 minutes. Add the meat and brown on all sides, about 3 minutes. Transfer to a bowl.

Add 2 tablespoons of the oil to the drippings left in the pan and heat over high heat until smoking. Add the dried eggplant, reduce the heat to medium-high and cook on one side for 3-4 minutes, until browned. Turn and cook for 3 minutes on the other side. Remove to a bowl and set aside.

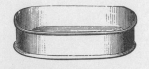

Add the remaining oil to the pan and heat on medium-high heat. Cook the onion and garlic in the pan until soft, about 3 minutes. Add the pine nuts, raisins and curry powder and cook for 4 minutes. Add the browned meat, along with any juices that have accumulated, and cook for 1 minute. Add the wine and boil until it has reduced by half, about 4 minutes. Stir in the chicken stock and parsley and bring to a boil, about 4 minutes. Cover the pan with the lid slightly ajar, reduce the heat and simmer for 1 hour. Add the browned eggplant and cook for 30 minutes longer without the lid.

Serve the stew with the rice on the side.

When he returned to Spain, he abandoned the fishing profession and opened a small restaurant featuring this special dish. He eventually earned such renown that the King invited him to court and asked him to cook his culinary masterpiece for all the nobility.

What follows is my version of this traditional Moroccan recipe.

Menu Suggestion
APPLE, GREEN BEAN
AND BELL PEPPER SALAD
MOROCCAN VEAL STEW
LEMON RICE PILAF
BREAD
PANNACOTTA

Wine Suggestion
VOUVRAY

Arista di Maiale
Roasted Pork Loin

This is a simple yet spectacular specialty from Tuscany that quite often graced the Stellino family gatherings at my grandmother's country house.

My father learned the basic recipe during his travels through Northern Italy. Its cooking was always a true family effort. Both my father and mother starred center stage as they tended the roast during its cooking in the wood burning oven. As the roast was pulled out of the oven to be basted with thick rosemary branches, the aroma would fill the air around us. All eyes were wide with anticipation. I loved watching my parents, little beads of sweat dotting their faces while they laughed and shared a glass of wine during their tasks. Sometimes, my Grandma Maria would catch me watching them, and she'd caress my head.

Serves 8

3 tablespoons chopped garlic
1 tablespoon chopped fresh rosemary
1 tablespoon chopped fresh sage
1 tablespoon chopped fresh thyme
1 tablespoon chopped fresh Italian parsley
½ teaspoon salt
¼ teaspoon black pepper
1 (3-pound) (1.4-kg) center-cut pork loin roast, tied
1 tablespoon olive oil
¼ cup Italian Bread Crumbs (see page 218)
½ cup white wine
1 ¾ cups Chicken Stock (see page 228)
2 tablespoons cornstarch mixed with 2 tablespoons chicken stock (slurry)

Preheat the oven to 500° F (260° C).

Place the garlic, rosemary, sage, thyme, parsley, salt and pepper on a chopping board and chop to a paste-like consistency. Make shallow 1- to 2-inch (2.5- to 5-cm) long slits randomly around the pork roast. Rub the roast with the olive oil, then fill the slits with the herb paste. Rub the remaining herbs on the outer surface. Roll the roast in the bread crumbs to coat it completely.

Place the roast in a lightly greased roasting pan (don't use a rack in the pan) and cook for 20 minutes in the preheated oven. At this point the roast will have formed a crust on the outside. Turn the roast over and reduce the oven heat to 350° F (180° C). Bake for 40-45 minutes, turning it every 15 minutes, until the internal temperature reaches 160° F (71° C). Remove the roast from the oven and transfer it to a plate. Cover it with aluminum foil and let rest for 15-20 minutes.

While the roast is resting, put the roasting pan on medium-high heat on the stove top and stir in the wine and chicken stock. Cook for 5 minutes, scraping up any brown bits from the bottom of the pan. Strain the juices into a saucepan and reduce on medium-high heat for 5 minutes. Remove from the heat and stir in the cornstarch slurry. Return to the heat and cook until the sauce clears and thickens, about 1 minute.

To serve, cut the strings from the roast, slice into thin slices and ladle some of the sauce over the meat.

Cook's Tip

Because of today's more sanitary methods of raising pigs and the fact that trichinosis has been almost eliminated, the recommended temperature for cooked pork has been lowered from 170° F (77° C) to 160° F (71° C). Pork roasts should be removed from the oven when the internal temperature reaches 155-160° F (68-71° C), depending on the size; larger roasts should be removed at the lower temperature and will continue cooking as they stand. At that stage of doneness, the meat will still be juicy and slightly pink.

Finally the moment came to sit down at the table and pass around a tray loaded with the succulent meat. My parents would be so proud, standing to one side and holding each other's waists while they watched the feeding frenzy.

Sometimes, it's difficult to think of our parents as being young and in love. But every time I prepare this pork roast, I think of my mamma and papá as two young people, holding hands, sharing wine, and cooking together. The same scene repeats itself now, when my wife and I cook this dish.

I ought to warn you that the same magic spell might come over you!

Menu Suggestion
PASTA WITH COLD TOMATO SAUCE
ROASTED PORK LOIN
COUNTRY STYLE ROASTED POTATOES
BREAD
FRESH FRUIT

Wine Suggestion
PETIT SYRAH

Costoletta di Maiale alle Erbe
HERBED PORK CHOPS

This is a truly simple recipe for a glorious dish.

One of the biggest challenges in cooking pork chops is to be able to flavor the meat all the way through. The marinating technique in this recipe allows a gentle yet complete flavoring of the pork meat. With each bite you take, your palate will be seduced by the sweet symphony of herbs: the subtle scent of the thyme to the aggressive aroma of rosemary. Each of their tastes will melt through like notes on a musical sheet.

As you appreciate the music of flavors in your mouth, you'll see how the combination of simple ingredients can give you a dish you never thought possible.

Menu Suggestion
RISOTTO WITH FOUR CHEESES
HERBED PORK CHOPS
GREEN BEANS WITH ALMONDS
BREAD
UPSIDE-DOWN APPLE PIE

Wine Suggestion
BRUNELLO DI MONTALCINO

SERVES 4
1 tablespoon chopped garlic
1 tablespoon chopped fresh rosemary
1 tablespoon chopped fresh thyme
1 tablespoon chopped fresh marjoram
½ tablespoon chopped fresh sage
1½ tablespoons chopped fresh Italian parsley
4 (¾-inch) (2-cm) thick pork chops, bone-in or boneless, fat trimmed
Salt and pepper to taste
¼ cup flour
3 tablespoons olive oil
½ cup white wine
1 cup Chicken Stock (see page 228)
1 tablespoon cornstarch mixed with 2 tablespoons chicken stock (slurry)

Heap the garlic, rosemary, thyme, marjoram, sage and parsley on a cutting board and chop to a fine consistency. Press the chopped herb mixture into both sides of the pork chops, wrap them in plastic wrap and refrigerate for at least 1 hour to let the flavors penetrate the meat.

Remove the plastic wrap and season the chops to taste with the salt and pepper. Sprinkle the chops with the flour, brushing off any excess.

Heat the oil in a large sauté pan set on medium heat. When the oil is hot, place the prepared chops in the pan and cook for 3-4 minutes on each side. Remove the chops to a serving dish and cover with foil to keep warm. Pour the oil from the pan and set it on high heat. Pour in the wine, stir up any brown bits from the bottom of the pan and boil until it has reduced by ½. Add the chicken stock and return to a boil. Remove the pan from the heat and stir in the cornstarch slurry. Return to the heat and cook, stirring, for 30 seconds. Season to taste with salt and pepper.

Pour the gravy over the chops and serve immediately.

Salsiccie Brasate col Cappuccio e le Mele

BRAISED SAUSAGE WITH CABBAGE AND APPLES

SERVES 4

2 tablespoons olive oil

1 pound (450 g) sweet Italian sausage (about 4 links)

½ onion, thinly sliced

4 garlic cloves, thickly sliced

2 apples, peeled, cored and thinly sliced

¼ teaspoon red pepper flakes

2 tablespoons flour

¾ cup sweet white wine

½ cup Chicken Stock (see page 228)

½ cup unsweetened applesauce

½ pound (225 g) cabbage, cored and thinly sliced

½ teaspoon salt

¼ teaspoon black pepper

Heat 1 tablespoon of the oil in a large sauté pan set on medium-high heat, until sizzling, about 2 minutes. Brown the sausage in the hot oil, about 2 minutes per side. Remove the sausages to a plate, cut into 1-inch (2.5-cm) pieces and set aside.

Add the remaining oil to the same pan set on medium-high heat and heat until sizzling, about 2 minutes. Add the onion, garlic, apples and red pepper flakes and cook for 3-4 minutes. Return the browned sausage to the pan along with the flour and stir well to mix the flour with the oil. Pour the wine into the pan, scraping up any brown bits from the bottom of the pan. Cook for 3 minutes. Add the chicken stock, applesauce, cabbage, salt and pepper. Reduce the heat and simmer, uncovered, for 7-10 minutes, until the sauce is slightly thickened and glossy.

The sausage and cabbage is now ready to be served!

Softly rolling hills covered in a patchwork of wild yellow daisies and waves of emerald grass, enchanted Nanci and me as we traveled through the Alsace region of France. Waving to a toothless old man who was driving a tractor home for lunch, we arrived at our own destination, a small restaurant in a rustic village called Chez Pepin.

The inside was crowded with patrons, mostly older men, enjoying their afternoon meal, talking animatedly, and smoking unfiltered French cigarettes. The wisps of pungent smoke, the clinking of glasses, the silverware glinting, made Nanci and I draw together, holding hands without talking, thoroughly enjoying this slice of life. What follows is my version of that delicious meal.

Menu Suggestion
BRAISED SAUSAGES
WITH CABBAGE AND APPLES
GARLIC MASHED POTATOES

Wine Suggestion
RIESLING

Salsiccie Brasate con Polenta

BRAISED SAUSAGES WITH POLENTA

During a vacation in Venice, Nanci and I found ourselves held hostage in our hotel room by a continuous torrent of rain that had no end in sight.

So at lunchtime, we armed ourselves with umbrellas and ventured outside. You know, Venice still sparkled with its own special beauty even through the darkest of rain clouds. As we continued to explore, the rain stopped, only to be replaced by an eerie fog bank that blanketed the streets. We were rescued by the neon light of a sign pointing to a trattoria. We rushed in through the glass paneled door and discovered a little slice of paradise.

Our host relieved us of our damp umbrellas and coats, then ushered us to a table that glowed with warmth from a rustic fireplace. We could hear the wind picking up outside, but a carafe of fresh wine just made us feel warmer.

SERVES 4

2 tablespoons olive oil

1 pound (450 g) sweet Italian sausage (about 4 links)

1 large carrot, thinly sliced

1 large stalk celery, thinly sliced

1 large onion, sliced

10 garlic cloves, peeled

1 cup red or white wine

2 tablespoons chopped fresh Italian parsley

1 tablespoon chopped fresh rosemary

2 cups Chicken Stock (see page 228)

¼ teaspoon black pepper

1 pound (450 g) potatoes, peeled and cut into 1-inch (2.5-cm) cubes

½ (13½-ounce) (390-g) package instant polenta

½ cup whipping cream (optional)

½ cup freshly grated Parmigiano Reggiano cheese (optional)

Heat the oil in a large nonstick sauté pan set on medium-high heat until it begins to sizzle, about 2 minutes. Add the sausages and brown on all sides, approximately 5 minutes. Remove the sausages from the pan and set aside.

In the same pan, cook the carrot, celery, onion and garlic over medium heat for 5 minutes, stirring several times. Cut the sausages into 2-inch (5-cm) pieces and add to the pan along with the wine, 1 tablespoon of the parsley and the rosemary. Cook over medium-high heat until the wine has reduced by half, about 3-5 minutes. Stir in the chicken stock, pepper and potatoes and bring to a boil. Reduce the heat to a simmer, cover the pan with the lid slightly ajar and cook for 15 minutes. Uncover and continue cooking for another 25 minutes, stirring occasionally. Stir in the remaining parsley just before serving.

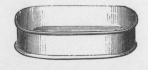

Five minutes before the sausages are done, cook the polenta according to package directions. If you wish, stir the cream and cheese into the finished polenta. Serve immediately, as the polenta sets up quickly.

To serve, spoon a mound of polenta in the center of each dinner plate and spoon the sausage mixture on top. Enjoy!

Cook's Tip

If you don't have whipping cream on hand for enriching the polenta, stir in 2-3 tablespoons of butter, instead.

As the time slowly ticked by, we found ourselves enjoying a series of delicious dishes, including this sausage with polenta. We enjoyed every bite, laughing and holding hands.

You don't need to be in Italy to be romantic, so the next time foul weather forces you inside, share this dish with someone you love, and soon enough I hope you will feel as if magically transported to a small trattoria in Venice.

Menu Suggestion
MIXED SALAD
WITH GREEN PEPPERCORN
HONEY VINAIGRETTE
BRAISED SAUSAGES WITH POLENTA
BREAD
POACHED APPLES

Wine Suggestion
CHARDONNAY

Polpettine d'Agnello col Sugo di Girgento
Lamb Meatballs with Girgento Sauce and Eggplant Timbales

It's a fact that while you see me romanticizing about the special moments in my life as if they were scenes from an epic movie, in reality, most of the years passed quietly by, leaving only a hint of their significance, until my thoughts wander back to them many years later.

The creation of this dish is a good example. Yes, the common ingredients of lamb, garlic, tomatoes and eggplant, combined in a few uncomplicated steps, brought about a synergy of celestial gourmand bliss. I can still remember the first time I made it, standing in my tiny home kitchen, improvising the steps and feeling the excitement of creation. The aromas of the food cooking, the color of the sauce, the consistency and shape of these delicate morsels of food, still stand out clearly in my mind. I was filled with anticipation.

Serves 8

Eggplant Timbales:

3 eggplants, about 1½ pounds (750 g) each

½ teaspoon salt

3 tablespoons olive oil

1½ cups Italian Bread Crumbs (see page 218)

4 eggs, separated

1 cup freshly grated Pecorino Romano cheese

Girgento Sauce:

2 cups Tomato Sauce (see page 225)

Roasted eggplant juice (reserved from cooked eggplant above)

2 teaspoons sugar

2½ tablespoons finely chopped fresh mint

Meatballs:

3 pounds (1.4 kg) ground lamb

2 tablespoons chopped garlic

1 teaspoon ground cumin

1½ teaspoons cinnamon

4 tablespoons sugar

½ teaspoon salt

½ teaspoon pepper

5½ tablespoons chopped fresh Italian parsley

3 tablespoons chopped fresh mint

1 cup freshly grated Pecorino Romano cheese

½ cup Italian Bread Crumbs (see page 218)

2 tablespoons olive oil

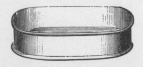

For the Eggplant Timbales

Preheat the oven to 425° F (220° C). Cut the stem ends off all the eggplants, then cut in half lengthwise and score the flesh with a sharp knife, making sure you don't cut through the skin. Rub the cut surfaces of the eggplants well with the salt. Set the eggplant halves aside on paper towels, cut-side-down, and let them drain for 20 minutes.

Line the bottoms of 2 (18 x 13-inch) (46 x 33-cm) baking sheets with parchment paper. Dry the cut surfaces of the eggplant halves and brush the parchment paper and eggplant with the olive oil. Place them on the baking sheets, cut-side-down, and bake in the preheated oven for 45-55 minutes. The eggplants are completely cooked when they dent easily as you poke the skin. Do not cook them more than 1 hour as they burn easily once they are cooked. Remove them from the oven and let cool for 15 minutes or longer.

Using a large spoon, scoop the flesh from the cooked eggplant halves. Discard the skin and place the flesh in a colander with a bowl underneath to catch the juices. Drain for 40 minutes, stirring once. You should have at least 1 cup of juices — if you don't, try putting a plate on the eggplant with weights on top to help squeeze the juices out. Reserve the juices for the sauce.

Preheat the oven to 400° F (200° C). Grease 8 small custard cups and use ½ cup of the bread crumbs to coat them. Set aside.

Mix the eggs yolks, the Romano cheese and 1 cup of the bread crumbs with the roasted eggplant flesh. Beat the egg whites until they form stiff peaks, then fold them gently into the eggplant mixture. Spoon the mixture evenly into the prepared custard cups and set the cups on a baking sheet. Bake the eggplant timbales in the oven for 20-25 minutes, until puffed and beginning to brown on top. Remove from the oven and immediately take the timbales out of the custard cups. They may be served immediately or cooled, wrapped in plastic wrap and refrigerated for 1-2 days. To reheat, cover each timbale with aluminum foil and bake in a preheated 375° F (190° C) oven for 20 minutes.

(Continued)

When my wife, Nanci, came home, she was treated to an unexpected candlelight meal. The smile in her eyes as she savored the flavor of each bite was all the approval I needed.

Like our first kiss, I will always remember this meal with Nanci as a special moment. My sincere wish is that it will bring you the same joy.

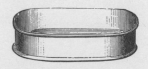

FOR THE GIRGENTO SAUCE

Liquefy the tomato sauce and the reserved roasted eggplant draining juice in a food processor or blender for 2 minutes. Stir in the sugar and mint and set aside until ready to use. The sauce can also be made 1-2 days in advance, just cover and refrigerate.

FOR THE MEATBALLS

In a large bowl, mix together the ground lamb, garlic, cumin, cinnamon, sugar, salt, pepper, 2½ tablespoons of the parsley, the mint, Romano cheese and bread crumbs. Mix well and form into meatballs that are slightly flattened for easier browning. Use about 2 heaping tablespoons of meat mixture for each meatball. This will yield about 30-38 meatballs. (Sometimes I like making larger meatballs, which will yield fewer — make them however you prefer.) Heat the remaining olive oil in a large sauté pan set on high heat. Brown the meat balls in 2 batches, for 2-3 minutes on each side. Remove them from the pan and drain them on paper towels or brown paper grocery bags (these work great!). Drain the grease from the pan. Put the meatballs back into the pan and pour the Girgento Sauce over them. Bring to a boil, reduce the heat to medium and cook for 15 minutes.

To serve, place an eggplant timbale in the center of each plate. Surround it with meatballs and pour some of the sauce over the meatballs. Garnish with the remaining chopped parsley.

COOK'S TIP

If you are short on time, but are just dying for meatballs, eliminate the eggplant timbales. When making the Girgento Sauce, substitute chicken stock for the roasted eggplant juices. Serve the meatballs and their sauce over pasta.

Menu Suggestion
GREEN SALAD
WITH BALSAMIC VINAIGRETTE
LAMB MEATBALLS
WITH GIRGENTO SAUCE
EGGPLANT TIMBALES
BREAD
STRAWBERRY ICE

Wine Suggestion
ZINFANDEL

Agnello a Scottadito con l'Aceto Balsamico e Rosmarino

Lamb Chops with Balsamic Vinegar, Garlic and Rosemary

Serves 6

2 (2-pound) (900-kg) racks of lamb, trimmed and cut into 18 chops
4 tablespoons chopped garlic
4 tablespoons chopped fresh rosemary
2 teaspoons salt
1 ¼ teaspoons black pepper
¼ cup olive oil
1 cup balsamic vinegar
2 tablespoons sugar

Place the lamb chops in a large dish. Whisk together the garlic, rosemary, salt, pepper, olive oil and vinegar and pour over the lamb chops. Cover with plastic wrap and marinate in the refrigerator for at least 2 hours or overnight, turning at least once.

Just before serving, remove the chops from the marinade, reserving the marinade separately. Cook the chops over hot charcoal or under a broiler for 3-5 minutes per side, until done to your liking.

While the chops are cooking. Pour the reserved marinade into a medium saucepan, stir in the sugar, bring to a boil and boil until reduced by half. The longer you reduce the marinade, the thicker and more intensely flavored it will become — you be the judge of how thick you want it to be. Pass the sauce in a sauceboat on the side to be poured over the lambchops.

Cook's Tip

This intensely flavored marinade/sauce is marvelous with other meats as well, such as pork or chicken.

Not only is this one of the easiest recipes in the book, it could easily elevate your culinary fame to legendary heights at the next family barbecue!

I think its secret lies in the marinating liquid of garlic, rosemary and balsamic vinegar. Not only does this tenderize the meat, you'll see how the lamb's flavor is magically altered to a whole new dimension, as if these little chops were putting on their Sunday best clothes just for your enjoyment.

So bring their poetry to your next barbecue menu, stand back, and wait for the compliments to come.

Menu Suggestion
Pasta with Artichokes, Leeks and Olives
Lamb Chops with Balsamic Vinegar, Garlic and Rosemary
Green Beans with Almonds
Zabaglione with Sparkling Wine

Wine Suggestion
Pinot Noir

Branzino al Forno

Baked Striped Bass with Garlic and Rosemary

One summer on the car ride back from my grandmother's house, we stopped for lunch at a little trattoria on the coast of Calabria. The sea was spectacularly blue and almost perfectly flat, with just a few waves breaking softly over the white sand. On the advice of a friend, my father had planned our return trip around this lunch stop.

The trattoria of Signore Fattore was a big hut built right over the sand to take advantage of the summer winds. Signore Fattore was a short dark-skinned man with curly hair and a pencil mustache. Wearing a spotted apron, a newspaper hat and a blue short-sleeved shirt, he darted quickly from place to place with purpose and determination. He and my father exchanged a few words and lunch was ordered. My brother, Mario, and I couldn't sit still; we just wanted to get undressed and go jump in the

SERVES 4

4 whole (1-pound) (450-g) striped bass, scaled, cleaned
and rinsed in salt water
¾ teaspoon salt
½ teaspoon black pepper
4 garlic cloves, sliced
4 (4-inch) (10-cm) rosemary branches
8 sprigs Italian parsley
8 whole basil leaves
4 lemon slices, ¼ inch (6 mm) thick
2 tablespoons chopped fresh Italian parsley
2 tablespoons chopped fresh basil
½ cup Chicken Stock (see page 228)
½ cup clam juice
½ cup dry white wine
1 tablespoon cornstarch mixed with 2 tablespoons clam juice (slurry)

Preheat the oven to 500° F (260° C). Season the fish inside and outside with ¼ teaspoon each of the salt and pepper. Stuff each fish with 1 sliced garlic clove, 1 rosemary branch, 2 sprigs of parsley, 2 basil leaves and 1 lemon slice. Place the fish in a greased 11 x 13-inch (28 x 33-cm) baking pan. Add the rest of the ingredients, except the cornstarch slurry, to the dish and bake in the oven, uncovered, for 15-20 minutes, turning once. (If you do not have a baking pan large enough to hold all 4 fish, then put 2 fish each in 2 (9 x 13-inch) (23 x 33-cm) baking pans and divide the sauce ingredients evenly between the two pans before putting them in the oven.) Transfer the cooked fish to a serving platter and keep warm.

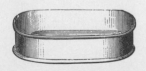

Pour the cooking juices into a saucepan, bring to a boil and add the remaining salt and pepper. Remove the pan from the heat, add the cornstarch slurry, return to the heat and cook, stirring, until thickened, about 30 seconds.

Pour a little of the sauce over the fish and serve the extra sauce on the side.

Cook's Tip

If striped bass is unavailable in your area, substitute whole rockfish or red snapper in this recipe. These fish will most likely be larger than the striped bass, so you will need to buy only 1 (3½- to 4-pound) (1.6- to 1.8-kg) fish to serve 4 people.

sea. But, when the appetizing aroma of the baked fish started to creep from the kitchen, as quickly as a magic potion, Mario and I were seduced back into our seats.

When Signore Fattore came to our table holding a huge whole baked fish on a silver tray, I knew I did the right thing by staying. This was an incredible dish. I don't know if my version will quiet your kids at dinner time, but I'm sure you'll love it. Its flavorful simplicity is something you'll want to share with more and more of your friends.

Menu Suggestion
STRIPED BASS
WITH GARLIC AND ROSEMARY
RICE PILAF
ARTICHOKE AND ZUCCHINI SAUTÉ
BREAD
MARINATED FRUIT SALAD

Wine Suggestion
VERNACCIA

Filetto di Pesce con la Salsa Fresca

Pan-Fried Chilean Sea Bass with Fresca Sauce

Before I was married, I brought my future wife, Nanci, to Sicily to meet my parents and take a tour of the island. The trip was a historical time in my life, as I rediscovered my birthplace through Nanci's eyes. Watching her eagerness to explore and experience my homeland, I found myself falling deeper in love with her and all the views around us.

Traveling late one evening, we arrived in the town of Gela. We found sleeping accommodations in an old pensione along the coast. In front of the building you could just read the sign "Ristorante." Nanci and I decided to take a chance on this place.

Inside we discovered a large round dance floor bordered by tables and chairs. An immense sequined ball hung over the center reflecting bullets of colored light all over the room. With the band playing a Benny Goodman tune, we felt like we had stepped back in time.

SERVES 4

FRESCA SAUCE:

1 (28-ounce) (790-g) can peeled Italian tomatoes, drained, chopped and juices discarded

¼ teaspoon sugar

½ teaspoon salt

⅛ teaspoon black pepper

½ cup olive oil

1 teaspoon balsamic vinegar

2 garlic cloves, finely chopped

1 tablespoon finely chopped fresh basil

SEA BASS:

4 (6- to 8-ounce) (175- to 225-g) Chilean sea bass fillets

1 teaspoon salt

½ teaspoon black pepper

1 tablespoon olive oil

Parsley sprigs for garnish

FOR THE FRESCA SAUCE

Combine the chopped tomatoes, sugar, salt and pepper in a medium bowl. Stir and let rest for 30 minutes for the flavors to combine.

FOR THE SEA BASS

Preheat the oven to 450° F (230° C). Sprinkle the fish with the salt and pepper. In an ovenproof nonstick sauté pan set on medium-high heat, cook the olive oil until sizzling, about 2 minutes. Add the fish, reduce the heat to medium and cook for 2 minutes on both sides, until well browned. Place the sauté pan in the preheated oven and cook for 8 to 10 minutes.

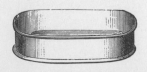

While the fish is cooking in the oven, finish the sauce by whisking together the ½ cup olive oil and the vinegar until well mixed and slightly thickened. Stir in the chopped tomato mixture, garlic and basil.

To serve, arrange the fillets on a beautiful serving dish, top with the sauce and garnish with sprigs of the parsley.

Cook's Tip

Buying sea bass can be very confusing as there are several kinds of fish sold under this name. Chilean sea bass is a richer and softer fleshed fish than other kinds of bass. If you are unable to find Chilean sea bass, regular sea bass will be fine to use. Other fish substitutes are red snapper and halibut.

We were the only people in the place, which made it magical to us at once.

After a beautiful banquet, Nanci and I took a spin around the dance floor. As I held her in my arms, looking around the big empty place, while dancing the perimeter of the dance floor, I felt the music fading into silence, the shimmering lights darting in the background. Looking at Nanci, all I could see were her eyes. I drew her close and we kissed.

As we were leaving, Don Santino gave us a hug and I kept the cork of the wine bottle, which we still have in our memory box.

Menu Suggestion
PASTA WITH ASPARAGUS
AND MUSHROOMS
PAN-FRIED CHILEAN SEA BASS
WITH FRESCA SAUCE
GREEN SALAD
WITH BALSAMIC VINAIGRETTE
FRESH FRUIT

Wine Suggestion
VERNACCIA

Filetto di Pesce con Carciofi e Funghi

Chilean Sea Bass Fillets with Artichokes and Mushrooms

La Signora Spiovento lived in the building behind us. Over the years, my mother met with her every morning as they hung their wash to dry on the balconies outside their kitchens. As they conducted this morning chore, they always managed to have a conversation at the same time.

The topics varied daily, ranging from television shows to politics, from friends to food. And although the two ladies never met socially, over the years through their morning meetings, they developed a bond that went beyond casual conversation and ventured into real friendship. As they discussed last night's episode of their favorite soap opera, they also came to know each others' family problems, marital disagreements, children's school problems, and personal wishes and aspirations.

Serves 4

4 tablespoons olive oil

4 (6- to 8-ounce) (175- to 225-g) Chilean sea bass fillets

1 ½ teaspoons salt

½ teaspoon + ⅛ teaspoon black pepper

8-10 fresh artichoke hearts (see page 14 for cleaning instructions), cut into 1-inch (2.5-cm) pieces

or 2 (9-ounce) (250-g) packages frozen artichoke hearts, thawed, leaf end trimmed and cut in half

4 ounces (115 g) sliced shiitake mushrooms

2 leeks, white part only, thinly sliced

4 tablespoons chopped shallots

4 garlic cloves, thickly sliced

¼ teaspoon red pepper flakes

¾ cup white wine

3 tablespoons chopped fresh Italian parsley

¾ cup Chicken Stock (see page 228)

3 Roma tomatoes, peeled and diced (optional)

Preheat the oven to 450° F (230° C). Heat 1 tablespoon of the olive oil in a large sauté pan set on medium-high heat until sizzling, about 2 minutes. Season the fish fillets with 1 teaspoon of the salt and ½ teaspoon of the pepper. Place the fish in the pan, reduce the heat to medium and cook for 2 minutes on each side, until well browned. Transfer the fillets to a plate and set aside.

Add the remaining olive oil to the same pan and raise the heat to high. Cook the artichoke hearts, mushrooms, leeks, shallots, garlic and red pepper flakes for 3-4 minutes, until the vegetables begin to brown. Pour in the wine and cook for 1 minute to reduce by ½, stirring up any brown bits from the bottom of the pan. Stir in the parsley, chicken stock and the remaining salt and pepper and cook for 2-3 minutes.

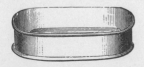

Pour the vegetable mixture into a 9 x 13-inch (23 x 33-cm) baking dish and place the fillets on top. Finish cooking the fish in the preheated oven for 8-10 minutes. Scatter the chopped tomatoes, if you wish, over the fish and serve immediately.

Cook's Tip

If you would like more sauce, double the amount of chicken stock to 1½ cups. To thicken it, combine ½ tablespoon each of butter and flour. Stir the mixture, a bit at a time, into the sauce and simmer it over low heat for 2 minutes.

As Mamma occasionally graced our dinner table with charming anecdotes from La Signora Spiovento, without even knowing her, she became a part of my world; especially when the two ladies exchanged recipes, many of which successfully survived my father's stern criticism.

When Signora Spiovento moved with her family to another city on account of her husband's work, my mother cried. That was the first time I understood the magnitude of their friendship.

What follows is my favorite recipe from La Signora Spiovento. I hope you share it with a good friend.

Menu Suggestion
PASTA WITH ARUGULA
CHILEAN SEA BASS WITH
ARTICHOKES AND MUSHROOMS
BREAD
COFFEE ICE

Wine Suggestion
VERDICCHIO

Il Tonno di San Vito

Peppered Tuna on a Bed of Lemony Limas

Sometimes in summer, my family would rent a small house close to the beach in the town of San Vito lo Capo. My father, of course, would immediately make the acquaintance of the local fisherman in order to secure a steady supply of fresh fish to grace our meals.

While not every single fish recipe met with the Stellino Brothers' seal of approval, the fiery heat of the pepper-studded tuna steak mingling with the bed of lemon-spiked lima beans in the following recipe seduced us into a state of culinary bliss and won our hearts. As a matter of fact, it became a symbol of that great summer together.

You do not have to wait for summer before you can enjoy this simple but flavorful dish. I guarantee that it will bring a summer breeze from the white sandy beaches of San Vito lo Capo, no matter what time of year it graces your table.

Serves 4

Lemony Limas:

6 tablespoons olive oil
4 garlic cloves, thickly sliced
½ onion, chopped
¼ teaspoon red pepper flakes
¼ cup lemon juice
Zest of 1 lemon, grated
½ teaspoon salt
¼ teaspoon black pepper
4 tablespoons chopped fresh Italian parsley
2 tablespoons chopped fennel leaves
1 fennel bulb, chopped
2 (15-ounce) (425-g) cans lima beans, drained

Tuna:

¼ cup coarsely ground black pepper
¼ cup Italian Bread Crumbs (see page 218)
4 (6-ounce) (175-g) tuna steaks, cut ¾ inch (2 cm) thick
4 tablespoons olive oil
4 sprigs fennel leaves for decoration

For the Lemony Limas

Heat 3 tablespoons of the olive oil and the garlic in a medium sauté pan set over medium-high heat until the garlic is sizzling, about 2 minutes. Add the onion and red pepper flakes and cook for 3-4 minutes, until the onion is soft and the garlic is beginning to brown. Remove from the heat. Transfer to a medium bowl and stir in 3 tablespoons of the remaining olive oil, the lemon juice, lemon zest, salt, pepper, parsley, fennel leaves, chopped fennel and lima beans. Cover and marinate for at least 2 hours or refrigerate overnight.

For the Tuna

Mix the coarsely ground black pepper and bread crumbs in a medium bowl. Coat the tuna steaks on all sides with the pepper/bread crumb mixture.

Heat the olive oil in a large sauté pan set on medium-high heat until sizzling, about 2 minutes. Put the tuna steaks in the pan and cook for 3-4 minutes on each side for medium-well steaks. The edges of the steaks should be nicely browned.

Place the beans on a large serving plate and lay the tuna steaks over them. Garnish with a sprig of fennel leaves.

Cook's Tip

If you don't have a pepper mill that will give you coarsely ground black pepper, there are a couple of different ways to do it. The simplest is to use a mortar and pestle. Another method is to put a small amount of peppercorns on a cutting board, place a flat-bottomed frying pan or saucepan on top and press down until the peppercorns crack. Repeat this process until you have the amount needed.

"The greatest dishes are very simple dishes."
Escoffier

Menu Suggestion
PEPPERED TUNA ON
A BED OF LEMONY LIMAS
GREEN SALAD
WITH BALSAMIC VINAIGRETTE
BREAD
WHITE CHOCOLATE MOUSSE

Wine Suggestion
VERNACCIA

Polpette di Tonno
Tuna Cakes with Spicy Mayonnaise

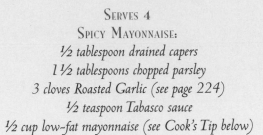

Serves 4
Spicy Mayonnaise:
½ tablespoon drained capers
1½ tablespoons chopped parsley
3 cloves Roasted Garlic (see page 224)
½ teaspoon Tabasco sauce
½ cup low-fat mayonnaise (see Cook's Tip below)

Tuna Cakes:
¾ cup Garlic Mashed Potatoes (see page 168)
2 (6½-ounce) (190-g) cans water-packed tuna, drained and flaked
¼ cup freshly grated Pecorino Romano cheese
¼ cup + ⅓ cup Italian Bread Crumbs (see page 218)
2 eggs
2 tablespoons chopped fresh Italian parsley
½ teaspoon salt
¼ teaspoon black pepper
⅓ cup flour
4-5 tablespoons olive oil

In the 12th century, King Federico the Second was, by all accounts, the most famous and beloved of all Sicilian kings. During his reign, he was able to successfully harmonize all the different ethnic and religious groups that characterized the population. So, while the rest of Europe burned in the fiery turmoil of political and religious wars, Sicily reached an apex of political and financial power never before seen. Christians, Jews and Muslims were able to practice their religion freely and to operate in a free market system that encouraged and rewarded the adventurous spirit of entrepreneurs.

When it came to food, King Federico was a passionate man and a true gourmand. Legend has it that while his wealth could afford him any culinary fancy he wished, he preferred a simpler, more peasant, kind of fare.

For the Spicy Mayonnaise
Process the capers, 1½ tablespoons of the parsley, the roasted garlic and the Tabasco sauce in a food processor or blender until coarsely chopped. Add the mayonnaise and pulse until thoroughly mixed. Transfer to a bowl, cover and refrigerate until ready to use.

For the Tuna Cakes
Thoroughly combine the mashed potatoes, flaked tuna, Romano cheese, ¼ cup of the bread crumbs, the eggs, the remaining 2 tablespoons of the parsley, the salt and pepper in a large bowl. Form the mixture into 12 patties, approximately ½ inch (1.5 cm) thick and 2½ inches (6.5 cm) wide. Combine the flour and the remaining bread crumbs on a plate. Roll the patties in the mixture to coat and set aside.

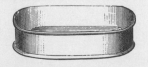

Heat 2 tablespoons of the oil in a large nonstick sauté pan set on medium heat until it starts to sizzle, about 2-3 minutes. (If you aren't using a nonstick sauté pan, you must increase the amount of oil used by 2-3 tablespoons.) Fry ½ of the cakes for 3 minutes on each side, or until nicely browned. Remove the cakes to a plate and place in a warm oven while cooking the remaining cakes. Add the remaining olive oil to the pan as needed.

Place 3 cakes on each plate with a dollop of the spicy mayonnaise on the side.

COOK'S TIP

There are many varieties of low-fat and nonfat mayonnaise on the market. The nonfat varieties tend to have a much stronger flavor and don't lend themselves as well to use as a base in sauces. Try several varieties yourself and decide which you prefer.

Maybe that's why the little trattoria in Palermo where I was eating named this dish "Federico the Second's Tuna Cakes." While I cannot draw you a direct historical link from the recipe to Federico, I can attest to the fact that I always feel like a king when I present this dish to my guests.

And, in truth, although King Federico might never have seen such a dish before, I believe he could not have resisted its charm. I dedicate this to the little king inside all of us.

Menu Suggestion
VEGETABLE BREAD SOUP
TUNA CAKES
WITH SPICY MAYONNAISE
ORANGES WITH CARAMEL SAUCE
AND VANILLA ICE CREAM

Wine Suggestion
TOCAI

Spadellata di Capesante

SCALLOPS WITH TOMATOES AND SAFFRON

SERVES 4

1 recipe Rice Pilaf with Lemon (see Cook's Tip, page 171)
1¼ pounds (560 g) sea scallops, cut in half
¾ teaspoon salt
¼ teaspoon black pepper
2 tablespoons flour
4 tablespoons olive oil
4 garlic cloves, thickly sliced
4 tablespoons chopped shallots
¼ teaspoon red pepper flakes
3 tablespoons chopped fresh Italian parsley
½ cup white wine
½ cup Chicken Stock (see page 228)
3 Roma tomatoes, peeled and diced
⅛ teaspoon powdered saffron

When I lived at home in Palermo, my brother Mario and I were always fighting. But once I came to America, so far from my family and friends, I started to miss the people who were left behind. I amazed myself by recounting stories to my college friends about that wild and crazy brother of mine.

Several years later, Mario came to America and joined me at college where we shared an apartment. It was then that I discovered that my pesky little brother had grown into a young man — more mature, very reflective. He reminded me of my father in his youthful years, in fact, the resemblance was uncanny.

One day Mario returned home looking very sad. He told me he had broken up with his girlfriend and proceeded to seclude himself in the apartment, quietly nursing his pain. I felt I had to do something.

Prepare the Rice Pilaf and keep warm.

Season the scallops with the salt and pepper and dust with the flour, shaking off any excess. Heat 2 tablespoons of the oil in a large sauté pan set on medium-high heat until sizzling, about 2 minutes. Cook the scallops in a single layer in the hot oil until well browned, about 1 minute on each side. Using a slotted spoon, transfer the scallops to a plate and set aside.

Pour the remaining oil into the same pan and over medium-high heat, cook the garlic, shallots, red pepper flakes and parsley until the shallots are brown, about 1-2 minutes. Stir the wine into the pan, scraping up any brown bits from the bottom, and cook for 1 minute. Add the chicken stock, tomatoes and saffron and cook for 3-4 minutes, until reduced by half. At this point the sauce should be slightly thickened and glossy. Return the scallops to the pan, along with any accumulated juices, and simmer for 1 minute to reheat the scallops.

To serve, place the warm rice pilaf in the center of each plate. Arrange the scallops around the rice and spoon the sauce over them.

COOK'S TIP

For a more elegant sauce, stir 2 tablespoons of cold unsalted butter, cut into pieces, into the hot sauce before serving it. Do this off the heat. This calorie busting approach will produce the ultimate glossing for the sauce.

So the next day I surprised him with a dinner cooked just in his honor. I remember eating and talking far into the late hours. His face had relaxed, and we laughed, recalling our mischievous adventures as young children. When I hugged my brother that night, I felt him close to my heart as never before, and that's where he has stayed all these years.

What follows is my recipe for the special dish I made that night. My wish is that it will take your mind away from worries and that with each bite you'll come closer to that smile inside of you, waiting to come out.

Menu Suggestion
SCALLOPS WITH TOMATOES
AND SAFFRON
LEMON RICE PILAF
GREEN SALAD
WITH BALSAMIC VINAIGRETTE
PANNACOTTA

Wine Suggestion
GAVI

Torta Rustica

LAYERED PICNIC PIE

SERVES 10 TO 12

1 recipe Pizza Dough (see pages 220-221)

3 tablespoons + ¼ cup olive oil

1 onion, chopped

4 garlic cloves, chopped

8 ounces mushrooms, sliced

2 tablespoons chopped fresh basil or 2 teaspoons dried basil

2 tablespoons chopped fresh oregano or 2 teaspoons dried oregano

1 teaspoon salt

½ teaspoon black pepper

½ teaspoon red pepper flakes

1 (10-ounce) (300-g) package frozen chopped spinach, thawed and squeezed dry

8 ounces (225 g) ricotta cheese

1 (1½-pound) (750-g) eggplant

1 pound (450 g) thinly sliced Black Forest ham or prosciutto

1 (13- to 15-ounce) (375- to 425-g) jar roasted red bell peppers, drained

1 pound (450 g) freshly grated provolone cheese

1 cup pitted Greek or Sicilian black olives, halved

1 egg, beaten

Now I must tell you that La Signora Pacis was absolutely amazing. None of us kids or even our parents in my Palermo neighborhood knew how she could, all by herself, dote with such care and attention on each of her six children. Not only was there basketball practice (which I shared with two of her sons), but piano lessons, swimming lessons, dance recitals, doctor appointments...I'll just let you imagine with six kids. But La Signora Pacis was invincible and always rose to the occasion.

I wish I could say the same for our basketball team, but we couldn't even boast an even win-loss record. After one Saturday afternoon game, we gathered for a potluck. I remember coming out of the locker room, tired and really ready to eat, to see a line of mismatched portable tables loaded with a beautiful display of food.

The day before serving, prepare the pizza dough. While the dough is rising, heat 3 tablespoons of the olive oil in a large sauté pan on medium-high heat until sizzling, about 2 minutes. Add the onion and garlic, reduce the heat to medium and sauté for 1 minute. Add the mushrooms, basil, oregano, ½ teaspoon of the salt, the pepper and red pepper flakes. Cook for 10 minutes, stirring occasionally, until the onions and mushrooms are limp and dry. Take off the heat and stir in the spinach and ricotta. Set aside.

Cut the eggplant lengthwise into ¼-inch (6-mm) slices. Sprinkle the slices with the remaining ½ teaspoon of the salt and place them in a colander to drain for 20 minutes. Pat the slices dry with a paper towel. Line the bottom of a baking sheet with parch-

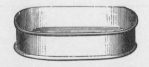

ment paper. Brush the eggplant slices with the remaining ¼ cup olive oil and bake in a 425° F (220° C) preheated oven for 10 minutes on each side. Remove from the oven and set aside.

Preheat the oven to 400° F (220° C). Roll out ¾ of the pizza dough to a 15-inch (38-cm) circle, approximately ½ inch (1.5 cm) thick. Place the dough into a 9 x 3-inch (23 x 8-cm) springform pan. You should have a 1-inch (2.5-cm) overhang all around the pan. Layer ½ of each ingredient in the pan in the following order: ham, spinach mixture, peppers, eggplant, cheese and olives. Repeat with the remaining ingredients.

Roll out the remaining dough into a circle to fit the top of the Torta Rustica. Lay it over the top and fold up the overhanging dough, crimping them together to seal the edges. Make 4 small slits in the top to let steam escape and brush with the beaten egg.

Place the Torta Rustica in the preheated oven and bake for 1 hour until the internal temperature in the middle reaches 120° F (49° C). About 20 minutes into the baking, cover the Torta Rustica with a tent of aluminum foil to keep the top from getting too brown. Remove from the oven, let cool for 1 hour, then cover with plastic wrap and refrigerate overnight.

Remove the Torta Rustica from the refrigerator about 1 hour before serving to bring to room temperature. Cut it into wedges and serve.

COOK'S TIP

If you prefer your Torta Rustica warmed, place the slices on a baking sheet. Warm in a preheated 400° F (200° C) oven for 5-8 minutes. Unless you enjoy crisp, browned edges, as I do, loosely cover it with a piece of foil.

But of all the lovingly prepared dishes, none stood out like Signora Pacis' Torta Rustica. It was tall, golden-brown, and brimming with colorful layers of good stuff.

No, we didn't win many games that season; but with all those potlucks the team grew quite a few inches and when we came back the next season, we were unbeatable.

Well, not really; but we did much better. And I'll always remember Signora Pacis with one or two of her children tugging at her skirt or hanging around her neck, standing beside her regal Torta Rustica. I hope you enjoy my version of that famous dish. It is the perfect meal for all little athletes on the go!

Menu Suggestion
MIXED SALAD WITH ORANGES,
ONION AND FENNEL
LAYERED PICNIC PIE
MARINATED FRUIT SALAD

Wine Suggestion
FRASCATI

Calzone con Verdure
VEGETABLE CALZONE

SERVES 4

1 (1-pound) (450-g) eggplant, cut into ½-inch (1.5-cm) dice

1½ teaspoons salt

3 tablespoons olive oil

1 zucchini, cut into ½-inch (1.5-cm) dice

1 sweet bell pepper (red, yellow or green), cut into ½-inch (1.5-cm) dice

4 Roma tomatoes, peeled and diced

2 tablespoons balsamic vinegar

2 teaspoons sugar

½ teaspoon black pepper

1 recipe Pizza Dough (see pages 220-221)

1 cup + 2 tablespoons Pizza Sauce (see page 224)

12 (¼-inch) (6-mm) slices fresh or smoked mozzarella cheese

4 tablespoons chopped fresh basil

This recipe pays homage to my mother and my Aunt Buliti who were driven by the incessant challenge of making vegetables palatable for their two diavoletti (little devils), my brother, Mario, and me.

I have expanded on my Aunt Buliti's prototype recipe by reducing the sauce to thicken it and heightening the contrast of sweet and sour. Even my brother, my cruelest critic, approves of this combination.

Never let it be said that vegetarian dishes have to be boring. Let this calzone's fabulous fireworks of texture and flavor mesmerize your taste buds into uncontrolled gluttony.

And remember, if Mario likes it, it has to be good.

Place the diced eggplant in a colander with a plate or bowl underneath. Sprinkle with 1 teaspoon of the salt. Put a small plate over the eggplant and place 2 cans of food on top as weights. Drain for 30 minutes. Pat the eggplant dry.

Preheat the oven to 400° F (200° C). In a large sauté pan, heat the olive oil over high heat until sizzling, about 2-3 minutes. Add the eggplant and zucchini and cook for 2 minutes until lightly browned on the edges. Add the bell pepper and cook 3 more minutes. Reduce the heat to low, add the tomatoes, balsamic vinegar, sugar, pepper and salt and cook for 2 minutes, tossing to mix well. Set aside and let the mixture cool for a few minutes.

Divide the pizza dough into 4 equal pieces and, on a floured board, roll out each ball of dough into an 8-inch (20-cm) circle.

Spread ¼ cup of pizza sauce on each round to within 1 inch (2.5 cm) of the edge. Put ¼ of the vegetable mixture on one side of each round and top that with 3 slices of the mozzarella and 1 tablespoon basil.

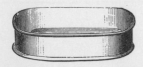

Fold the circle in half and seal the edges by pressing them with a fork. Place the calzones on a greased baking sheet (it's best to use one with edges in case the calzones leak). Brush each calzone with the remaining pizza sauce. Bake 30-40 minutes until puffed and golden brown.

COOK'S TIP

You can make 3 small cuts in the top of each calzone before baking to release the steam while it cooks. The calzone will not puff up as much when you cut steam vents.

"A man taking basil from a woman will always love her."

SIR THOMAS MORE

Menu Suggestion
PASTA WITH RAPINI
VEGETABLE CALZONE
MIXED SALAD WITH
ORANGES, ONION AND FENNEL

Wine Suggestion
MERLOT

Calzone con Prosciutto Cotto

HAM CALZONE

SERVES 4

1 recipe Pizza Dough (see pages 220-221)

1 cup + 2 tablespoons Pizza Sauce (see page 224)

4 Roma tomatoes, peeled and diced

12 (¼-inch) (6-mm) slices fresh or smoked mozzarella cheese

½ pound (225 g) thinly sliced ham

4 tablespoons chopped basil

½ teaspoon salt

Pepper to taste

Preheat the oven to 400° F (200° C). Divide the pizza dough into 4 equal pieces. On a floured board, roll out each ball of dough into an 8-inch (20-cm) circle.

Spread ¼ cup of pizza sauce over each circle to within 1 inch (2.5 cm) of the edges. On ½ of each round, place 1 chopped tomato, 3 slices mozzarella, 2 ounces ham, 1 tablespoon basil, ⅛ teaspoon salt and a pinch of pepper.

Fold each calzone in half and seal the edges by pressing them with a fork. Place the calzones on a greased baking sheet and use the remaining pizza sauce to brush the tops. Bake for 30-40 minutes until golden brown.

You may not be surprised to learn that my daily walk to school was dictated by culinary fancy. You see, I could always take the bus, which would get me to school in fifteen minutes. But if I budgeted my time judiciously, I could walk to school in the same amount of time, stopping by the Panificio or bread bakery of Signora Rosa, and buy a ham calzone. Furthermore, I could time my arrival at Signora Rosa's in order to get the hot calzones just out of the oven.

It has long been my ambition to reproduce a calzone as good as the ones from that bakery. I'll let you be the judge; but if I've done the job right, you'll hear the whistling of Little Nick as he struts through the streets of Palermo in anticipation.

Menu Suggestion
MOZZARELLA, TOMATO
AND BASIL SALAD
HAM CALZONE
COFFEE ICE

Wine Suggestion
MERLOT

Sfincione
Sicilian Style Pizza

Serves 4

2 teaspoons olive oil
1 recipe Pizza Dough (see pages 220-221)
1 small white onion, thinly sliced
2 cups hot water
1 recipe Pizza Sauce (see page 224)
4 tablespoons freshly grated Pecorino Romano cheese
4 tablespoons Italian Bread Crumbs (see page 218)

Grease a 9 x 13 x 2-inch (23 x 33 x 5-cm) rectangular glass baking dish with the olive oil. Stretch the pizza dough (which has risen for 1 hour) to fit the pan. Cover the pan and let the dough rise for 1 hour.

While the dough is rising, soak the onions for 1 hour in the hot water. This will reduce the pungency of strongly flavored onions. Drain the onions well and pat dry with a towel.

Preheat the oven to 400° F (200° C). Top the raised pizza dough with ½ of the pizza sauce, spreading it to cover the entire crust. Top with the drained onions, the remaining pizza sauce, the cheese and bread crumbs. Bake for 45 minutes. Remove the pizza from the oven and let it rest for 10 minutes. Cut into 4 pieces and serve on warm plates.

Some memories of food play into my mind as a medley of music from the past, evoking times, people and places that I had long forgotten.

Sfincione is one of those foods. It makes me remember my junior high school years, rushing out at lunch break, straight to the street vendors and their carts of earthly delights.

Don Pasquale Mirabella was the King of Calzone. His cart (a scooter-drawn hot box) was painted with colorful scenes from famous Italian operas. Don Pasquale, himself, was a short, stout man with a tenor voice. He would sing arias while selling slices of his sfincione. His cart was always mobbed and often sold out of sfincione.

So, put some opera music on and enjoy this recipe.

Menu Suggestion
Artichoke Caponata
Sicilian Pizza
Fruit Compote

Wine Suggestion
Zinfandel

Pizza con Cipolle
ONION PIZZA

"La crema di cipolle" or onion reduction, is a little known ingredient in America. But when cooked properly, it yields amazing results.

Legend has it that onion reduction was a very secret recipe developed by a monastery of Benedictine monks in the hills overlooking my hometown of Palermo.

I have used this concept before in my Onion Glazed Pot Roast. I have found this recipe to be a very popular snack and a great hit at dinner parties, especially cut into small rectangular slices next to a selection of Italian cheeses.

SERVES 6

2 tablespoons olive oil
1 recipe Pizza Dough (see pages 220-221)
½ recipe Onion Purée (2 cups) (see page 219)
½ cup Italian Bread Crumbs (see page 218)
⅓ cup freshly grated Pecorino Romano cheese

Preheat the oven to 375° F (190° C). Brush 1 tablespoon of the olive oil over the bottom of a 14- to 15-inch (35- to 38-cm) round pizza pan. On a floured surface, roll the pizza dough out into a 16-inch (41-cm) circle, approximately ¼ inch (6 mm) thick. Place the dough in the prepared pan and roll the edges of the dough under to form a lip around the edge.

Brush the remaining olive oil over the dough, making sure not to miss the edges. Spread the onion purée over the dough. Sprinkle with the bread crumbs and Romano cheese.

Bake for 35 minutes or until the crust in golden brown. Cut the pizza into wedges and serve hot.

Menu Suggestion
GREEN SALAD
WITH BALSAMIC VINAIGRETTE
ONION PIZZA
ASSORTED CHEESES
STRAWBERRY GRANITA

Wine Suggestion
PINOT GRIGIO

Pizza con Patate
Potato Pizza

Serves 6

¾ pound (350 g) unpeeled small red new potatoes, thinly sliced
1 tablespoon chopped garlic
1 tablespoon chopped fresh rosemary
1 tablespoon chopped fresh oregano
1 tablespoon chopped fresh thyme
½ teaspoon salt
¼ teaspoon black pepper
4 tablespoons olive oil
1 recipe Pizza Dough (see pages 220-221)
⅓ cup freshly grated Pecorino Romano cheese

Preheat the oven to 375° F (190° C). In a large bowl, gently toss the potato slices, garlic, rosemary, oregano, thyme, salt, pepper and 2 tablespoons of the olive oil until the potatoes are completely coated.

Brush 1 tablespoon of the olive oil on the bottom of a 14- to 15-inch (35- to 38-cm) round pizza pan. On a floured surface, roll the pizza dough out into a 16-inch (41-cm) circle, approximately ¼ inch (6 mm) thick. Place the dough in the pan and roll the edges of the dough under to form a lip around the edge.

Brush the remaining olive oil over the dough, making sure not to miss the edges. Arrange the potato slices on the pizza dough, overlapping them like fish scales. Sprinkle the cheese over the top and bake for 35 minutes until the edges are golden brown. Cut into wedges and serve hot.

After a huge family dinner at my Grandmother Maria's house in Alcamo, we were sent home with the usual care package of leftovers that, in this instance, contained a gargantuan amount of rosemary roasted potatoes. With her usual adventurous culinary spirit, my mother, Massimiliana, pushed the edge of the envelope trying to use up all these potatoes. Some were clearly disasters, while others, like this pizza, were an overwhelming success.

I know you will appreciate the daring spirit of my mom and be inspired to experiment with dishes of your own.

Menu Suggestion
Potato Pizza
Tuna Salad
with Caper Vinaigrette
Strawberry Ice

Wine Suggestion
Orvieto

Contorni

Side Dishes

Polenta

Cornmeal Pudding

I remember my Grandmother Adele standing over a big copper pot stirring polenta. In her family, polenta (a dense cornmeal pudding) was like bread that accompanied every meal.

There is a very simple reason for polenta's popularity: it's inexpensive, easy to make and naturally versatile. Of course, before the days of instant polenta, this dish required a long time of constant attention and continuous stirring. For my family this was an opportunity for sharing stories that make food magic.

Sure, you can use the instant polenta that will be ready in just a few minutes — and let me tell you, it tastes great. But at least once, try making polenta the old fashioned way, surrounded by your family. Maybe a little bit of magic will take place and you'll start sharing stories from your family's past.

Serves 4

4 cups water
1 teaspoon salt
1 cup cornmeal or imported polenta

Bring the water and salt to a boil in a 3- to 4-quart (2.75- to 3.75-l) saucepan. Slowly stir in the cornmeal with a whisk to avoid lumps. Once the cornmeal has all been whisked in, begin stirring with a long-handled wooden spoon. (The polenta will spatter, so you might want to wear an oven mitt to protect yourself from burns.) Turn the heat down to medium and stir continuously for 30-40 minutes until the polenta is thick and comes away from the sides of the pan. Serve immediately.

Cook's Tip

If you want to prepare the polenta a few hours in advance, but still serve it soft, place the covered saucepan into a larger pan with 1 inch (2.5 cm) of simmering water in the bottom and stir occasionally. If it is a little too firm at serving time, vigorously stir in a bit of chicken broth or milk.)

A great variation on the basic polenta recipe is Broiled Polenta. To prepare, cook 1 recipe of polenta as directed above (or ½ of a 13-ounce (375-g) package of instant polenta), spread it in a greased 9 x 9-inch (23 x 23-cm) baking pan and set aside for at least 30 minutes until firm. Sprinkle the top with 4 tablespoons of grated Parmigiano Reggiano cheese. Place under the broiler for 7-10 minutes, until the cheese is melted and lightly browned. Cut into 4 squares and then cut each square in half to make 2 triangles. Serve 2 triangles per person.

Fagiolini Verdi con le Mandorle

Green Beans with Almonds

Serves 4

4 tablespoons olive oil

1 pound (450 g) green beans, ends trimmed and parboiled for 3 minutes

½ teaspoon salt

⅛ teaspoon black pepper

3 tablespoons chopped fresh Italian parsley

5 garlic cloves, thickly sliced

½ cup blanched, slivered almonds

1 tablespoon freshly grated Parmigiano Reggiano cheese

Heat 2 tablespoons of the olive oil in a large nonstick sauté pan set on high heat until it begins to sizzle, about 2 minutes. Add the green beans and cook for 2 minutes. Stir in ¼ teaspoon of the salt, the pepper and parsley and cook for 1 minute. Transfer the cooked beans to a dish.

Add the remaining olive oil to the same pan and cook over medium heat for 1 minute. Add the garlic and almonds and cook for 2-3 minutes, until the garlic and almonds start to brown.

Return the cooked green beans to the pan, add the remaining salt and cook for 5 minutes, tossing until well mixed. Remove from the heat, add the Parmigiano Reggiano cheese, toss well and serve immediately.

Cook's Tip

If you would prefer not to parboil the green beans, they can be steamed for 4 minutes instead. This method can be used with all the green bean recipes in the book.

Somebody once said, "Inside the almond beats the heart of Sicily." This could explain the almost fanatical appreciation of almonds in Sicilian culinary traditions, from marzipan, a favorite sweet almond paste, to the almonds with green beans in this recipe.

My Uncle Mimi's wife, Ciccina, was the one that introduced me to this combination. Uncle Mimi and my father had gone together to the town square of Alcamo, where it was customary for produce buyers and sellers to meet and barter. The smiles, eyebrow raising and eventual handshakes, were the steps of an intricate ballet set to this musical background. The finale to this performance was a magical moment around the dinner table of Aunt Ciccina over a plate of green beans and almonds.

With a bravo to my father, uncle and aunt, I present this dish to you.

Fagiolini Verdi Salati con Pomodori e Aglio

Green Beans with Tomatoes and Garlic

O ne of my mother's missions in life was to provide her children with a balanced diet which would include a variety of vegetables. Her often heroic failures live on in the Stellino family folklore. In one memorable episode, my brother, Mario's, distinct dislike of broccoli was visually displayed with an airborne projectile ejected from his mouth with a force that made a distinct green spot behind the refrigerator.

The tomato was the answer to my mother's prayers. This common ingredient provides a flavor spike that makes even the most odious vegetable acceptable. This dish became one of my brother's and my favorites. I can never thank my mother enough for tricking me into eating it!

Serves 4

5 tablespoons olive oil
1 pound (450 g) green beans, ends trimmed, parboiled for 3 minutes
½ teaspoon salt
⅛ teaspoon black pepper
5 garlic cloves, thickly sliced
⅛ teaspoon red pepper flakes
1 (15-ounce) (425-g) can stewed tomatoes, drained and chopped, juices reserved separately
3 tablespoons chopped fresh basil

Heat 3 tablespoons of the olive oil in a large sauté pan set on high heat until sizzling, about 2 minutes. Add the beans and cook for 2 minutes. Stir in ¼ teaspoon of the salt and the pepper, mix well and cook 1 more minute. Transfer the beans to a dish with a slotted spoon and set aside.

Pour the remaining olive oil into the same pan set on medium heat. Add the garlic and red pepper flakes and cook until the garlic begins to brown, about 2 minutes. Stir in the chopped tomatoes and basil and cook 3 more minutes. Return the beans to the pan along with the remaining salt and the reserved tomato juices. Cook until most of the juices have been absorbed, about 3-5 minutes. The beans are now ready.

Cook's Tip

Fresh basil is a delicate herb that has a short shelf life when refrigerated. To keep the leaves from turning brown, place them in a glass of cold water and cover loosely with a plastic bag. Store in the refrigerator.

Fagiolini Verdi Salati al Limone e Menta

GREEN BEANS WITH LEMON, MINT AND GARLIC

SERVES 4

3 tablespoons olive oil

1 pound (450 g) green beans, trimmed, cut in half and parboiled for 3 minutes

1 tablespoon chopped garlic

2 tablespoons chopped fresh mint

¼ teaspoon salt

⅛ teaspoon black pepper

3 tablespoons lemon juice

Heat the oil in a large nonstick sauté pan set over medium-high heat until sizzling, about 2 minutes. Add the green beans and cook for 5 minutes, stirring occasionally, until just beginning to brown. Reduce the heat to medium, toss in the garlic, mint, salt and pepper and cook for 2 minutes. Stir in the lemon juice and cook for 2 minutes longer. Serve warm or at room temperature.

Sometimes you have to go for your dreams, even if the people around you doubt your vision. For instance, I have to confess that I developed this recipe over my wife, Nanci's, protestations. But I'm happy to report to you that she now says that this dish is the best thing she's ever tasted!

While food will not change your life, I hope this dish reminds you that life is a series of small victories and defeats. Be encouraged, your next victory could be around the corner.

Cavoli Gratinati

CAULIFLOWER AU GRATIN

My father once told me and my brother Mario, about a small village that holds a feast once each year in honor of cauliflower. This whole idea appeared to us as a foolish waste of time, and we showed very little interest in his story.

But as we had our first bites of the dish that my father had prepared, I was suddenly struck by how the tender bites of cauliflower were permeated with intense flavors. Mario and I couldn't believe that the object of our finicky culinary affection was one of our least liked vegetables — the cauliflower!

I must tell you that in hindsight my father's most persuasive tool in this case was not his story of the cauliflower feast, but in the dish, itself. But please feel free to make up a story of your own about your favorite foods if you feel the need. After all, everybody likes a good story.

SERVES 4

4 tablespoons olive oil
1 tablespoon anchovy paste
1 tablespoon drained capers
4 garlic cloves, thickly sliced
1 ½ teaspoons chopped fresh rosemary
¼ teaspoon red pepper flakes
⅛ teaspoon black pepper
1 tablespoon + 1 teaspoon chopped fresh Italian parsley
1 pound (450 g) cauliflower florets, cut into 1-inch (2.5-cm) pieces, parboiled for 3-4 minutes and patted dry
3 tablespoons Italian Bread Crumbs (see page 218)
3 tablespoons freshly grated Pecorino Romano cheese

Preheat the broiler. Heat the oil in a large sauté pan set on medium-high heat until sizzling, about 2 minutes. Add the anchovy paste, capers, garlic, rosemary, red pepper flakes, black pepper, and 1 tablespoon of the parsley and cook for 2-3 minutes, until the garlic is browned. Toss the cauliflower into the pan and stir to coat well. Cook the cauliflower for 2 minutes on each side to brown.

Transfer the cauliflower to a small 8 x 8-inch (20 x 20-cm) baking dish. Combine the bread crumbs and cheese and sprinkle over the cauliflower. Place under the broiler for 5-6 minutes, until the bread crumbs and cheese are browned. Sprinkle with the remaining parsley and serve.

COOK'S TIP

To save time when preparing this recipe, parboil the cauliflower the day before serving and keep refrigerated until you're ready to cook.

Melanzane Saltate alla Menta

Eggplant with Tomatoes and Mint

SERVES 4

¾ teaspoon salt

1 pound (450 g) eggplant, cut into 1-inch (2.5-cm) cubes

5 tablespoons olive oil

5 garlic cloves, thickly sliced

3 tablespoons chopped fresh mint

⅛ teaspoon red pepper flakes

1 (1-pound) (450-g) can peeled Italian tomatoes,
drained and chopped, juices reserved separately

½ teaspoon sugar (optional)

Sprinkle ¼ teaspoon of the salt over the cubed eggplant. Place in a colander, top with a plate and 2 cans of food to weight it down. Drain for 15-20 minutes with a bowl underneath, then pat the eggplant dry with a towel and set aside. Discard the drained eggplant juice.

In a large nonstick sauté pan set on high heat, heat 3 tablespoons of the oil until sizzling, about 2 minutes. Add the drained eggplant and cook for 5 minutes, tossing twice. The eggplant should be nicely browned, which will increase the flavor of the dish. Add the garlic, mint and red pepper flakes and cook for 2 more minutes. Add the chopped tomatoes, sugar (if you wish; see Cook's Tip below) and the remaining salt and cook 3 minutes, tossing twice. Add the reserved tomato juices, reduce the heat to medium and let cook, uncovered, for 8 to 10 minutes, stirring occasionally.

Transfer to a serving dish and serve immediately or refrigerate overnight and serve the next day at room temperature.

COOK'S TIP

The sweetness of canned tomatoes varies greatly. The amount of sugar used in this recipe can be adjusted up or down, depending on the sweetness of the tomatoes.

One day I borrowed my father's car to take a group of friends to attend a beach party in the coastal town of Terrasini. I suggested that we take the mountain road instead of the usual car route, and enjoy the vistas.

Unfortunately, my sense of adventure did not compare with my sense of direction. After a series of unfortunate twists up and down the tortuous mountain roads, I had to tell my passengers that we were lost.

Finally we reached the town of Montelepre and I thought we should stop and eat something. We sat down at a little trattoria and ordered this appetizer, big bowls of pasta and fresh country wine. We took our time and a sensation of peace came with our meal.

When we continued with our journey, I thanked my lucky star for discovering this delicious dish. Of course, I paid for lunch; that was the least I could do.

Zucchine con la Zagara

Orange Zucchini

Occasionally we call the orange blossom "ciuri d'ammuri" (the flower of love).

I first discovered this dish at a little trattoria in Palermo where it was called "Zucchine Nammurate" (Zucchini in Love). While I cannot endorse its romantic powers, I'm in love with its intricate flavor. Try this recipe and let yourself fall in love.

Serves 4

2 tablespoons olive oil
4 medium zucchini, cut into 3 pieces widthwise,
then cut into ¼-inch (6-mm) sticks, parboiled for 1 minute and patted dry
3 tablespoons chopped garlic
2 tablespoons chopped fresh mint
Zest of 1 orange, finely grated
¾ teaspoon salt
½ teaspoon black pepper
3 oranges, peeled and separated into sections, each section cut into thirds

Cook the olive oil in a large nonstick sauté pan set on high heat until sizzling, about 2 minutes. Throw in the zucchini and sauté for 2 minutes until lightly browned. Add the garlic, mint and orange zest, reduce the heat to medium-high and cook for 3 minutes. Gently stir in the salt, pepper and orange pieces, mix well, and cook for 2 minutes. Transfer to a serving dish and the zucchini is ready to serve.

Cook's Tip

Orange or lemon zest should be removed from the fruit just shortly before cooking. The zest is rich in oils that dissipate quickly and are lost if allowed to sit too long.

Zucchine con Porcini e l'Aceto Balsamico

Zucchini with Porcini Mushrooms and Balsamic Vinegar

SERVES 4

5 zucchini, cut into ½-inch (1.5-cm) slices

1 teaspoon salt

2 tablespoons olive oil

½ cup sliced fresh porcini mushrooms or ½ ounce (15 g) dried porcini,
softened for 30 minutes in 1 cup of hot chicken stock

1 tablespoon chopped garlic

1 tablespoon chopped fresh Italian parsley

1 tablespoon chopped fresh rosemary

¼ teaspoon black pepper

2 tablespoons balsamic vinegar

1 tablespoon sugar

Sprinkle the zucchini slices with ½ teaspoon of the salt and place in a colander or on paper towels to drain for 15 minutes. Pat the slices dry with a towel and set aside.

Cook the oil over high heat in a large sauté pan until sizzling, about 2 minutes. Add the drained zucchini and cook for 2 minutes on each side, until well browned. Add the porcini, garlic, parsley, rosemary, the remaining salt and the pepper, reduce the heat to medium and cook for 5 minutes, tossing once.

Bring the balsamic vinegar and sugar to a boil in a small saucepan and cook until syrupy, about 3 minutes. Add to the zucchini, stir well and cook 3 minutes.

The zucchini is ready to be served.

The following recipe was developed by Gino Tortorella after a particularly abundant hunt for wild mushrooms. He was one of my dad's acquaintances who would often join us on these hunts right after the first spring rains.

The beauty of this dish lies in its ultimate simplicity. If you're blessed with the opportunity to obtain fresh porcini mushrooms, you could basically make this your main course by increasing the proportions a bit and serving it with a big bowl of Polenta (see page 150). Of course, let's not forget a glass of good red wine. Soon you will understand my father and Signore Tortorella's anticipation every time they went to the woods looking for these beautiful mushrooms.

Carciofi con Zucchine

Artichoke and Zucchini Sauté

Serves 6 to 8

4 tablespoons olive oil

1 golden zucchini, halved lengthwise, cut into ½-inch (1.5-cm) slices

4 garlic cloves, thickly sliced

2 (9-ounce) (250-g) packages frozen artichoke hearts, thawed at room temperature
or run under warm water, cut into 1-inch (2.5-cm) dice

½ onion, diced

3 tablespoons drained capers

2 ounces (½ cup) (60 g) pitted black Greek or Sicilian olives, sliced

2 ounces (½ cup) (60 g) oil-packed sun-dried tomatoes, chopped

Zest of 1 lemon, grated

1 tablespoon chopped fresh basil

1 tablespoon chopped fresh Italian parsley

½ teaspoon salt

¼ teaspoon black pepper

I've told you in other stories how I used to be afraid of artichokes. Well, once I made it over this fear, I discovered a new dimension of flavor that artichokes can bring to many dishes.

Today I like to think of the artichoke as "Gioconda's" enigmatic smile. No, I don't believe that when Leonardo da Vinci painted this pictorial masterpiece he was thinking about artichokes.

But as the slow crescendo of flavors begins to grow on you, you might soon find yourself grinning. And then, with soft laughter, you'll understand the connection between the artichoke's flavor sensations and the mysterious smile of the "Gioconda." And if you don't? Look at it this way: as the worst case scenario, you will still have discovered a fabulous new dish.

Heat 1 tablespoon of the olive oil in a large sauté pan set on high heat until sizzling, about 2 minutes. Add the zucchini and garlic and sauté for 2 minutes on each side, to lightly brown. Transfer to a medium bowl and set aside.

Place the same pan back on high heat, add 1 tablespoon of the remaining olive oil and cook the artichoke hearts for 3 minutes to lightly brown. Add to the zucchini in the bowl.

In the same pan, set on medium-high heat, cook the remaining olive oil, onion, capers, olives, sun-dried tomatoes and lemon zest for 2 minutes. Stir in the basil, parsley, salt and pepper and cook for 1 more minute. Return the cooked artichokes and zucchini to the pan, stir thoroughly and heat through.

Serve warm or at room temperature.

Cook's Tip

Many cooks feel that curly parsley and Italian flat parsley are interchangeable in recipes, but the flavor of the Italian is more intense and adds more flavor to the dishes in which it is used. My preference is obvious since I always ask you to use it in my recipes.

Caponata di Carciofi

Artichoke Relish

Serves 6

5 tablespoons olive oil

12 fresh artichoke hearts (see page 14 for cleaning instructions),
cut into 1-inch (2.5-cm) dice

or 2 (9-ounce) (250-g) packages frozen artichoke hearts,
cut into 1-inch (2.5-cm) dice

1½ cups diced onion

1 tablespoon chopped garlic

1 cup finely diced celery, parboiled for 2 minutes

¼ teaspoon red pepper flakes

¼ cup drained capers

4 ounces (115 g) pitted Greek or Sicilian black olives, halved

2 cups Tomato Sauce (see page 225)

3 tablespoons chopped fresh basil

¼ teaspoon unsweetened cocoa powder

2 tablespoons balsamic vinegar

1 tablespoon sugar

Heat 2 tablespoons of the olive oil in a large sauté pan set on medium-high heat until sizzling, about 2 minutes. Add the artichokes and cook until browned, about 3 minutes on each side. Using a slotted spoon, transfer the artichokes to a bowl, leaving as much oil in the pan as possible. Reduce the heat to medium, add the remaining oil and the onion, stir until well coated and cook for 5-8 minutes. Add the garlic, celery, red pepper flakes, capers and olives and cook for 3-5 minutes. Stir in the tomato sauce and basil. Heat until the sauce is bubbling and cook for 3 minutes. Stir in the cocoa powder and cooked artichokes until well mixed and simmer for 5-8 minutes.

In a small saucepan on high heat, boil the vinegar and sugar until reduced by half and quite syrupy, about 2 minutes. Stir into the cooked vegetables, mix well and simmer on very low heat for 3-5 minutes. Remove from the heat, transfer to a bowl and refrigerate overnight. Bring to room temperature before serving.

This dish also makes a wonderful appetizer spread to serve on garlic toast. Coarsely chop the artichokes instead of cubing.

This recipe is a practical demonstration of the artichoke's eclectic culinary personality. Caponata is traditionally prepared with eggplant. But by substituting the artichoke, even though the basic ingredients remain the same, the final result is completely different. It's like two ballerinas dancing their most imaginative steps to the same music: while the melody remains the same, their interpretations are different.

Ultimately, the personalization of recipes is the beauty about cooking. You can use your favorite ingredients and spices to discover whole new personalities for recipes. But after your first bite of this dish, you'll care very little about this whole philosophical dissertation — you'll be too busy enjoying and sharing with your friend this fabulous new dish.

Carciofi Ripieni al Forno
Stuffed Artichoke Hearts

The truth about this dish is that it came about during one of my daily trips to the grocery store. Maybe this is uncommon for you, but like my mother, I do my shopping each day. Most of the time I don't know what I'll have for dinner until I get inspired by some fresh ingredients.

My wife usually accompanies me on these daily trips, and my habit is to talk aloud in a constant stream, telling her what my ideas are for each food I see. Anyway, one day I went babbling on about all the ingredients, until I turned around and came face-to-face with a complete stranger, who said, "Mister, I don't know who you are, but I sure like that recipe."

So, be cautious about judging the next person you meet who talks to himself. He might just be under the influence of culinary genius.

SERVES 8
6 cups Chicken Stock (see page 228)
8 fresh artichoke hearts (see page 14 for cleaning instructions)
½ recipe Vegetarian Stuffing (see page 214)
1 cup Tomato Sauce (see page 225)

Bring the chicken stock and artichoke hearts to a boil in a medium saucepan. Reduce the heat and simmer for 5-6 minutes, until a knife inserts easily. Drain the artichokes, reserving the chicken stock separately, and cool. Return the chicken stock to high heat and boil until reduced to ½ cup. This will take 25-30 minutes.

Preheat the oven to 350° F (180° C). Place the artichoke hearts into a 9 x 13-inch (23 x 33-cm) baking dish and mound each one with the stuffing. Pour the tomato sauce and the ½ cup of reduced chicken stock around the stuffed artichoke hearts in the dish and bake in the oven for 20 minutes.

To serve, place a stuffed artichoke heart on a serving dish and spoon the sauce around it.

Pomodori Fritti

Fried Tomatoes

SERVES 4

6 Roma tomatoes
¼ + ⅛ teaspoon salt
¼ teaspoon black pepper
½ teaspoon sugar
1 teaspoon dried oregano
6 tablespoons olive oil
3 garlic cloves, thickly sliced
2 tablespoons drained capers
¼ cup chopped Greek or Sicilian black olives
1 tablespoon chopped fresh basil
1 recipe Tossed Green Salad with Balsamic Vinaigrette (see page 38)

Each food has many different personalities which show themselves through different cooking methods. Once you try this recipe, you will discover a whole new frontier of tomato cooking.

The frying technique brings out a new sweetness in this familiar vegetable. My favorite menu combines it with Steak Salad (see page 47).

Cut the tomatoes in half crosswise, sprinkle the cut sides with ¼ teaspoon of the salt and place cut-side-down on paper towels or a rack to drain for 20 minutes. Pat the cut side dry. Sprinkle with the remaining salt, the pepper, sugar and oregano.

Heat 3 tablespoons of the oil in a large sauté pan set on high heat until sizzling, about 2 minutes. Put the tomatoes in the pan cut-side-down and cook for 1½-2 minutes, until browned. Turn them over and cook for 1½-2 minutes on the other side. Remove to a plate.

Add the remaining oil to the same pan along with the garlic and cook over medium-high heat until the garlic begins to brown, about 1 minute. Add the capers, olives and basil and cook for 1 more minute. Remove from the heat.

Place 3 tomatoes on each plate and spoon ¼ of the pan juices over them. Serve the tossed green salad alongside the tomatoes. Garlic toast is a great accompaniment for this dish.

Pomodori Arrosti Ripieni di Tonno
Stuffed Tomatoes with Tuna Sauce

My paternal grandfather, Don Nicola Stellino, was a man of few words. He had a very difficult life because his own father died when he was a young teenager. To provide for his family, he took over his father's duties, working the fields and raising a small herd of sheep.

He was a gifted young man who, having abandoned his studies because of necessity, found his means of self expression through his work. Nobody was a more ambitious farmer or a more aggressive livestock trader. His business acumen allowed him to succeed at a young age, but having spent so much time alone in the fields among his farm animals, Don Nicola was a man who lacked the social graces. However his heart was not immune to the temptation of love, and according to my father, he was head over heels in love when he married my Grandmother Maria.

Serves 4

4 medium tomatoes (3½- to 4-inches wide) (9- to 10-cm)
½ teaspoon salt
4 tablespoons olive oil
¼ teaspoon red pepper flakes
4 garlic cloves, thickly sliced
½ onion, chopped
2 teaspoons drained capers
¼ cup pitted Greek or Sicilian black olives, coarsely chopped
1 (14½-ounce) (415-g) can stewed tomatoes,
drained, chopped and juices reserved separately
½ cup uncooked medium-grain white rice
1 tablespoon sugar
1 tablespoon white wine vinegar
1 (6-ounce) (175-g) can water-packed white tuna, drained and flaked
1 cup frozen peas, thawed
4 tablespoons freshly grated Parmigiano Reggiano cheese
½ recipe Tuna Sauce (see page 226)

Slice the tops off the tomatoes and reserve. Using a very sharp paring knife, remove and discard the ribs and seeds from the insides of the tomatoes, being very careful not to puncture the skin. Sprinkle the salt inside the tomatoes and place them upside down on paper towels to drain for 10 minutes.

In a large sauté pan set on medium-high heat, cook the olive oil, red pepper flakes and garlic for 1 minute. Add the onion, capers and olives and cook for 3-5 minutes, stirring well. Stir in the drained tomatoes, rice, sugar, vinegar and tuna and cook for 3 minutes. Pour in the reserved tomato juice and bring to a boil. Reduce the heat to low and simmer, covered, for 10 minutes. At this point, most of the juices should be absorbed by the rice, which will be just tender. Transfer the rice to a large bowl, stir in the peas and cheese and set aside.

Preheat the oven to 400° F (200° C). Brush the bottom and sides of an 8 x 8-inch (20 x 20-cm) baking dish and the drained tomatoes with the remaining olive oil. Lightly stuff the prepared tomatoes with the rice mixture and place in the baking dish. Don't stuff them too tightly or they'll split during cooking. Place the tops on the tomatoes.

Bake for 45 minutes. Serve immediately with 2 tablespoons of Tuna Sauce on the side (and more available in a sauceboat, because your guests will always ask for more!). I also recommend this dish for picnics and buffets, because it's delightful served at room temperature.

My father remembers a tender, rare moment he witnessed between my grandparents. As was customary in those days, my grandmother would take a packed lunch to my grandfather while he was working in the fields. As they all sat in the shade, they enjoyed the bountiful spread she had laid out over a checkered tablecloth thrown over the grassy ground. While they were eating and drinking some wine, they started talking together and sharing a few laughs. As the cool autumn breeze blew by, my father witnessed Don Nicola embracing Nonna Maria and kissing her tenderly. That was the only time my dad saw such a display of affection, a moment that he treasured forever in his heart. He still believes that the cause of such magic was in a certain special dish greatly favored by my grandfather; but I would like to believe that it was love.

What follows is the recipe of that magical dish.

Ragù di Verdure

Asparagus, Peppers and Mushrooms with Polenta

This dish was created by my grandmother Adele during World War II. Even though meat was in short supply, Nonna Adele was determined to make her family dinners a festive and alluring affair. She decided that she needed a garden, but the only land available was a small strip of rocky ground.

My mother still remembers how Nonna recruited the entire family to remove the rocks, till the soil, and carry in buckets of water by hand to irrigate the plants. And I can tell you that Nonna's little piece of ground, fostered by the care of the Boccato family, grew and flourished beyond their wildest expectations. It really brought a ray of sunshine to everyone's heart during one of Italy's darkest moments.

What follows is my version of Nonna Adele's "Vegetarian Ragù." It always reminds me of the power of her love to create a green oasis for my family.

SERVES 4

1 recipe Broiled Polenta (see Cook's Tip, page 150)
4 tablespoons olive oil
1 pound (450 g) asparagus, thin stalked, cut into 1-inch (2.5-cm) pieces
1 large red bell pepper, cut into 1-inch (2.5-cm) dice
4 garlic cloves, thickly sliced
4 tablespoons chopped shallots
6 ounces (175 g) shiitake or button mushrooms, sliced
1 tablespoon chopped fresh Italian parsley
2 tablespoons chopped fresh basil
1 tablespoon chopped fresh thyme
¼ teaspoon red pepper flakes
½ cup white wine
½ cup Chicken Stock (see page 228)
½ cup sliced oil-packed sun-dried tomatoes
½ teaspoon salt
¼ teaspoon black pepper

Prepare the Broiled Polenta and keep warm in the oven.

Heat the oil in a large sauté pan set on medium-high heat until sizzling, about 2 minutes. Add the asparagus, bell pepper and garlic and cook until they begin to brown, about 2-3 minutes. Add the shallots, mushrooms, parsley, basil, thyme and red pepper flakes and cook until the shallots are soft and translucent and the mushrooms are limp, about 2-3 minutes. Pour in the wine, chicken stock, sun-dried tomatoes, salt and pepper. Bring to a boil, reduce the heat and simmer until the liquid is reduced by half, about 5-8 minutes.

To serve, spoon the vegetables onto serving plates and top with triangles of broiled polenta.

Torta di Polenta con Spinaci

Polenta Spinach Pie

SERVES 8

3 tablespoons olive oil

8 ounces (225 g) sliced mushrooms

1 (10-ounce) (300-g) package frozen chopped spinach, thawed and squeezed dry

¾ cup pesto (store bought is fine)

1 recipe Polenta (see page 150)

or ½ a 13-ounce (375-g) package instant polenta

¾ cup freshly grated Parmigiano Reggiano cheese

4 ounces (115 g) chopped oil-packed sun-dried tomatoes

This is a very easy recipe that shows the versatility of polenta. Once you master this dish, there is no limitation to the type of filling you can create to customize your own polenta pie.

Heat the oil in a large nonstick sauté pan set on medium-high heat until sizzling, about 2 minutes. Add the mushrooms and cook for 5 minutes, stirring occasionally. Remove from the heat and stir in the spinach and pesto. (If you are using packaged pesto and the oil has settled to the top, stir well before measuring out the ¾ cup needed for the recipe.)

Cook the polenta according to directions. Remove from the heat and stir in the cheese and sun-dried tomatoes. Pour half the polenta into a greased 9-inch (23-cm) pie pan. Spread the spinach mixture over the polenta and top with the remaining polenta, spreading with a knife to distribute evenly. Let the pie sit for 5-10 minutes before cutting into wedges.

The dish can be made ahead, refrigerated overnight and reheated before serving. Simply cover with foil and bake in a 375° F (190° C) oven for 1 hour.

COOK'S TIP

For a more colorful presentation, serve the wedges of pie on a bed of tomato sauce or with a dollop of pesto on top.

Puré di Patate Speziate

HERBED MASHED POTATOES

Is there anything more comforting than a serving of mashed potatoes to accompany your favorite foods? As a child, I was a fanatic about this dish: everything with sauce had to be nestled next to mashed potatoes.

Of course, by now you may have noticed that it is not in my nature to leave a good thing alone; and unlike other experiments (which shall remain nameless), my quest for the perfect mashed potato variation was, I believe, quite successful.

So have fun and share these recipes with your family and friends. Then sit back and watch the magic that takes place around your table when you present your guests with such good food.

SERVES 4 TO 6

2 pounds (900 g) Russet potatoes, peeled and quartered
1 large shallot (2 ounces) (60 g), peeled and quartered
¾ teaspoon salt
¼ teaspoon black pepper
¼ cup cold butter, cut into pieces
1 tablespoon chopped fresh sage
1 tablespoon chopped fresh rosemary
1 tablespoon chopped fresh thyme
3 tablespoons freshly grated Pecorino Romano cheese

Put the potatoes and the quartered shallot into a large saucepan with enough cold water to cover by 2 inches (5 cm). Cover the pot and bring to a boil. Once the water reaches the boil, uncover, reduce the heat to medium-low and cook for 15-20 minutes, until the potatoes and shallot are so soft they will break with pressure from the back of a spoon. Drain well and return the potatoes and shallot to the pan. Mash the potatoes with the shallot, mixing well to incorporate the shallot throughout. Add the remaining ingredients and mix well with a wooden spoon. Serve immediately.

COOK'S TIP

To save time when preparing this recipe, keep some herb/butter mixture on hand in the freezer. Simply stir the chopped herbs into room temperature butter, shape into a log and wrap with plastic wrap. Place in a freezer bag and freeze for up to 2-3 months. To use, remove from the freezer, thaw in the refrigerator, cut into chunks and stir into hot mashed potatoes along with the cheese, salt and pepper.

Puré di Patate all'Ungherese

Sour Cream Chive Mashed Potatoes

Serves 4 to 6

2 pounds (900 g) Russet potatoes, peeled and quartered
¾ teaspoon salt
¼ teaspoon black pepper
3 tablespoons freshly grated Parmigiano Reggiano cheese
¼ cup sour cream
3 tablespoons chopped fresh chives

Put the potatoes into a large saucepan with enough cold water to cover by 2 inches (5 cm). Cover the pot and bring to a boil. Once the water reaches a boil, uncover, reduce the heat to medium-low and cook for 15-20 minutes, until the potatoes are so soft they will break with the back of a spoon. Drain well and return the potatoes to the saucepan. Mash the potatoes well, add all the other ingredients and mix with a sturdy, wooden spoon.

"I declare that a meal prepared by a person who loves you will do more good than any average cooking."

Luther Burbank

Puré di Patate con l'Aglio
Garlic Mashed Potatoes

SERVES 4 TO 6

2 pounds (900 g) Russet potatoes, peeled and quartered
1 head garlic, broken into individual peeled cloves
⅛ teaspoon garlic powder (optional)
¾ teaspoon salt
¼ teaspoon pepper
¾ teaspoon Aromat (Knorr Aromatic Salt, either chicken or meat base)
3 tablespoons freshly grated Parmigiano Reggiano cheese
¼ cup whipping cream

Put the potatoes and garlic into a large saucepan. Fill with cold water at least 2 inches (5 cm) over the potatoes. Cover the pot and bring to a boil over medium heat. Once it reaches a boil, uncover, reduce the heat to medium-low and cook for another 15-20 minutes, until the potatoes and the garlic cloves are so soft that they will break with pressure from the back of a spoon. Drain well and pour back into the saucepan. Mash the potato mixture well, add all the other ingredients except the cream and mix with a sturdy, wooden spoon.

Place the saucepan over medium-low heat and add the cream, stirring constantly until it is incorporated. Turn off the heat and it is ready to be served.

COOK'S TIP

Make mashed potatoes with roasted garlic or garlic roasted in oil, in place of the garlic head, in this recipe.

For mashed potatoes with Roasted Garlic (see page 224), prepare the roasted garlic as directed and add the garlic pulp to the mashed potatoes. Continue with the original recipe.

For Garlic Roasted in Oil, add the peeled cloves from 1 head of garlic to 2 cups of simmering olive oil. Simmer gently for 30 minutes, until the garlic cloves are completely cooked and very soft. Surprise — you've just made garlic olive oil! Add the soft cloves to the mashed potatoes and continue with the original recipe.

> *"We owe much to the fruitful meditation of our sages, but a sane view of life is, after all, elaborated in the kitchen."*
>
> JOSEPH CONRAD

Patate Arroste

COUNTRY STYLE ROASTED POTATOES

SERVES 4

3 pounds (1.4 kg) Russet potatoes, peeled and thickly sliced
1 ½ large heads garlic, separated into cloves, unpeeled
1 teaspoon salt
½ teaspoon pepper
1 tablespoon chopped fresh rosemary
1 tablespoon chopped fresh thyme
1 tablespoon chopped fresh sage
6 ½ tablespoons olive oil
1 small white onion, thinly sliced

This recipe is a variation of my traditional roasted potatoes using a different combination of herbs to change the character of the dish. I hope this will inspire you to experiment with the herb mixture in some of your own recipes.

Preheat the oven to 425° F (220° C). Place the potatoes and garlic in a large pot, cover with water, place the lid on and bring to a boil. Boil for 10 minutes. Uncover, reduce the heat to medium and cook for 10 minutes. The potatoes should still be a bit hard. Drain. Transfer the garlic cloves to a glass of cold water. When they are cool enough to handle, peel them by simply squeezing them out of their softened skin.

Place the potatoes and garlic purée in a large bowl. Sprinkle with the salt, pepper, rosemary, thyme, sage and 4½ tablespoons of the olive oil and mix until well coated.

Grease the bottom of a large baking tray with the remaining 2 tablespoons of olive oil. Place the potatoes on the greased baking tray and roast for 20 minutes, turning once. Spread the sliced onions on top of the potatoes and roast until the potatoes are well browned, about 20 minutes, turning once. If you like them extra crispy, cook for 10 more minutes.

COOK'S TIP

If you're making this potato dish together with a roasted meat, add 3 tablespoons of the defatted roasting juices to the potatoes during the last 5 minutes of cooking. Mix to coat well and cook for 5 minutes. Serve proudly alongside your roast.

Soufflé di Patate Dolci
Sweet Potato Soufflé

I created this dish for my guests on the occasion of a "Thanksgiving dinner." I was trying to take the "same old sweet potatoes" and turn them into something exciting and fun to eat. It's a perfect example of what I mean by improvising in the kitchen and letting your passions flow. I hope that with every bite you take of this dish, you'll find yourself struck by its flavorful delicacy, and your mind will wander into culinary projects of your own.

Go ahead and go for it!

Serves 8 to 10

1½ pounds (750 g) (3 medium) sweet potatoes or yams
5 eggs, separated
8 ounces (225 g) cream cheese
¾ teaspoon salt
¼ teaspoon black pepper
2 tablespoons + ½ cup honey (optional)
½ cup freshly grated Parmigiano Reggiano cheese
2 tablespoons chopped fresh thyme

Preheat the oven to 325° F (170° C). Bake the unpeeled sweet potatoes for 1-1½ hours, until easily pierced with a knife. Let them cool completely, then peel and cut into large chunks. Set aside.

Preheat the oven to 325° F (170° C). Cream the egg yolks and cream cheese in a food processor or with an electric mixer until creamy and pale yellow, about 3 minutes. Add the cooked sweet potatoes and process for 2-3 minutes, until smooth. Add the salt, pepper, 2 tablespoons of the honey, the cheese and thyme and process for 1 more minute, until well mixed. Pour into a large bowl (if you've been using a food processor) and set aside.

Beat the egg whites with an electric mixer until they form stiff peaks, about 3-4 minutes. Fold the egg whites into the sweet potato mixture ⅓ at a time, being careful not to over mix. Pour into a lightly greased 9 x 13-inch (23 x 33-cm) baking dish. Bake for 30-40 minutes, until the top is lightly browned and beginning to crack.

Serve drizzled with the remaining ½ cup honey, if you wish a sweeter soufflé.

Riso al Forno

Rice Pilaf

SERVES 4

4 tablespoons olive oil

1 cup finely chopped onion

2 garlic cloves, thickly sliced

1 bay leaf

1 cup long-grain white rice

½ cup white wine

1 ½ cups Chicken Stock (see page 228)

¼ teaspoon salt

⅛ teaspoon black pepper

2 tablespoons chopped fresh Italian parsley

Heat the oil in a large nonstick sauté pan over medium-high heat until sizzling, about 2 minutes. Add the onion, garlic and bay leaf and cook for 3-4 minutes, until the onion is soft. Stir in the rice and cook for 2 minutes. Add ¼ cup of the white wine, stir to scrape up any brown bits from the pan bottom and cook for 1 minute until the wine is absorbed. Stir in the remaining wine, the chicken stock, salt, pepper and parsley and bring to a boil. Cover the pan with a tight-fitting lid, reduce the heat to low and simmer for 20 minutes. Remove from the heat and let sit for 5 minutes. Stir the rice to fluff and remove the bay leaf.

COOK'S TIPS

This is a great basic rice pilaf recipe. Feel free to experiment with the ingredients — if you don't have white wine, use all chicken stock or beef stock. Stir in 1 teaspoon of a chopped fresh herb, such as thyme or oregano, at the same time as the parsley, to complement the dish you'll be serving the pilaf with. Spices such as curry powder or cumin are also great additions — simply stir in ½ tablespoon of curry powder or 1 teaspoon cumin when you add the rice to the pan.

For a great Lemon Pilaf, stir in the grated zest of 1 lemon after the 20 minutes of cooking and then let it sit, covered, for 5 minutes.

I assure you that no pre-packaged mixture matches the flavor of homemade pilaf. The recipe is really quite simple and once you master the basic technique, you'll be able to create any number of personalized versions with whatever seasonings are on hand in your pantry.

In fact, after a few tries, it will take you the same time to prepare rice pilaf from scratch as it does to prepare the boxed version. Of course, once you've tasted the powerful fresh flavors of homemade, it will be very hard to go back to the "stuff" in the box.

DOLCI

DESSERTS

Melone Stile Esotico
Canteloupe with Apple Rosemary Syrup

Serves 4 to 6
2 medium cantaloupes
2 cups apple juice
1 cup sugar
5 (4-inch) (10-cm) sprigs fresh rosemary

Cut the canteloupes in half. Scoop out the seeds and using a melon baller, scoop out the flesh into a medium bowl.

Heat the apple juice, sugar and 3 of the rosemary sprigs to the boiling point in a small saucepan over medium-high heat. Pour the juice over the melon balls and chill for at least 2 hours or overnight.

Serve in glass goblets decorated with the remaining rosemary sprigs.

My mother often ran into our longtime neighbor, La Signorina Giovanna, doing our daily food shopping. Waiting in line together at the bread shop, delicatessen, or fruit stand for so many years fostered a unique bond. La Signorina Giovanna knew everything about Mario's and my schoolwork, as we did about her sister, Margherita, and her little French poodle, Cicero.

As an exuberant single woman, La Signorina Giovanna had many exciting travel adventures. Through her stories we were magically transported to exotic lands. She also loved to share new recipes for foods she discovered on her trips.

The following dish is based on La Signorina Giovanna's personal interpretation. I think it illustrates the ebullient spirit of a life full of culinary adventure. I'm sure you'll enjoy passing it on to one of your friends, the next time you're standing together in a long line, just as La Signorina Giovanna did with my mother.

Mele Cotogne
Poached Apples

Serves 4
2 cups apple juice
2 cups fruity white wine, such as Chenin Blanc
1 ½ cups sugar
1 vanilla bean, split
1 cinnamon stick, 3-4 inches (8-10 cm) long
4 apples
2 tablespoons lemon juice
4 Amaretti cookies, crushed

Combine the apple juice, wine and sugar in a saucepan just large enough to fit the apples in a single layer. Bring to just below a simmer, add the vanilla bean and cinnamon stick, cover and simmer until the apples are ready to cook.

Peel and core the apples. Cut a thin slice from the bottom of each apple and put in a large bowl of water to which the 2 tablespoons of lemon juice has been added to prevent browning. When all the apples are peeled, put them in the hot liquid and bring the temperature back to just below simmering. If the liquid doesn't cover the apples by ½ inch (1.5 cm), add more wine and water, sweetening with 6 tablespoons of sugar to each cup of liquid. If the apples are simply floating in the liquid, cover them with a piece of parchment paper or aluminum foil, put a small plate or saucer on top of that to weigh the apples down and cover with the lid. Cook for 25-35 minutes (the size of your apples will determine how long it will take), until tender when pierced with a skewer. Remove from the heat and let cool for 30 minutes while the apples continue to absorb the liquid's flavor.

Transfer the apples to a plate. Return the pan with the liquid to the heat, bring to a boil and cook until reduced to 2 cups, with a thickened, syrup-like consistency, about 40-45 minutes.

Serve the apples warm or at room temperature, with the warm syrup drizzled over them and the crushed Amaretti cookies sprinkled on top.

"Non voguo la frutta voglio un dolcino!" (I don't want fruit, I want pastry!)

This was one of my brother, Mario's, and my favorite war cries. In fact, we launched a daily full-speed-ahead campaign to convince my mother that she should make dessert as the finale for every evening meal. But, as you probably realize by now, my mother was not the type to crumble under her children's pressure. However, when she did make dessert, she wanted it to be the healthiest possible, which often translated into "any kind of dessert with fruit" that Mario and I would eat.

The following is one of her most successful "healthy desserts." It seduced Mario and me into eating many, many apples and I'm sure will be a favorite of even the most stubborn of your children.

Frutta Sciroppata

FRUIT COMPOTE

Ending a meal with fruit as dessert is a Mediterranean tradition that just wasn't part of my Stellino genes. In fact, I am a confessed "chocolate pastry kind of guy" when it comes to dessert. But I must tell you that sampling this simple fruit combination was, as in true love, a sweet surrender. Do not be misled by its apparent simplicity: the subtle contrasts of sweet and tangy yield a surprisingly satisfying ending to any meal.

*Note: If you're unable to find fresh peaches or pears, using canned fruit in light syrup is an acceptable alternative. Simply drain the fruit and add to the syrup at the same time as the grapes — they don't need the 5-10 minutes poaching time.

SERVES 4

1 ½ cups Port wine
1 ½ cups water
2 teaspoons vanilla
1 (6-inch) (15-cm) piece cinnamon stick
½ cup sugar
Zest of 1 lemon, grated
2 pears (1 ½ pounds) (750 g), peeled, cored and sliced into 8 pieces*
2-3 peaches (1 ½ pounds) (750 g), peeled and sliced into 8 pieces*
1 cup green grapes, cut in half
3 tablespoons cornstarch mixed with 3 tablespoons Port wine (slurry)
1 cup blueberries or raspberries, fresh or frozen

In a large saucepan set on high heat, bring the wine, water, vanilla, cinnamon stick, sugar and lemon zest to a boil. Reduce the heat to medium-high and add the pear and peach slices. Cook for 5-10 minutes, until the fruit is easily pierced with a knife. Add the grapes, remove the pan from the heat and let sit for 15 minutes. With a slotted spoon, remove the fruit to 4 glass goblets or bowls.

Stir the cornstarch slurry into the cooking liquid, return the pan to the heat and bring to a boil to clear and thicken the juices, about 1 minute.

To serve, spoon the sauce over the fruit and top with the berries. This dish can be made ahead of time — it will keep well in the refrigerator for 3 to 4 days and can be served warm or chilled.

COOK'S TIP

A wonderful way to serve this dish is over Sweetened Polenta. In the recipe for Polenta (see page 150), add ¼ cup of sugar to the water and salt before bringing it to a boil. Then proceed with the recipe as directed. Place the cooked polenta into a 9 x 9-inch (23 x 23-cm) baking dish and allow it to cool. At serving time, cut the polenta into slices and top with the Fruit Compote.

Macedonia di Frutta
MARINATED FRUIT SALAD

SERVES 8

2 oranges, peeled, cut into sections and diced
2 apples, peeled, cored and diced
2 peaches, peeled and diced
2 bananas, peeled and cut into ½-inch (1.5-cm) pieces
2 cups (approximately 1 pound) (450 g) red or green grapes
Juice of 3 lemons
½ cup Italian grappa or vodka
3 tablespoons sugar

Place all the fruit in a large bowl. Combine the lemon juice, grappa and sugar and stir until the sugar is dissolved. Pour over the fruit and gently stir to coat well. Marinate in the refrigerator for 1½-2 hours. Serve chilled in fruit cups or over ice cream.

COOK'S TIP

Canned fruit can be substituted for any of fruits that are out of season or you can let your imagination go and try it with whatever fruits are available fresh.

Grappa is a brandy distilled from the solids left after the fermentation of wine. Unaged grappa is identifiable by its crystal clarity and should be served ice cold, while aged grappa has a golden amber color and should be served at room temperature, like a fine brandy.

Some of you may be surprised to know that "Frutta Fresca" (fresh fruit) is often listed in an Italian restaurant's dessert list. Indeed, the following dish is a very common restaurant offering. It is a variation on the basic bowl of fresh fruit, marinated until it reaches its highest culinary interpretation.

In northern Italy, the cold winter weather inspires many trattoria chefs to come up with their personal favorites. The addition of grappa or vodka adds a fascinating new dimension to this mix of fresh fruit.

This recipe warms the body and the mind on those cold winter nights when the wind is howling outside your windows as you sit by the fireplace enjoying every bite of this delicious dessert.

Pere al Cioccolatto

Pears with Chocolate Sauce

This is one of my mother's best "no fuss" desserts: something ready in minutes to please the sweet tooth of her two sons.

This dish is lifted from the ordinary by the chocolate sauce, which is based on a reduction of the canned pear's syrup, until it arrives at its most flavor-packed essence. The pear essence combined with the chocolate is a match made in heaven.

Like a simple black dress, you can make this dessert as elegant as you wish, with fresh whipped cream piped on top in an intricate design and sprinkled with toasted hazelnuts. But my loyalty remains with its humble origins as a mother's heaven-sent solution to her family's desire for a comforting sweet treat for the conclusion of dinner.

Serves 6

2 (1-pound) (450-g) cans pears in heavy syrup,
drained and syrup reserved separately
4 tablespoons dark rum
4 ounces (115 g) milk chocolate baking chips or bar
½ cup whipping cream, whipped with 3 tablespoons sugar
or 3 cups vanilla ice cream
6 mint sprigs for decoration (optional)

In a medium saucepan set on medium to medium-high heat, cook the pear syrup until reduced to ½ cup. This will take about 25 minutes. Stir in the rum and cook for 1-2 minutes longer. Add the chocolate and stir until the chocolate is melted and completely incorporated. Remove from the heat. Let the sauce sit for 10-15 minutes to cool slightly and thicken.

To serve, place 2 pear halves on a plate with the cut-side-down. Drizzle with the chocolate sauce and top with a dollop of the whipped cream and a sprig of the mint, if you wish. (If using ice cream instead of whipped cream, put a scoop of ice cream next to the pears and then drizzle with the chocolate sauce.)

Cook's Tip

For a more elegant presentation, puddle the chocolate sauce on the plate. Cut the pears into fans and place on the sauce. Decorate with the whipped cream and mint.

Pere al Forno con Ricotta
Baked Pears with Sweetened Ricotta

Serves 8

4 firm pears, preferably Bartlett, peeled, halved, cored
and brushed with lemon juice

2 cups water

2 cups sweet Marsala wine

1 cup sugar

½ cup low-fat cream cheese

½ cup low-fat ricotta

3 tablespoons powdered sugar

1 ounce (30 g) semisweet chocolate, grated

4 tablespoons chopped, toasted hazelnuts or almonds

Preheat the oven to 400° F (200° C). Place the pears in a deep baking dish, approximately 6 x 6 x 4 inches (16.5 x 16.5 x 10 cm). In a small saucepan, bring the water, Marsala wine and sugar to a boil over high heat to dissolve the sugar. Pour the boiling Marsala mixture over the pears and bake in the oven, uncovered, for 30 minutes. They are done when a knife easily pierces the pear. Remove the pears from the oven and let them rest in the liquid for 30 minutes to cool slightly; then refrigerate for at least 2 hours or overnight.

Beat the cream cheese until soft. Beat in the ricotta and powdered sugar, mixing well. Set aside.

Remove the pears from the cooking liquid and set aside. In a medium saucepan set on medium-high heat, reduce the cooking liquid to 1 cup, about 15 minutes.

To serve, cut a slice from the bottom of each pear half to make them lie flat. Place a chilled pear half, cut-side-up, on a serving plate. Spoon 2 tablespoons of the ricotta mixture on top and drizzle with the reduced cooking liquid. Sprinkle with the grated chocolate and chopped nuts.

This is a favorite dessert throughout Italy where pears and wine are common staples for every Italian family.

My Sicilian version features an irresistible hint of Marsala wine. It's roots lie in the tradition of "cucina povera" (poor man's cooking) which relies on simple and inexpensive ingredients prepared in flavorful combinations.

I always break into a smile when I think how restaurants turn these simple dishes into exclusive haute cuisine. Share this dessert with a dear group of friends and toast with a glass of Sicilian Marsala wine the person who first came up with this dessert combination.

Arance Candite

Oranges with Caramel Sauce

Makes ¾ cup sauce

Serves 4

¾ cup sugar

¼ cup orange juice

½ cup whipping cream

1 tablespoon Triple Sec or other orange-flavored liqueur

Zest of 1 orange, grated

2 large oranges, peeled and cut into sections (see Cook's Tip, page 183)

1 pint (500 ml) vanilla ice cream

You must first know that with this recipe, my mother believed that she had created the best caramel sauce in the world. Her only problem then was finding something that was worthy of this culinary gem. Let me assure you that short of pasta, she tried everything, so I know for a fact that the following combination is the perfect caramel dessert.

Today when I find myself caught in a burst of cooking enthusiasm, and up to my neck in pots and pans, I think of my mother searching for that perfect caramel culinary combination. Suddenly I flash a smile and softly move my head from side to side. Now, after so many years, I understand what she was looking for, and I laugh aloud saying, "I'm just like my mother."

Enjoy this simple dessert with your family. My mother and I will be happy to know how much you've enjoyed it.

Heat the sugar and orange juice in a medium saucepan over medium heat, until the sugar is dissolved. Increase the heat to medium-high and boil, without stirring, for 8-10 minutes, until the mixture is a rich amber color. Reduce the heat to medium, add the cream (the mixture will bubble up) and cook until the caramel is smooth and slightly thickened, stirring occasionally, about 5-7 minutes. Remove from the heat and stir in the orange liqueur and orange zest. The sauce can be prepared one day ahead. Reheat gently before serving.

To serve, place ¼ of the orange slices in each dish, top with 2 small scoops of the ice cream and spoon some of the caramel sauce over the top.

Arancia con Cioccolatto Bianco e Menta
ORANGES WITH WHITE CHOCOLATE AND MINT

SERVES 4

4 oranges, peeled and cut into sections (see Cook's Tip below)
¾ cup Triple Sec or other orange-flavored liqueur
¾ cup packed light brown sugar
Zest of 1 orange, grated
3 ounces (90 g) good quality white chocolate
4 (1-inch) (2.5-cm) slices pound cake
2 tablespoons chopped fresh mint
4 tablespoons toasted sliced almonds

This dessert is a marvel of simple flavors, blended together in a concert that is light and tasty. I believe it both pleases the palate and satisfies the soul of the sweet tooth inside all of us.

You don't believe me? Well, you'll just have to try it!

Marinate the orange sections in the Triple Sec for 30 minutes. Strain the liqueur into a small saucepan. Set the oranges aside until ready to assemble the dessert.

Stir the brown sugar and orange zest into the Triple Sec in the saucepan and bring to a boil. Reduce the heat to medium and simmer for 5 minutes — do not stir. Set the syrup aside to cool.

Just before serving, melt the chocolate in a small bowl in the microwave on high for 1½-2 minutes. (If you don't have a microwave, melt the chocolate over hot water in a double boiler.)

To serve, put 1 piece of the pound cake on a each dish and spoon 1 tablespoon of the syrup over it. Arrange ¼ of the orange sections on the pound cake, drizzle with the melted chocolate and sprinkle with the mint and almonds.

COOK'S TIP

To section oranges (or any other citrus fruits), cut both ends from the oranges. Place an orange, cut-side-down, on a cutting board. With a thin-bladed knife, cut down the sides of the orange to remove the pith and peel. Don't worry if you cut away some of the flesh. Holding the orange over a bowl, carefully cut down alongside the membrane between each section. Remove the whole sections and place in the bowl.

Fagottini di Ricotta e Pere
Little Purses with Pears and Ricotta

I can still see myself as a little boy holding tightly to my mother's hand gazing at the wonders of Don Carmelo's pastry shop. This dimly lit establishment was a mecca to me, its old refrigerated shelves laden with a king's ransom of irresistible pastries, tortes and cakes. Even as a tiny child, I felt as rich as Ali Baba in the treasure room.

Although it could not boast the glamorous trappings of the newer uptown stores, nobody could beat the quality of Don Carmelo's product. He was also a great charmer who would greet each customer with a noble title, like Countess or Baroness, and punctuate the point by executing an elaborate kiss on the hand. Children were not excluded from the royal treatment. None of us ever left his store without a special treat.

Serves 6

¼ cup sweet Marsala wine
⅓ cup golden raisins
1 ½ cups ricotta cheese
3 tablespoons sugar
2 eggs
2 (16-ounce) (450-g) cans pears packed in heavy syrup, drained and syrup reserved separately
¼ cup toasted pine nuts
1 (17-ounce) (480-g) package frozen puff pastry, thawed
2 tablespoons brandy
Whipped cream (optional)

Heat the Marsala wine in a small saucepan or in the microwave. Soak the raisins in the warm Marsala until plumped, about 15-30 minutes. Drain well and set aside. Discard the Marsala.

Stir together the ricotta, sugar and 1 of the eggs in a large bowl. Coarsely chop the pears and add to the ricotta along with the pine nuts and plumped raisins, mixing well.

Preheat the oven to 400° F (200° C). Place one of the sheets of puff pastry on a lightly floured cutting board and cut into thirds along the fold lines, then cut each of those pieces in half. Repeat this process with the second square of puff pastry. You will have 12 pieces of puff pastry when you are finished. Roll each of the puff pastry pieces into a rectangle approximately 4 x 5 inches (10 x 13 cm) in size.

Place about ½ cup of the ricotta filling in the center of 6 of the puff pastry rectangles and brush the edges with water. Cover the filling with another piece of puff pastry and crimp the edges with a fork to seal. Repeat with the remaining 5 filled rectangles.

Mix the remaining egg with 1 teaspoon of water. Brush the tops of the pastries with the egg wash and place on a lightly greased baking sheet. Bake in the preheated oven for 15-20 minutes, until golden brown. Let cool for at least 15 minutes. (The pastries can be made early in the day and refrigerated after they have cooled. Remove from the refrigerator 1 hour before serving to allow them to come to room temperature.)

While the pastries are baking, put the reserved pear syrup in a small saucepan. Bring to a boil over medium-high heat, reduce the heat to keep at a slow boil and reduce by half, about 5-7 minutes. Remove from the heat and stir in the brandy.

To serve, place a pastry on a serving plate and drizzle 1-2 tablespoons of the pear-brandy syrup over it. If you're like me, you won't be able to resist a spoonful of whipped cream on top.

COOK'S TIP

Stir 1-2 tablespoons of butter into the reduced sauce to make it thicker and give it a shinier finish.

Don Carmelo worked in his shop well into his late seventies. While the passage of time whitened his hair, thickened his eye glasses, and brought a small shake to his hands, it could never take away from the regal way he treated his customers.

One sad day we read about Don Carmelo's passing in the newspaper obituaries. Together with my mother, we drove to his shop to leave some flowers. We were not alone. Just like a true king, the innumerable "princesses, countesses and baronesses" that he had served all his life came to offer their last respects to the kind man and master baker who brought a little bit of fantasy into all our lives.

What follows is my rendition of one of Don Carmelo's specialities. A small way of giving to others what he gave to me.

Crostata di Pere e Noci

Pear and Walnut Tart

This recipe is particularly close to my heart as it represents the first time I successfully created a dessert recipe of my own. Well, not quite.

While this dessert is the sum of my training and experience, I have to admit to plenty of "borrowing." It would also be easy for me to tell you that while under the influence of a creative trance I simply took a part of my culinary vision and cooked it neatly into reality. But the truth is that just like my mother, and probably my grandmother, I became so possessed with the goal of creating a new dish that I turned my kitchen into a battlefield.

On this occasion, my wife returned from work to find the kitchen in a state of chaos and me covered from head to toe in flour. Various prototypes in differing degrees of burning lay on every counter with the smell of burning crust lingering in the air. Not to mention the

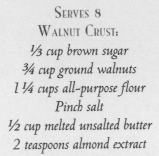

SERVES 8
WALNUT CRUST:
⅓ cup brown sugar
¾ cup ground walnuts
1 ¼ cups all-purpose flour
Pinch salt
½ cup melted unsalted butter
2 teaspoons almond extract

FILLING:
¼ cup raisins
¼ cup dark rum
3 pears, peeled, cored and thinly sliced
2 tablespoons sugar
¼ cup chopped walnuts
3 Amaretti cookies, crushed (optional)
2 tablespoons butter, chilled and sliced into thin pieces
⅓ cup apple jelly or apricot preserves
1 tablespoon powdered sugar

FOR THE WALNUT CRUST

Preheat the oven to 350° F (180° C). Mix the sugar, walnuts, flour and salt in a large bowl. Combine the butter and almond extract and pour over the dry ingredients, mixing well with a wooden spoon.

Press the dough into the bottom and up the sides of a 9-inch (23-cm) fluted tart pan and bake in the oven for 10-12 minutes. (This particular type of crust does not require any weights during cooking.) Let cool completely before filling. You can make this crust 2 days ahead of time, if you wish. Simply cover with plastic wrap and refrigerate.

For the Filling

Soak the raisins in the rum for 1 hour. Drain, reserving the raisins and rum, separately.

Preheat the oven to 350° F (180° C). Arrange the pear slices over the bottom of the baked tart crust. Scatter the sugar, soaked raisins, walnuts, Amaretti (if you wish) and butter pieces evenly over the pears. Bake for 35-40 minutes. Remove from the oven and let cool for 10 minutes.

While the tart is cooking, heat the reserved rum in a small saucepan set on medium-high heat and boil until it reduces to about 2 tablespoons, about 3-5 minutes. Add the jelly or preserves, stir well, and cook until the jelly melts. Pour the jelly over the top of the warm baked tart, using a pastry brush to gently and evenly coat.

Once the tart has completely cooled, sprinkle with the powdered sugar and serve!

blast furnace temperature of the kitchen itself from continuous operation of the oven.

When I finally came up with this final version, there was a sigh of relief from my wife. And since then, this beautiful tart has graced many of our dinners. Nanci always enjoys recounting its tumultuous birth and I must say that there is nothing better than good laughter to accompany a "mighty fine" slice of Nick's homemade Pear and Walnut Tart.

Crostata di Mele
Apple Custard Tart

Every time my father got into some kind of trouble with my mom, he would bring home this Apple Custard Tart from the Magri Pastry Shop. It was my mom's favorite dessert in the whole world and its healing power earned it the stature as the perfect peace offering for everything that spelled trouble. I remember bringing home a warm slice nicely wrapped by Mr. Magri himself to give to my mother along with my report card from school.

However, the most satisfying moment came when I first personally prepared this recipe for mom. As she chewed softly, critically savoring every little nuance of the tart's delicate texture, she turned to me and said, "Let me have the 'pagella' (report card). I'm ready to sign it now."

Then she looked at me with a smile so typical of my mother, and standing there, I felt like a proud little boy.

Serves 8
½ recipe Pie Dough (see pages 222-223)
1 baking apple, peeled, cored and thinly sliced
3 tablespoons apple jelly

Custard:
1 cup milk
¼ cup + ½ tablespoon sugar
Pinch salt
3 egg yolks
1 teaspoon vanilla
2 tablespoons cornstarch

Line an 8 or 9-inch (20 or 23-cm) fluted tart pan with the pie dough and prick the bottom with the tines of a fork. Cover the pie shell with plastic wrap and refrigerate for 30 minutes or more.

Preheat the oven to 375° F (190° C). Cut a square of lightweight aluminum foil 4 inches (10 cm) larger than the diameter of the pan. Line the unbaked pie shell with the aluminum foil, draping it over the top edge to keep it from browning too fast. Fill with beans or pie weights and bake for 15 minutes, then remove the foil and bake for another 10 minutes or until the crust is golden brown. Cool completely before filling.

For the Custard
Heat the milk, 2 tablespoons of the sugar and the salt in a large saucepan set on medium-high heat. While the milk is heating, beat the egg yolks with 2 tablespoons of the remaining sugar and the vanilla, until foamy and the sugar dissolved, about 2 minutes. Beat in the cornstarch a little at a time. Slowly drizzle the hot milk into the eggs, whisking constantly. When the milk has all been whisked in, pour the mixture back into the pan set on medium heat, whisking constantly until it begins to thicken, about 1 minute.

Remove from the heat immediately and continue whisking until it has a thick pudding-like consistency, about 2-3 minutes. Let cool for 10 minutes, then pour into the prebaked pie shell and smooth the top.

Preheat the broiler. Arrange the apple slices over the custard, overlapping them in a spiral pattern. Sprinkle with the remaining ½ tablespoon sugar and broil for 7-8 minutes, until the apples are beginning to brown on the edges. (If the top edges of the crust are becoming too brown, cover them with aluminum foil.) Remove from the oven and let cool for 10 minutes.

Melt the apple jelly in a small saucepan or in a bowl in the microwave and brush over the top of the tart. Serve warm or at room temperature.

"Good apple pies are a considerable part of our domestic happiness."

JANE AUSTEN

Crostata di Pompelmo
Grapefruit Custard Tart

My father was not what you'd call a "dessert kind of guy." Faced with a table laden with pastries, he'd usually choose the fresh fruit. Mario and I never discussed this with him; we just thought that he must be trying to teach us some kind of weird adult control technique that we'd understand when we were older.

But one August, all this came to an abrupt end. The hot sirocco winds had blown all week. It was particularly uncomfortable at night, and I would toss and turn in bed. One evening, I was so fidgety, I got up thinking that I would find relief by standing in front of the refrigerator's open door.

Imagine my shock when I got to the refrigerator and found my father, sitting in front of the open refrigerator door, holding a plate of leftover tart in one hand, while the other forked huge bites into his mouth! With stunning clarity

Serves 8 to 10
½ recipe Pie Dough (see pages 222–223)
3 grapefruit
3 tablespoons apple jelly

Custard:
1 cup milk
¼ cup + 1½ tablespoons sugar
Pinch salt
3 egg yolks
1 teaspoon vanilla
2 tablespoons cornstarch

Line an 8 or 9-inch (20 or 23-cm) fluted tart pan with the pastry and prick the bottom with the tines of a fork. Cover the pie shell with plastic wrap and refrigerate for 30 minutes or more.

Preheat the oven to 375° F (190° C). Cut a square of lightweight aluminum foil 4 inches (10 cm) larger than the diameter of the pan. Line the unbaked pie shell with the aluminum foil, draping it over the top edge of the crust to keep it from browning too fast. Fill with beans or pie weights and bake for 15 minutes, then remove the foil and bake for another 10-12 minutes, until the crust is golden brown. Cool completely before filling.

For the Custard

Heat the milk, 2 tablespoons of the sugar and the salt in a large saucepan, set on medium-high heat. While the milk is heating, beat the egg yolks with 2 tablespoons of the remaining sugar and the vanilla, until light yellow in color, about 2 minutes. Beat in the cornstarch a little at a time. Slowly drizzle the hot milk into the eggs, whisking constantly to keep the eggs from cooking.

When the milk has all been whisked in, pour the mixture back into the pan set on medium heat, whisking constantly until it begins to thicken, about 1 minute. Remove from the heat immediately and continue whisking until it has a thick pudding-like consistency, about 2-3 minutes. Let cool for 10 minutes, then pour into the prebaked pie shell and smooth the top.

Cut both ends from the grapefruit. Place the grapefruit, cut-side-down, on a cutting board. With a thin-bladed knife, cut down the sides of the grapefruit to remove the peel and pith. Don't worry if you cut away some of the flesh. Holding the grapefruit over a bowl, carefully cut down alongside the membrane between each section. Remove the whole sections to a strainer and drain well. Lay the sections on paper towels and pat dry before assembling the tart.

Preheat the broiler. Lay the grapefruit sections on the custard, beginning with a circle around the outside edge of the tart. Place the next circle inside the first and continue in this manner until the top has been covered. The pattern of the grapefruit will resemble a flower. Sprinkle the remaining sugar over the top of the tart and place under the broiler for 7-10 minutes until the grapefruit is beginning to brown on the edges. Let cool for 10 minutes.

Melt the apple jelly in a bowl in the microwave or in a small saucepan set on medium heat. Brush the top of the tart with the warm jelly and serve. Refrigerate if not serving immediately.

I suddenly realized that it wasn't my brother, Mario, who'd been polishing off the dessert leftovers all those years!

Without losing a bit of his composure, Dad waved me over to his side. Then we sat together, in the light of the refrigerator, laughing and eating the last few slices together with ruthless abandon.

Years later, my mother told me that she, too, had tiptoed to the kitchen that night to steal a bit of leftover tart, but the sight of Dad and me eating together was the best dessert of all. Following is my version of the tart that brought my father and me together on a hot August night by the light of an open refrigerator door.

Tart Tatin
Upside-down Apple Pie

Serves 6 to 8
¼ cup unsalted butter
1 cup sugar
6 apples, peeled, cored and cut into eighths
1 sheet frozen puff pastry, thawed (store bought is just fine)
1 pint (500 ml) vanilla ice cream

You might ask yourself, what's this dish doing in an Italian cookbook? Indeed, this is a traditional French dessert, which according to legend, was created by the Sisters Tatin in a small country restaurant.

Occasionally I justify my passion for something so blatantly non-Italian by telling a little fib about the Sisters Tatin. According to my sources, the sisters changed their name from "Tatino" after they emigrated from Italy. Once established in France, they made their fame and fortune by making this pie recipe given to them by their mother, Concetta.

Of course, none of this is true. And whenever I tell this story (o.k., most of the time), I confess my historical re-creation. I'm sure that somewhere in France there is a little rascal of a chef who makes up a few stories, just like me, about the origin of certain foreign dishes.

Preheat the oven to 400° F (200° C). In a large sauté pan set on medium-high heat, melt the butter. Add the sugar and stir for 3 minutes with a wooden spoon until the sugar mixture is a golden caramel brown color, but still somewhat grainy in texture. Add the apple slices, stirring well to coat each slice. Reduce the heat to medium and cook for 10 minutes, uncovered, stirring often. Cover and cook 10 minutes longer. Remove from the heat and let cool slightly.

Roll the sheet of puff pastry out until it's large enough to cut a 10-inch (25-cm) circle. Arrange part of the apple slices in a decorative circular pattern in the bottom of a 9-inch (23-cm) pie pan. When you eventually serve this "upside-down," this will be the top of the tart, so make this as pretty as possible. (If the sauté pan in which the apples were cooked is ovenproof, it is not necessary to transfer them to a pie pan.) Pile the remaining slices on top along with any of the juices remaining in the pan. Place the circle of puff pastry over the apples and tuck the excess dough down inside the pan.

Bake for 12 minutes, until the pastry is golden brown, puffed and crispy. Using oven mitts, carefully invert the pie onto a large serving plate. The caramel sauce is very hot, so be careful not to get it on yourself.

Serve the pie hot with vanilla ice cream.

Torta di Zucca

PUMPKIN CHEESECAKE

SERVES 8 TO 10
1 recipe Walnut Pie Crust (see page 186)
16 ounces (450 g) cream cheese
8 ounces (225 g) ricotta cheese
1½ cups canned pumpkin
1 cup light brown sugar
¼ teaspoon nutmeg
1 teaspoon vanilla
3 eggs
Whipped cream (optional)

Make the walnut pie crust and pat the mixture over the bottom and ⅔'s of the way up the sides of a 9-inch (23-cm) springform pan.

Preheat the oven to 350° F (180° C). With an electric mixer, beat the cream cheese and ricotta cheese in a large bowl until light and fluffy, about 2 minutes. Add the pumpkin and beat well. Mix in the brown sugar, nutmeg and vanilla. Add the eggs, one at a time, beating well after each addition. Pour the batter into the prepared crust and bake for 1¼ hours, or until a knife inserted in the center comes out clean. Remove from the oven, let cool completely on a baking rack, then, refrigerate for 4 hours or overnight.

To serve, remove the cheesecake from the refrigerator, place on a serving dish, remove the side ring and cut into wedges. Serve with a dollop of the whipped cream on top.

COOK'S TIP

If you would prefer not to garnish the cheesecake with whipped cream, an alternative is to drizzle 1 or 2 tablespoons of Caramel Sauce (see page 182) over the top, or garnish each slice with a whole walnut or a chocolate covered coffee bean.

This is my Sicilian idea of the perfect way to end the traditional American Thanksgiving dinner.

It's funny, but my wife Nanci seems to request this dish most during the hot Los Angeles summer. She tells me that with the weather peaking at its warmest temperatures of the year, this creamy dessert is a lovely reminder of the fall season just ahead. As she takes each bite, she can imagine the caress of the autumn breeze gently stirring a whisper through falling leaves.

Nanci smiles as she paints this picture with her words. Suddenly, I am transported to autumn, even as the ceiling fan buzzing overhead is pushing down the warm air of the sweltering summer night.

While other Los Angelenos are sitting by their fans wiping their browns, Nanci and I are riding through the Vermont country roads on a cool November day — try it!

Torta di Noci

Three Nut Tart

Serves 8

½ recipe Pie Dough (see pages 222-223)

¼ cup butter, room temperature

¼ cup brown sugar

½ cup honey

¼ teaspoon salt

3 eggs

⅓ cup sliced almonds

⅓ cup chopped walnuts

⅓ cup chopped hazelnuts

The following recipe has been a great success for many of my dinners at home. You'll be amazed how changing a tart's main ingredient to something simple but unexpected, like the hazelnut, brings a very familiar concept to new heights of enjoyment. Even my mom approved of this dish, which as you know, is no easy task. So next time you're ready for something different, give this dessert a try.

Line an 8- or 9-inch (20- or 23-cm) fluted tart pan with a removable bottom with the dough and prick the bottom with a fork. Cover the tart shell with plastic wrap and refrigerate for at least 30 minutes.

Preheat the oven to 375° F (190° C). Cut a square of aluminum foil 4 inches (10 cm) larger than the diameter of the pan. Remove the tart shell from the refrigerator, discard the plastic wrap and line the tart shell with the foil, draping it over the edges to keep them from browning too fast. Fill with dried beans or pie weights and bake for 10 minutes. Remove the foil and cool completely before filling.

Preheat the oven to 350° F (180° C). Beat the butter and sugar until creamy with an electric mixer. Add the honey and salt and beat well. Beat in the eggs, one at a time, beating well after each addition. Mix in the nuts. Pour the filling into the partially baked tart shell and bake for 25-30 minutes, until the top and crust are well browned and a knife inserted into the center of the tart comes out clean.

Let cool to room temperature before serving.

Mousse di Cioccolatto Bianco
White Chocolate Mousse

SERVES 8 TO 10

1 envelope unflavored gelatin
2 tablespoons cold water
8 ounces (225 g) good quality white chocolate
3 cups whipping cream
3 tablespoons sugar
2 teaspoons almond extract
Fresh mint sprigs for garnish (optional)

Put the gelatin powder and cold water in a small dish and let sit for 10 minutes to soften.

Melt the chocolate and ½ cup of the whipping cream in the top of a double boiler, stirring well. Stir in the softened gelatin, mixing well, then transfer the mixture to a large bowl to cool until just warm, about 10 minutes. Don't let sit too long or the chocolate/gelatin mixture will become too firm.

Chill a large bowl and a whisk or mixer beaters in the freezer 30 minutes before you are going to whip the cream. Whip the remaining cream in the bowl with the whisk or electric mixer for 2 minutes. Gradually add the sugar and the almond extract and continue beating until the beater leaves soft traces on the surface and the cream holds its shape when lifted with the beater, about 2-3 minutes.

Stir ¼ of the whipped cream into the chocolate mixture to lighten it, then fold in the remaining cream, ⅓ at a time, being careful not to over blend. Spoon the mousse into individual dessert bowls and chill for at least 1 hour before serving. To serve, decorate each serving with a sprig of the mint, if you wish.

When I became a teenager, my father took me to a business event held at the Villa Buscemi. This baroque palace possessed one of the most spectacular ballrooms I'd ever seen.

Even though I was awed by the villa's opulence, underneath my new blue suit and designer tie beat the heart of a teenager, and my attention was soon caught by a buffet table spread lavishly with irresistible desserts.

I remember mounting an assault on those sweets with almost military precision. Since I systematically tasted them all, I can assure you that it was the velvety flavor of the white chocolate mousse that won my heart that evening.

Riding home in the car, I had to sit with my pants unbuttoned. The last thing I remember before I fell asleep was my father's hand caressing my head. I dozed off in a whirl of dreams, the full moon obscured by puffy clouds of white chocolate mousse.

Crema Caramella al Mocha

MOCHA CREME CARAMEL

When Aunt Buliti made coffee, it was with religious devotion to details: the beans ground just so, carefully mixed with water and frothed through an espresso machine. She followed the Neapolitan School of Coffee, making a "coppetta" or paper cone, and placing it at the spout of the espresso pot to retain most of the steam in the brewing coffee. Then, with great ceremony, Aunt Buliti poured her "brewed nectar" into her favorite demitasse cup, stirred in an exact amount of sugar and drank it in two quick gulps. The ceremony now almost complete, she chased it with a quick sip of chilled water.

Mario and I noted all of this as children, standing on tiptoe and barely able to see over the kitchen table. We were fascinated by Aunt Buliti, and it was our devotion to attending to every detail of her

SERVES 8

1 ½ cups sugar
⅓ cup water
3 eggs
3 egg yolks
1 teaspoon vanilla
1 cup half-and-half cream
1 ½ cups milk
2 tablespoons instant espresso powder
3 ounces (90 g) semisweet chocolate
3 ounces (90 g) milk chocolate
Fresh berries for decoration (optional)
8 mint sprigs for decoration (optional)

Stir 1 cup of the sugar and the water together in a medium saucepan. Bring to a simmer over medium-high heat, swirling the pan over the heat to dissolve the sugar — don't stir the mixture. Cover the pan tightly and boil for 4-5 minutes, until the bubbles are thick and large. Uncover and continue boiling, while swirling the pan in a circular motion. Once the color begins to darken, continue to cook for approximately 1 more minute, until light brown in color. Remove from the heat and keep swirling the pan, as the caramel will continue to darken. Pour equal amounts of the caramel into 8 custard cups and swirl to cover the bottom and halfway up the sides. Place the custard cups into a baking dish or roasting pan just large enough to hold them all. Set aside.

Preheat the oven to 325° F (170° C). Mix together the eggs, egg yolks, vanilla and the remaining ½ cup sugar in a large bowl. Stir the eggs rather than whipping, as you don't want them to become foamy. Set aside.

In a medium saucepan, mix together the half-and-half, milk and espresso powder. Heat over medium-high heat until steaming, but not boiling. Slowly add the hot milk to the egg mixture, a little at a time, stirring constantly. Pour the custard mixture into the prepared custard cups. Carefully pour hot water into the baking dish so that it comes halfway up the sides of the custard dishes. Bake for 30 minutes, until the custard has set — it will be slightly jiggly in the center. Remove the custard cups to baking racks to cool at room temperature for 1 hour.

Melt both the chocolates in a small saucepan and spread a thin layer over the top of each custard. Refrigerate, uncovered, for at least 4 hours or overnight.

Just before serving, run a small knife around the edges of the chocolate and custard. Invert onto a small serving dish and garnish with fresh berries and a mint sprig, if you wish.

morning ritual that I believe inspired Aunt Buliti to create this fabulous dessert. It was something we could enjoy together while Aunt Buliti savored her favorite coffee.

I must confess that my version of this dish just doesn't taste the same as when Aunt Buliti made it. After all, nobody could ever match Aunt Buliti's love for her two nephews, even though she was the one that nicknamed us "mascarati" (rascals). But maybe that's just what she loved most about us!

*"Coffee is
a fleeting moment
and a fragrance."*

CLAUDIA RODEN

Budino di Riso con Ciliege

CHERRY ALMOND RICE PUDDING

My entire family had been invited to attend the opening of my father's business associate's new restaurant. Unfortunately, the food at this establishment was nothing to get excited about, but Mario and I still held out hopes for "the pudding" we heard was planned for dessert, imagining dense chocolate piled high with whipped cream.

When the waiter presented us with "rice pudding," we were disappointed; but youthful appetites being what they are, we still dove right in, and let me tell you, our faces beamed like candles on a birthday cake. Mom and Dad caught our enthusiasm and soon our table was filled with laughter as we pointed out pudding drops on each other's faces.

It was at that moment, as I looked at my mom and dad laughing away like little kids, that I felt a sense of togetherness. I hope it will bring you and your family many happy moments to remember.

SERVES 6 TO 8

4 cups milk

⅔ cup uncooked arborio rice

Pinch of salt

3 egg yolks

⅓ cup sugar

2 teaspoons almond extract

1 teaspoon vanilla

1 (8-ounce) (225-g) can dark cherries, drained, cut in half and juice discarded

Bring the milk, rice and salt to a boil in a 2-quart (2-l) nonstick saucepan set on medium-high heat. Reduce the heat to medium and keep at a slow boil for 10 minutes, stirring often.

In a medium bowl, mix the egg yolks, sugar, almond extract and vanilla, stirring to dissolve the sugar. With a glass measuring cup or ladle, remove about 1 cup of the milk/rice mixture from the pan and gradually whisk it into the egg mixture in the bowl. Slowly pour the egg mixture into the pan with the remaining milk/rice mixture and stir until thoroughly mixed. Continue cooking over medium heat for 5 minutes, stirring constantly to prevent the pudding sticking to the bottom of the pan. The pudding should become thick and coat the back of a spoon. Stir in the cherries and pour the pudding into a large serving bowl or individual dessert bowls.

If you wish to serve the pudding warm, let it cool at room temperature for 15-20 minutes and serve. To serve chilled, refrigerate for at least 2 hours or overnight, covered.

Pannacotta
ITALIAN CREAM PUDDING

SERVES 8 TO 10
1 envelope unflavored gelatin
2 tablespoons cold water
8 ounces (225 g) semisweet chocolate
1½ cups whipping cream
3 tablespoons sugar
1½ cups milk
2 teaspoons vanilla
Fresh berries for decoration (optional)
Mint sprigs for decoration (optional)

Sprinkle the gelatin powder over the water in a small dish. Let sit for 10 minutes to soften the gelatin.

Melt the chocolate, ½ cup of the whipping cream and the sugar in the top of a double boiler, stirring well. Make sure the chocolate has melted completely and that the mixture doesn't look grainy — it should be shiny and thick. Slowly whisk in the remaining cream and the milk. Heat just until steaming — do not boil. Stir in the softened gelatin and the vanilla, stirring just until the gelatin is completely dissolved. Pour the mixture into individual small custard cups or dessert molds. Chill in the refrigerator for 4-5 hours or overnight.

To serve, dip the custard cups or molds into hot water for 20-30 seconds to loosen the edges. Turn out onto small serving dishes and garnish with fresh berries and a sprig of the mint, if you wish.

"Pannacotta" translates as cooked cream and is the Italian answer to the French dessert called Creme Caramel. Having "professionally tested" both of them, I can point out a few differences.

First, the pannacotta uses gelatin instead of egg yolks as its support structure, making its preparation much simpler. The gelatin is also the base for a texture that will seduce your taste buds at once.

But the choice between pannacotta and creme caramel will always be a tough one. On a recent trip to America, I remember my mother asking me which of these two dishes I wanted for dessert. "I want them both, Mom," I quickly replied. She looked at me sharply and said, "Nick, you're looking pudgy. I think you need some fresh fruit for dessert."

I should have known better than to try to sneak one by her, but at least I took my best shot.

Tiramisú con i Frutti di Bosco

Raspberry Tiramisu

Tiramisú is often presented as the ultimate Italian dessert, a national treasure. Now many people would say, "if it isn't broken, don't fix it;" and many times, they are right. But life without adventure, culinary or otherwise, is stagnant. So, what can I tell you? Under the influence of a higher creative inspiration (or was it just childish flight of fancy?), I set out to create a new tiramisú.

For all of the adventurous souls out there, this recipe is the answer to your prayer. Once you try the delectable contrast of the sweet, creamy tiramisú with the tart, red raspberries, you'll see there is no limit to the many combinations yet to be discovered.

My father Vincenzo always said, "L'ispirazione viene mangiando!" (The inspiration arrives while you eat!) I've always liked that, especially when it comes to tiramisú.

Serves 8

1¼ cups sugar

⅓ cup hot water

½ cup cold water

4 tablespoons Triple Sec or other orange-flavored liqueur

14 ounces (400 g) ladyfingers or savoiardi

16 ounces (450 g) fresh or frozen raspberries, thawed

4 eggs, separated

½ teaspoon vanilla

1 pound (450 g) mascarpone cheese

4 ounces (115 g) semisweet chocolate

3 tablespoons toasted sliced almonds

Stir ¼ cup of the sugar into the hot water until completely dissolved, then stir in the cold water and orange liqueur. Lay the ladyfingers or savoiardi out on a baking sheet and brush both sides with the orange liqueur syrup. They should be moist on the outside but still crunchy on the inside.

Place the raspberries in a medium bowl and stir in ¼ cup of the remaining sugar. Set aside.

In a large bowl, beat the egg yolks, 6 tablespoons of the remaining sugar and the vanilla with an electric mixer until the mixture is thick enough to form a long ribbon when you lift the beaters, about 5 minutes. Add the mascarpone cheese, beat for 3 minutes then set aside.

Clean the beaters of the electric mixer carefully and in a clean bowl, beat the egg whites until soft peaks form, 3-4 minutes. Add the remaining 6 tablespoons of sugar and beat until they form stiff peaks and have a glossy finish, about 1-2 minutes longer.

Fold the beaten egg whites into the mascarpone mixture,
⅓ at a time. Make sure you fold the egg whites in completely to
avoid a coarse texture, but don't overmix or you'll lose the lightness.

Cover the bottom of a 7 x 11-inch (18 x 28-cm) baking dish
with a single layer of the soaked ladyfingers. Cut the remaining
ladyfingers in half and stand up around the edges of the dish.
Spread with the raspberries, ½ of the cheese mixture, the grated
chocolate and the remaining ½ of the cheese mixture. Sprinkle
the toasted almonds over the top. Lightly cover the dish with
plastic wrap and refrigerate for four hours or overnight. Serve
chilled.

Cook's Tip

Make sure that your mixer beaters are thoroughly cleaned
after beating the egg/cheese mixture and before beating the egg
whites. If there is even the slightest bit of oil left on them, the
egg whites won't whip properly.

*"Delight in cooking
is one of the oldest
and dearest things
in the world.
We have not made
mud pies for nothing.
If a cook is simply
willing to look at what
he is doing, there is hope."*

Robert Farrar Capon

Zabaglione con lo Spumante
ZABAGLIONE WITH SPARKLING WINE

There is a French proverb that goes, "There is laughter in each bubble of a glass of champagne." What better match could you think of than the joyful personality of champagne teamed with the velvety sweet texture of zabaglione?

It's a match made in heaven!

"I feel the end approaching. Quick, bring me my dessert, coffee and liqueur."

PIERETTE, AUNT OF
BRILLAT-SAVARIN

SERVES 4
4 egg yolks
¼ cup sugar
½ cup sparkling wine
1 pound (450 g) mixed fresh or frozen berries
(use a combination of raspberries, blueberries, blackberries or strawberries)
4 sprigs fresh mint for decoration (optional)

In the top half of a double boiler, whisk the egg yolks and sugar to a creamy consistency. Place the egg mixture over hot water in the bottom of a double boiler, making sure it doesn't touch the water. Beat the mixture well with a whisk, until it starts to thicken, about 5 minutes. Be careful not to beat too long or you will cook the eggs. Remove from the heat and stir in ¼ cup of the wine, whisking until well incorporated. Return to the double boiler and whisk until thickened, 3-5 minutes. Remove from the heat and set aside.

Divide the berries among 4 wine glasses or dessert bowls and spoon 1 tablespoon of the remaining wine over each. Top with the custard and decorate with a mint sprig, if you wish. It can be eaten warm immediately or refrigerated and eaten chilled later.

Biscotto di Cannella al Cioccolatto

Cinnamon Sugar Cookies with Chocolate

Makes 5 dozen cookies

1 cup (2 sticks) unsalted butter, room temperature
¾ cup sugar
2 egg yolks
2 teaspoons vanilla
2½ cups all-purpose flour
½ teaspoon baking powder
⅛ teaspoon salt
1 teaspoon cinnamon
4 ounces (115 g) semisweet chocolate

Beat the butter and sugar in a large bowl with an electric mixer until creamy. Add the egg yolks one at a time, beating well after each addition. Mix in the vanilla. In another bowl, stir together the flour, baking powder, salt and cinnamon. Gradually add the dry ingredients to the butter mixture, blending thoroughly. Divide the dough into 3 pieces and form into logs 1½ inches (4 cm) in diameter. Refrigerate for at least ½ hour or overnight.

Preheat the oven to 350° F (180° C). Slice the chilled logs ¼ inch (6 mm) thick on the diagonal to make oblong cookies. Place the slices on an ungreased cookie sheet, spacing them about 1 inch (2.5 cm) apart. Bake 10-12 minutes or until the edges are lightly browned. Transfer to racks to cool.

Melt the chocolate in a double boiler. Dip one end of the cooled cookies into the melted chocolate, leaving the other end bare. Place on waxed paper and refrigerate for ½ hour, until the chocolate has set.

Cook's Tip

For a variation on the basic sugar cookie, sprinkle the tops of the uncooked cookies with chopped nuts of your choice or turbinado sugar.

Cookie making at the Stellino household was a family affair. Mario would stand on a stool, helping my mother with the mixing of the dough. I'd stand next to her, adding the ingredients to her large bowl as she asked for them.

I remember Mario mixing away in his little bowl, his tiny fingers wrapped tightly around the small wooden spoon. He stirred with great intensity and the dough flew everywhere. I would catch myself looking at his long blond curls spilling over as he licked the dough right off the spoon. Then, looking up at my Mother and me, with the dough still stuck to his rosy cheeks he'd say, "Look Mom. It's ready." He looked so cute that I felt proud.

Even today when I see my brother Mario, a strapping figure of a man, I can't help remembering him as that cute little boy with the golden curls.

Torta di Nocciole

Hazelnut Cake

SERVES 12

HAZELNUT CAKE:

1 cup (2 sticks) unsalted butter, at room temperature
½ cup sugar
1 cup semolina flour
6 eggs
2 teaspoons vanilla
1 cup all-purpose flour
1 tablespoon baking powder
½ cup milk
1 cup ground toasted hazelnuts

SYRUP:

3 cups water
2 cups sugar
2 thick lemon slices
Whipped cream (optional)
Fresh strawberries (optional)

You must realize that having a husband who is always following his creative visions to come up with new recipes has its ups and downs. Trust me — you, my reader, only get to see the very best results of my experiments. There are also plenty of disasters and my wife Nanci gets to taste them all.

So, when Nanci is inspired by a creative vision which moves her to the kitchen, I must confess, although I may not always look forward to being the designated "Taste Tester," I feel it is my duty.

Unfortunately, as a dessert eater, I'm most habitual in my choices. And when Nanci announced we were having hazelnut cake, well, this was way beyond my traditional comfort zone. I approached the table as a condemned man walking into prison with no way out.

Preheat the oven to 350° F (180° C). Grease a 9 x 13-inch (23 x 33-cm) baking dish. In a large mixing bowl, cream the butter and sugar with an electric mixer until lightened in color and fluffy, about 2-3 minutes. Beat in the semolina flour a little at a time. Add the eggs, one at a time, beating well after each addition. Beat in the vanilla. In another bowl, combine the all-purpose flour and baking powder. Stir the dry ingredients into the batter, alternating with the milk. Stir in the hazelnuts. Pour the batter into the greased pan and smooth the top with a spatula. Bake until the top is golden brown, about 25-30 minutes.

While the cake is baking, make the syrup. Combine the water, sugar and the lemon slices in a medium saucepan and bring to a boil over medium-high heat. Boil for 15 minutes and remove from the heat. Set aside and let cool slightly.

Remove the cake from the oven and prick the top with a knife or skewer in several places. Spoon the syrup over the cake and let cool completely.

Cut the cake into diamond-shaped pieces. Serve with a dollop of whipped cream and top with a strawberry, if you wish.

Nanci served me a slice of cake and sat right next to me, anxiously waiting for my response. I held my fork firmly, took my first bite, closed my eyes and waited for the worst.

Nanci tells the story from this point on with great relish. She says I started humming a little melody, and keeping hold of the plate with my left hand, I continued eating the cake with my right hand, all the while directing an imaginary orchestra! After consuming every last crumb on my plate, I rose spontaneously to my feet and gave Nanci a standing ovation. I was applauding not just the cake, but her boldness in pursuing her vision over my limited culinary horizons.

Like my Uncle Giovanni always said, "In life, always follow the dream within."

Granita di Caffé
COFFEE ICE

My family traveled to Alcamo every weekend to spend time with my grand-parents. I remember my grandfather, Don Nicola, and my father taking me for special walks which always ended at the local coffee bar for a cup of granita. Don Nicola's big calloused hands held my cup and he roared with laughter, telling me how he would buy me a horse and teach me how to run a farm. Here, sharing granita, my father saw a man he had seldom met before: soft, sensitive and loving.

Don Nicola died before he got a chance to buy me that horse. But my father and I kept going to that same coffee bar for a cup of granita, and there he told me many stories about my grandfather.

Don't wait to visit Sicily before you try granita, but do plan for an evening with family members. Then it can work its magic on you.

SERVES 6
1 cup water
½ cup sugar
¼ cup whipping cream
1 cup strong espresso or strong coffee
Whipped cream (optional)

Combine the water and sugar in a small saucepan and heat over medium-high heat until it comes to a boil and the sugar is dissolved. Stir in the cream and coffee, then transfer the mixture to a shallow dish, large enough that the liquid will be no more than 1½ inches (4 cm) deep – a 7 x 11-inch (18 x 28-cm) baking dish works well. Cool to room temperature, about 15 minutes, then place in the freezer, uncovered, for 3 hours, stirring every hour.

The finished granita will be a loose mixture of ice particles. If you're not going to serve it at this point, be sure to stir it every hour to keep the ice particles small.

To serve, spoon the granita into stemmed glasses or bowls and top with a dollop of whipped cream, if you wish.

Granita di Limone
Lemon Ice

SERVES 6
½ cup sugar
2 cups water
1 cup lemon juice
6 sprigs fresh mint

Heat the sugar and 1 cup of the water in a small saucepan over medium-high heat until the sugar is dissolved, about 4 minutes. Stir in the remaining water and lemon juice. Pour the mixture into a shallow glass dish large enough that the liquid in no more than 1½ inches (4 cm) deep – a 7 x 11-inch (18 x 28-cm) baking dish works well – and let cool for 15 minutes. Place the mixture into the freezer, uncovered, for 3 hours, stirring every hour. Stirring every hour helps to break the granita up into flakes and keeps the texture light.

Spoon the granita into small glass bowls and garnish with a sprig of the mint, if you wish. If you don't have mint on hand, use thin slices of lemon or lemon peel. Flowers also make a beautiful garnish against the pale color of the granita.

COOK'S TIP

For a beautiful and fun serving idea, cut the tops from 6 large lemons. Using a grapefruit knife, cut between the pulp and the skin and remove the pulp with a small spoon or melon baller, scraping the inside clean. Fill the lemon shells with the frozen granita and return to the freezer until ready to serve. To serve, place the filled shells in small glasses or cups and garnish with a sprig of mint. If you prefer to serve these on plates, cut a small slice from the bottom of the lemon shell before filling so they will stand by themselves.

*"Too much
of a good thing
can be wonderful."*
MAE WEST

Granita di Fragole

STRAWBERRY ICE

SERVES 6

1 (10-ounce) (300-g) package frozen sweetened strawberries, thawed*
1 cup water
2 tablespoons lemon juice
6 whole strawberries for garnish

Purée the strawberries in a blender or food processor until smooth. Strain the purée through a fine sieve into a shallow dish that is large enough that the liquid will be no more than 1½ inches (4 cm) deep — a 7 x 11-inch (18 x 28-cm) baking dish works well. Stir in the water and lemon juice, then place in the freezer, uncovered, for 3 hours, stirring every hour.

To serve, spoon the granita into stemmed glasses and garnish with a strawberry.

COOK'S TIP

For a festive occasion, prepare the granita as directed and freeze for 2-3 hours, until almost firm. (It's not necessary to stir every hour using this method, which will produce a smoother, less grainy ice.) Transfer the ice to the bowl of a food processor and process until smooth. Return the ice to the shallow dish and freeze until firm, another 3-4 hours.

To serve, use a small ice cream scoop to scrape along the surface of the ice. Place 2 or 3 scoops into stemmed glasses and pour ¼ cup of champagne or 2 tablespoons of Grappa over each serving.

*NOTE: The tartness of sweetened strawberries varies greatly. Taste the mixture before freezing to see if additional sugar is needed.

> *"So much of our future lies in preserving our past."*
>
> PETER WESTBROOK

Sugo di Fragole
STRAWBERRY SAUCE

MAKES 2⅔ CUPS
2 quarts (2 l) fresh or thawed frozen unsweetened strawberries
½ cup + 2 tablespoons sugar
2 tablespoons lemon juice
6 tablespoons Cassis liqueur

If using fresh strawberries, wash, hull and slice into quarters. Place the strawberries in a medium saucepan with the sugar and lemon juice and heat to boiling. If using fresh strawberries, boil for an additional 5-8 minutes, until soft. Remove from the heat and purée in a food processor or blender. Strain into a bowl to remove the seeds. Stir in the Cassis. Serve over ice cream.

The sauce will keep for 4-5 days in the refrigerator or may be frozen for up to 6 months.

You will be totally surprised by the smooth texture and elegant appeal of this very simple sauce. You'll ask yourself, how can something so easy taste so good? Well, try it and surprise yourself!

*"I would eat
my own father
with such a sauce."*

GRIMOD DE LA REYNIERE

Ricette Fondamentali

Basics

Farcito Vegetariano
VEGETARIAN STUFFING

Use this recipe to stuff whatever strikes your fancy: zucchini to chickens. Of course, you can always enjoy it just by itself as a side dish. Either way you can't go wrong.

MAKES 2 TO 2½ CUPS

2 tablespoons olive oil
½ red onion, finely chopped
4 garlic cloves, thickly sliced
⅛ teaspoon red pepper flakes
¾ pound (350 g) white button mushrooms, sliced
1 bay leaf
¾ cup white wine
1 (14½-ounce) (415-g) can stewed tomatoes,
drained and chopped, juices reserved separately
1 tablespoon chopped fresh Italian parsley
1 tablespoon chopped fresh basil
1 large egg
¾ cup Italian Bread Crumbs (see page 218)
½ cup freshly grated Pecorino Romano cheese

Pour the olive oil into a nonstick sauté pan and cook the onion over medium-low heat until soft, about 3 minutes. Add the garlic and red pepper flakes and continue cooking for 5 minutes. Increase the heat to high, add the sliced mushrooms and the bay leaf and cook for 2 minutes, stirring well to prevent sticking.

Add the wine and cook until it has all evaporated, 3 more minutes. Stir in the chopped tomatoes, reduce the heat to medium and cook for 2 minutes. Add the parsley and the basil, stirring well. Pour in the reserved juice of the stewed tomatoes and cook over medium-low heat for 5 minutes, stirring occasionally. The mixture should be fairly thick and almost dry. If it is very watery, cook for 3 more minutes.

Transfer the mixture to a large mixing bowl. Add the egg, bread crumbs and cheese and mix well. The stuffing should be very thick and fairly moist. If it is still watery, add more cheese and bread crumbs.

Farcito con le Salsiccie

SAUSAGE STUFFING

MAKES 2½ TO 3 CUPS
2 tablespoons olive oil
10 ounces (300 g) hot Italian sausage, out of the casing
1 white onion, finely chopped
4 garlic cloves, thickly sliced
⅛ teaspoon red pepper flakes
¾ pound (350 g) mushrooms, finely sliced
1 bay leaf
¾ cup white wine
1 (14½-ounce) (415-g) can stewed tomatoes,
drained and chopped, juices reserved separately
1 tablespoon chopped fresh Italian parsley
1 tablespoon chopped fresh basil
2 eggs
1 cup Italian Bread Crumbs (see page 218)
¾ cup freshly grated Pecorino Romano cheese

Use this to stuff any type of meat or fowl. Choose the sausage that fits your taste and have fun.

Pour the oil into a nonstick sauté pan set on medium heat and brown the sausage for 3 minutes, crumbling it with the back of a wooden spoon. Transfer the sausage to a plate lined with paper towels and set aside.

Discard all but 3 tablespoons of the fat left in the sauté pan. On medium heat, cook the onion for 3 minutes. Add the garlic and red pepper flakes, reduce the heat to low and cook for 5 minutes. Increase the heat to high, add the sliced mushrooms and bay leaf, stir well and cook 2 minutes. Add the wine and cook until it has almost evaporated, about 3 minutes. Stir in the chopped tomatoes, reduce the heat to medium and cook 2 minutes. Add the parsley, basil, reserved juices and cooked sausage, stir well, and cook for 5 minutes, stirring occasionally. The mixture should be fairly thick and almost dry. If it is very watery, cook for 3 more minutes. Transfer the mixture to a large mixing bowl.

Add the eggs, bread crumbs and cheese and mix well. The stuffing should be very thick and fairly moist. If it is still watery, add more cheese and bread crumbs to your taste.

Farcito Arrosto

Roasted Stuffing

This preparation turns stuffing into a brand new dish with a soufflé-like finish that has a singular personality of its own. In my household, it's served with cheese melted on top and tomato sauce on the side.

Serves 4 to 6

2 tablespoons olive oil
10 ounces (300 g) hot Italian sausage, out of the casing (optional)
1 white onion, finely chopped
4 garlic cloves, thickly sliced
⅛ teaspoon red pepper flakes
¾ pound (350 g) mushrooms, finely sliced
1 bay leaf
¾ cup white wine
1 (14½-ounce) (415-g) can stewed tomatoes,
drained and chopped, juices reserved separately
1 tablespoon chopped fresh Italian parsley
1 tablespoon chopped fresh basil
3 eggs
1½ cups Italian Bread Crumbs (see page 218)
¾ cup freshly grated Pecorino Romano cheese

Preheat the oven to 350° F (180° C). Pour the oil into a nonstick sauté pan and brown the sausage, if you wish, over medium heat, about 3 minutes, crumbling it with the back of a wooden spoon. Transfer the sausage to a plate lined with paper towels and set aside.

Discard all but 3 tablespoons of the fat left in the sauté pan. Sauté the onion in the reserved fat for 3 minutes over medium heat. Add the garlic and red pepper flakes to the pan, reduce the heat to low and cook 5 minutes. Increase the heat to high, add the sliced mushrooms and bay leaf, stir well and cook 2 minutes.

Add the wine and cook until it has all evaporated, 3 minutes. Stir in the chopped tomatoes, reduce the heat to medium and cook 2 minutes. Add the parsley and basil and toss well. Add the juices of the stewed tomatoes and the browned sausage and cook over medium-low heat for 5 minutes, stirring occasionally. The mixture should be fairly thick and almost dry. If it is very watery, cook for 3 minutes more. Transfer the mixture to a large mixing bowl.

Separate the egg whites and yolks. Add the yolks to the stuffing mixture along with 1 cup of the bread crumbs and cheese. Beat the egg whites until they have almost a meringue-like consistency. Fold them into the stuffing.

Coat the bottom and sides of baking ramekins or a small baking dish with butter, coat well with the remaining bread crumbs and fill with the stuffing mixture. Bake in the preheated oven for 20-25 minutes if using ramekins or 35-40 minutes for a single baking dish. Run a sharp paring knife around the edges of the ramekins to loosen the stuffing. Turn the ramekins upside down over a dinner plate and the baked mixture will slide right out.

*"Give me
eggs of an hour,
bread of a day,
wine of a year,
a friend of thirty years."*

Italian Proverb

Pane Grattugiato Condito
ITALIAN BREAD CRUMBS

As you can well imagine, the typical Italian household has a lot of leftover bread. It's recycled in every possible form: dessert, fritters, stuffing and soup. Although it's now possible to buy excellent Italian seasoned bread crumbs at your local supermarket, nothing matches the love and the passion that you add to a homemade version.

The following recipe is a very simple method that is the perfect base to create your own versions, adding whatever flavoring agents strike your fancy. Who knows — you might get so good at it that I'll find your personal brand at the grocery store one day!

MAKES 1½ CUPS

½ teaspoon olive oil
1 cup plain bread crumbs
1 tablespoon finely chopped fresh basil
1 tablespoon finely chopped fresh Italian parsley
⅛ teaspoon salt
⅛ teaspoon black pepper
2 tablespoons freshly grated Pecorino Romano or Parmigiano Reggiano cheese

Brush a nonstick sauté pan with the olive oil and cook over medium heat for 1 minute. Add the bread crumbs and cook, stirring, until brown, about 2 minutes.

Transfer to a bowl, add all the remaining ingredients and mix well. Store in an airtight container or reclosable plastic bag.

Crema di Cipolle
Onion Purée

MAKES 4 TO 5 CUPS
5 large onions, peeled and thinly sliced
1 bay leaf
1 teaspoon thyme
¼ teaspoon salt (see Cook's Tip)
¼ teaspoon pepper
1 cup dry Marsala wine
2 quarts (2 l) Chicken or Beef Stock (see page 228 or 230)

Place all the ingredients in a 3- to 4-quart (2.75- to 3.75-l) stockpot. Bring to a boil, reduce the heat to medium and cook for 1-1½ hours, stirring every 15 minutes. Cook until all the liquid has evaporated and the onions have cooked down to a very thick consistency with a pungent flavor.

Remove the bay leaf. Put the onions in the food processor and process until creamy. Place in ice cube trays and freeze. When frozen, take out of the trays and place in freezer bags.

The frozen cubes of onion purée will be used as a flavoring agent in other recipes.

COOK'S TIP

This recipe will be very salty if you make it with regular canned stock. In order to avoid this, bring the canned stock to a boil, put in 2 medium peeled and quartered potatoes and boil for 20 minutes. The potatoes will absorb much of the salt from the stock. Strain the stock and discard the potatoes.

You should also eliminate the salt from the recipe if you are using canned stock.

This is a real flavor booster. You'll experience powerful flavor enhancement with just a couple of spoonfuls in any dish.

Remember, it used to be a secret recipe of a Benedictine monastery near Palermo. Just one taste and you'll understand why this culinary elixir was kept such a closely guarded secret.

Impasto per la Pizza
Pizza Dough

This recipe comes from a fellow chef and dear friend, Antonio Coppola. His pizzas are legendary: a culinary composition blending perfection and romance. Although Antonio cooks his pizza in a wood burning oven, this recipe will work equally well in a gas or electric oven.

MAKES 1 (14-INCH) (35-CM) PIZZA OR 4 CALZONES

2 packages active dry yeast
3 teaspoons sugar
½ cup warm water
½ cup milk
1 whole egg
2 tablespoons olive oil
3½ cups all-purpose flour
2 teaspoons salt

In a small bowl, mix together the yeast, ½ teaspoon of the sugar and ¼ cup of the warm water. Let the yeast mixture proof for 10 minutes until it becomes foamy.

In a another bowl, whisk together the milk, egg and 1 tablespoon of the olive oil. In a large bowl, beat 3 cups of the flour, the remaining sugar and the salt with an electric mixer on low speed for 5-10 seconds. Add the proofed yeast and the egg/milk mixture and beat until all the ingredients are well mixed, scraping down the sides of the bowl as needed. With the mixer on medium speed, add the remaining ¼ cup of water in a slow stream and beat until the dough forms a soft ball.

If making the dough by hand, combine the yeast mixture and the egg/milk mixture in a large bowl. Mix the dry ingredients, 1 cup at a time, into the wet ingredients, stirring to get all the lumps out.

Sprinkle some of the remaining ½ cup of flour on a work surface. Remove the dough from the bowl and flatten it into a disk. Sprinkle the dough with a little flour and knead for 3-5 minutes, folding the dough over on itself and pushing it out with the heels of your hands. Turn the dough ¼ turn and repeat the folding and pushing process.

Keep kneading until the dough is smooth, satiny and elastic, adding more flour if it starts sticking. (If the dough was mixed by hand, knead for 8-10 minutes.) Grease a large bowl with the remaining olive oil, place the dough in it and cover with plastic wrap. Let the dough rise in a warm place for 1 hour. Punch the dough down and it is ready to use.

Cook's Tip

Pizza dough freezes very well and it's such a treat to have on hand. To freeze, punch the dough down after it has risen and form into a ball. Wrap in plastic wrap and then place in a freezer bag or over-wrap with aluminum foil. It can be frozen for up to 6 months. Thaw in the refrigerator and then bring to room temperature. When it is at the point of beginning to rise again, simply form and bake it according to your recipe.

"The discovery of a new dish does more for the happiness of mankind than the discovery of a star."

Brillat-Savarin

Pasta Frolla
PIE DOUGH

You'll treasure this as one of the easiest and most effective pie dough recipes. It's a versatile crust that spans uses from savory meat pies to all the fruit-filled desserts.

Be careful not to spoil your family with an over-abundance of homemade pies — it will undoubtedly become the expected finale to every meal. But if this should happen, you can follow my mom's example. She taught Mario and me how to do it ourselves, and said, "You guys have gotten so good I think I'll rest for a while. What's for dessert tonight?"

MAKES 2 (8 OR 9-INCH) (20 OR 23-CM) TARTS
OR 1 COVERED (8-INCH) (20-CM) TART

1 ¼ cups all-purpose flour
¼ teaspoon salt
2 tablespoons sugar
1 egg yolk
4 ounces (115 g) (1 stick) cold unsalted butter,
quartered lengthwise and cubed
3 tablespoons ice water

Place the flour, salt, sugar and egg yolks in a food processor fitted with a steel blade and pulse for 5 seconds to mix. Add the butter and pulse about 15 times, until the butter is the size of small peas. With the machine running, slowly add the water until the dough has formed a ball, about 10-15 seconds. Transfer the dough to a floured work surface and lightly knead, about 1 minute. (It is important not to over-knead the dough. When properly blended, the baked crust will be light and flaky.)

To make by hand, place the flour, salt and sugar into a bowl and stir to mix. Cut the butter into the flour mixture with a pastry blender or two knives, until the mixture resembles a coarse meal. Slowly stir in the egg yolks and then the ice water, mixing thoroughly. Turn the dough out onto a lightly floured work surface and gather it together. Knead the dough roughly and briefly until the dough comes together.

At this point the dough may be patted into place in a tart pan and baked after chilling for 30 minutes in the refrigerator. If you're not patting the dough into the pan, shape it into a flat disk, approximately 1 inch (2.5 cm) thick, wrap in plastic wrap and refrigerate for at least 45 minutes before rolling it out.

Unwrap the dough and divide it in half for 2 (8-inch) (20-cm) tarts or into ⅔ and ⅓ pieces for a covered tart. Place the larger piece of dough on a floured work surface and roll it out into a circle large enough to fit the pan. Ease the dough into the pan and trim the edges or form a decorative edge.

For a partially-baked tart shell, prick the shell with a fork. Line it with aluminum foil, draping it over the edges to keep them from browning too much and fill with dried beans or pie weights. Bake in a preheated 375° F (190° C) oven, for 15 minutes, then remove the foil and cool on a rack.

For a pre-baked shell, continue baking for 10 minutes longer or until the shell is golden brown. Cool completely before filling.

*"The art of dining well
is no slight art,
the pleasure
not a slight pleasure."*
MONTAIGNE

Sugo per la Pizza
PIZZA SAUCE

In my opinion, most tomato sauces are too watery for pizza. This preparation will give you what I believe to be exactly the right consistency and flavoring without making your crust soggy. However, I can assure you that any type of sauce will work — experiment and make your own decision.

YIELDS 2¼ CUPS
1 ¾ cups Tomato Sauce (see page 225)
½ cup tomato paste
¼ teaspoon garlic salt
½ teaspoon dried oregano
½ teaspoon dried basil
1 ½ teaspoons sugar

Place all the ingredients in a food processor or blender and process for 15 seconds or until it reaches a smooth consistency.

Aglio Arrosto
ROASTED GARLIC

Use this fabulous ingredient to kick-up the flavor in lots of your dishes, especially sauces and vegetables. Once you get started, you won't be able to stop.

MAKES APPROXIMATELY ¼ CUP
1 large head garlic
1 teaspoon olive oil

Slice the top ⅓ off the head of garlic, brush with the olive oil and place the sliced tops back on. Wrap the garlic in aluminum foil and bake in a 400° F (200° C) oven for 35 minutes. When cool enough to handle, hold the head of garlic at the bottom and squeeze to force the pulp out. You can also remove individual cloves and squeeze them one at a time.

Sugo di Pomodoro
Tomato Sauce

Makes 5¾ cups
4 tablespoons olive oil
4 whole garlic cloves
¾ cup finely chopped onions
2 (28-ounce) (800-g) cans peeled Italian tomatoes
10 fresh basil leaves

Pour the oil into a 3-quart (2.75-l) pot on medium-high heat and cook the garlic and onion for 3-5 minutes. Reduce the heat to a simmer and cook until the onions are soft and start to brown, about 10 minutes, stirring occasionally.

While the onions are cooking, put the tomatoes and their juices in a blender or food processor and purée until smooth. Add the tomato purée to the onion mixture, raise the heat to high and bring to a boil for 5-8 minutes. Reduce the heat, add the basil and simmer for 25 minutes, stirring occasionally.

Cook's Tip

I can't stress enough the importance of using Italian tomatoes because they're naturally sweeter. If you have to use American tomatoes, double the amount of chopped onions and add 2 tablespoons of oil.

Remember, this is a plain, unsalted sauce, which is great as an ingredient in other finished sauces. If you want to use this as a garnish for your pasta, I'd suggest you add ¼ teaspoon of salt for each 2 cups, according to your taste.

This recipe is a simple and efficient way to prepare a basic sauce that can be used for all the recipes in this book.

"Contented belly
A clement heart
Empty belly
Heart of stone."
Italian Proverb

Sugo Tonnato
Tuna Sauce

Makes 2 cups

1 (6-ounce) (175-g) can water-packed white tuna, drained and flaked
½ cup Chicken Stock (see page 228)
¾ cup fat-free mayonnaise
2 teaspoons drained capers
¼ teaspoon salt
1 tablespoon freshly squeezed lemon juice
1 tablespoon anchovy paste

Place all the ingredients in a food processor or blender and purée for 15 seconds. Transfer to a covered container and store in the refrigerator until ready to use, for up to 3-4 days.

Legend has it that this sauce was developed as the result of a crisis. It seems that somewhere around the 14th century, tuna had become scarce throughout Italy. A young Sicilian chef named "Palicchio" (Little Paul) developed this sauce. He would spread it over thinly sliced pieces of veal round or fillet which had been braised in water. Marinated for a few hours, the veal tasted like tuna.

Trust me, you're bound to hear this tale over and over when preparing this dish, with the name of the chef changed according to his native region. But as far as I'm concerned, this is still Palicchio's sauce.

Ragù di Carne
BOLOGNESE MEAT SAUCE

SERVES 4 TO 6

5 tablespoons olive oil

¼ teaspoon red pepper flakes

½ cup finely chopped celery

½ cup finely chopped carrots

½ cup finely chopped onion

4 garlic cloves, thickly sliced

1 large bay leaf

1 tablespoon chopped fresh sage

2 tablespoons chopped fresh basil

2 ounces (60 g) finely diced prosciutto

¼ pound (115 g) ground veal

¼ pound (115 g) ground lamb

¼ pound (115 g) ground beef

⅓ cup red wine

½ cup Tomato Sauce (see page 225)

2 tablespoons tomato paste

2 cups Chicken or Beef Stock (see page 228 or 230)

Salt and pepper to taste

Heat the oil in a large saucepan set on high heat until sizzling, about 2 minutes. Add the red pepper flakes, celery, carrots, onion, garlic, bay leaf, sage, and basil and cook for 2 minutes, stirring constantly. Reduce the heat to medium-low and cook 10 minutes more, stirring occasionally.

Raise the heat to high, add the prosciutto, veal, lamb and beef and cook, stirring constantly, for 2 minutes. Add the wine, reduce the heat to medium and let it cook until almost evaporated, about 5 minutes. Raise the heat to high, add the tomato sauce, tomato paste and stock and bring to a boil. Reduce the heat to a simmer, cover and cook for 45 minutes, stirring twice.

If you like your sauce thicker, remove the cover during the last 15 minutes of cooking. Taste for salt and pepper.

Now you can see why this sauce makes the town of Bologna, Italy, where it is said to have originated, famous. I kindly but energetically urge you to try it at least once. The flavor is explosive, increasing as you reduce the sauce over a low simmer. My Grandma Adele is responsible for the addition of the cinnamon. In my house it was used to top my favorite pasta, potato gnocchi, but it works well with any kind of pasta, especially my Baked Pasta Wrapped in Eggplant Slices (see page 68).

I must say that Parmigiano Reggiano cheese is the only one that truly works in this sauce. In fact, my Grandma Adele used to save all her Parmigiano Reggiano crusts leftover from grating cheese to place in the sauce while it simmers — a great added dimension of flavor.

Brodo di Pollo

CHICKEN STOCK

MAKES 2 QUARTS (2 L)

1 (3-pound) (1.4-kg) whole chicken, without the liver
2 small carrots, peeled and quartered
2 celery ribs, cut into 2-inch (5-cm) pieces
2 medium white onions, quartered
1 small fresh rosemary branch, about 4 inches (10 cm) or ½ teaspoon dried
3 sprigs fresh Italian parsley
10 leaves fresh basil
3 sprigs fresh thyme or ½ teaspoon dried
1 tablespoon black peppercorns
2 eggs, beaten well, egg shells reserved
1 cup white wine
¾ tablespoon salt
3¼ quarts (3.25 l) water

Place all the ingredients, including the egg shells, in a large stockpot and bring to a boil. Reduce the heat and simmer, with the cover slightly ajar, for 2 hours. Skim any foam that rises to the top every 30 minutes.

Remove the chicken and set aside to use in another recipe. Strain the stock through a fine sieve lined with cheesecloth. Place in the refrigerator until the next day. All the fat will rise to the top, harden and become solid white. Skim it off and discard.

The stock will keep up to 4 days refrigerated and for 1 month if frozen.

"The destiny of nations depends on their manner of eating."

BRILLAT-SAVARIN

Brodo Tinto
ENHANCED CHICKEN STOCK

MAKES 8 TO 9 CUPS

1 pound (450 g) sliced mushrooms
1 ounce (30 g) dried mushrooms, porcini or shiitake
8 cups Chicken Stock (see page 228)
4 tablespoons chopped fresh Italian parsley
1 stalk celery
1 carrot
1 leek (white part only)
½ teaspoon dried thyme
¼ teaspoon dried marjoram
4 whole garlic cloves, peeled
½ cup Tomato Sauce (see page 225)
1 cup dry Marsala wine

Place all the ingredients in a large stockpot and bring to a boil. Simmer, with the lid ajar, for 2 hours. Strain the stock and discard the vegetables. Return the liquid to the pot and simmer for 40 minutes longer.

Transfer to a bowl and refrigerate for up to 4 days, until ready to use or freeze for up to 1 month.

This is only for those who want to venture into new realms of taste. Save it for one of those rainy weekends when you have a little time to play around. But be warned, once bitten by its taste, you turn into a vampire, but you'll definitely be a believer. Use it wherever you use plain chicken stock.

Brodo di Carne
BEEF STOCK

MAKES 2 QUARTS (2 L)
5 pounds (2.4 kg) beef or veal bones, preferably shin bones
3 tablespoons tomato paste
1 tablespoon flour
1 large carrot, cut into 1-inch (2.5-cm) pieces
1 large onion, quartered
1 large celery rib, cut into 1-inch (2.5-cm) pieces
1 teaspoon black peppercorns
5 whole cloves
2 bay leaves
1½ teaspoons dried thyme or 2 fresh sprigs
5 sprigs fresh basil
5 fresh sage leaves
2 sprigs fresh rosemary, about 3 inches (8 cm) each
1 gallon (3.75 l) water

"Pleasantest of all
is the tie
of host and guest."

AESCHYLUS

Preheat the oven to 400° F (200° C). Place the bones in a large ovenproof pan and bake until well browned, turning twice, about 20-30 minutes. Remove from the oven.

In a large bowl, mix the tomato paste, flour, carrot, onion and celery. Spoon this mixture on top of the browned bones and roast in the oven for 15 minutes.

While the bones are cooking, make a cheesecloth pouch and place all the herbs and spices inside. Tie it securely with kitchen twine and put at the bottom of a large stockpot.

Transfer the cooked vegetables and bones into the stockpot with the pouch of herbs. Be careful not to pour in the fat that has accumulated in the bottom of the pan. Cover with the water, bring to a boil, reduce the heat to a simmer and cook for 6-8 hours with the lid ajar, without stirring. When the water level has reduced by ⅓ (about half way through the simmering), add 3 cups of cold water.

Strain the stock, discarding the bones and vegetables. Let come to room temperature then refrigerate overnight. The next day, discard any of the fat that has congealed on the top. Refrigerate the stock for up to 5 days or freeze for up to 1 month.

Brodetto di Gamberi
SHRIMP STOCK

MAKES 2½ CUPS
2 tablespoons olive oil
Shells from 1 pound (450 g) shrimp
2 whole garlic cloves
1½ tablespoons chopped onion
1½ tablespoons chopped celery
1½ tablespoons chopped carrot
1 tablespoon tomato paste
1 tablespoon chopped fresh Italian parsley
1 teaspoon thyme
¼ cup white wine
4 cups clam juice
¼ teaspoon salt
¼ teaspoon black pepper

My father used to say, "A true chef never wastes anything."

The following recipe will show you his gifted vision as it pertains to culinary recycling. I don't think you'll throw away your shrimp shells anymore. I can't believe my own ears — I'm starting to sound just like my father!

Cook the olive oil in a medium saucepan set on medium heat until sizzling, about 2 minutes. Add the shrimp shells, garlic, onion, celery, and carrot and cook for 5 minutes. Add the tomato paste, parsley, and thyme, increase the heat to high and cook for 2 minutes, stirring well. Add the wine and cook until it evaporates, about 3 minutes. Add the clam juice, bring to a boil, and simmer, uncovered, for 30 minutes. Taste for salt and pepper.

Strain the stock through a fine mesh strainer. Let come to room temperature, then refrigerate. It will keep for 4 days in the refrigerator or 1 month in the freezer.

A

W

Z

"Nicolino, non farti, mai fregare dalla paura!"

"Ci provo, Papá, ci provo."

"Little Nick, don't ever let fear get the best of you!"
"I try Dad, I try."